Augustin Cournot: Modelling Economics

Cournot Centre for Economic Studies

(formerly the Saint-Gobain Centre for Economic Studies)

Series Editor: Robert Solow, *Emeritus Professor of Economics, Massachusetts Institute of Technology; President of the Cournot Centre for Economic Studies, Paris, France*

Conference Editor: Jean-Philippe Touffut, *Director of the Cournot Centre for Economic Studies, Paris, France*

Augustin Cournot: Modelling Economics

Edited by

Jean-Philippe Touffut

Director of the Cournot Centre for Economic Studies, Paris, France

THE COURNOT CENTRE FOR ECONOMIC STUDIES SERIES

Edward Elgar
Cheltenham, UK • Northampton, MA, USA

Published by
Edward Elgar Publishing Limited
Glensanda House
Montpellier Parade
Cheltenham
Glos GL50 1UA
UK

Edward Elgar Publishing, Inc.
William Pratt House
9 Dewey Court
Northampton
Massachusetts 01060
USA

A catalogue record for this book
is available from the British Library

Library of Congress Cataloguing in Publication Data
Augustin Cournot : modelling economics / edited by Jean-Philippe Touffut.
    p. cm. — (The Cournot Centre for Economic Studies series)
    Includes bibliographical references and index.
    1. Cournot, A. A. (Antoine Augustin), 1801–1877. 2.
    Economics—Mathematical models—History—19th century. 3.
    Economics—France—History—19th century. I. Touffut, Jean-Philippe.

    HB105.C65A94   2007
    330.01'5195—dc22

                                                            2007025582

ISBN 978 1 84720 586 5 (hardback)
ISBN 978 1 84720 654 1 (paperback)

Typeset by Manton Typesetters, Louth, Lincolnshire, UK
Printed and bound in Great Britain by MPG Books Ltd, Bodmin, Cornwall

Contents

Contributors

Robert J. Aumann is a professor of mathematics at the Hebrew University of Jerusalem, where he is also a founding member of the Interdisciplinary Center for Rationality. His wide-ranging and innovative contributions to game theory have been decisive in shaping contemporary economic theory and the study of strategic interactive behaviour. In 2005, Aumann shared with Thomas Schelling the Bank of Sweden Prize in Economic Sciences in Memory of Alfred Nobel.

Alain Desrosières is an administrator at the Institut National de la Statistique et des Études Économiques (INSEE) and a member of the International Statistical Institute. He teaches the history of statistics at the École Nationale de la Statistique et de l'Administration Économique and at the Alexandre Koyré Centre. His fields of research are the sociology of quantification and the comparative history of public statistical systems since 1950.

Jean Magnan de Bornier is a professor of economics at the Université Paul Cézanne Aix–Marseille. His research interests are Austrian theory, in particular capital theory, the theory of cultural development, and the history of theories of imperfect competition. Magnan de Bornier has published widely on the reception of Cournot's work in economics, with particular emphasis on his contributions in the domains of the theory of markets and value theory.

Thierry Martin is a professor of philosophy of science at the Université de Franche-Comté, Besançon. He is a researcher at the Institute for History, Philosophy of Science and Technology. He is head of the Laboratory for Philosophical Research on the Logic of Action. Martin is a co-editor of the complete works of Augustin Cournot. His main area of research is the history and philosophy of probability theory and mathematics in the social sciences. Professor Martin is a member of the Scientific Committee of the Cournot Centre for Economic Studies.

Glenn Shafer is a professor at Rutgers University, New Jersey, and at the Computer Learning Centre, Royal Holloway College, University of London. Shafer is the author of five books and numerous research papers that have appeared in journals of statistics, philosophy, history, psychology, computer science, economics, engineering, accounting and law.

Robert M. Solow is Institute Professor Emeritus at the Massachusetts Institute of Technology. In 1987, he received the Bank of Sweden Prize in Economic Sciences in Memory of Alfred Nobel for his contributions to economic growth theory. He is Robert K. Merton Scholar at the Russell Sage Foundation, where he is a member of the advisory committee for the Foundation's project on the incidence and quality of low-wage employment in Europe and the USA. Professor Solow is President of the Cournot Centre for Economic Studies.

Bernard Walliser is a professor at the École Nationale des Ponts et Chaussées and a director of studies at the École des Hautes Études en Sciences Sociales. He was formerly in charge of the Cognitive Economics Research Group of the Centre National de la Recherche Scientifique (CNRS) and is now at the Paris School of Economics. His works examine the connections between game theory, economics, cognitive science and epistemology.

Jean-Philippe Touffut is co-founder and director of the Cournot Centre for Economic Studies. His research interests include probabilistic epistemology and the exploration of evolutionary games from a neurological and economic perspective.

Preface

This volume is one of a series arising from the conferences organized by the Cournot Centre for Economic Studies, Paris. The aim is to explore contemporary issues in economics. This conference, entitled 'Augustin Cournot, Economic Models and Rationality', was unique in that it focused on the pioneering work of nineteenth-century mathematician Antoine Augustin Cournot – namesake of the Cournot Centre – in the fields of economics, game theory, sociology and epistemology of probability and statistics. The contributors are from backgrounds as diverse as economics, mathematics, philosophy, statistics and history.

The conference, the Cournot Centre's eighth, was held on 1–2 December 2005.

NA

Acknowledgements

My warmest thanks go to Therrese Goodlett, Anna Kaiser and Timothy Slind, who greatly contributed to this book, from the organization of the conference from which these proceedings originated through to putting on the final touches. Special thanks go to Richard Crabtree for translations and to Stephanie Mansion for her help with the formatting of the texts and references. A heartfelt thanks to all of them.

The editor is grateful to The Nobel Foundation for permission to reprint Robert J. Aumann's Prize lecture 'War and peace'. ©The Nobel Foundation 2006.

About the series

Professor Robert Solow

The Cournot Centre for Economic Studies is an independent French-based research institute. It takes its name from the pioneering economist, mathematician
and philosopher Antoine Augustin Cournot (1801–77).

Neither a think-tank nor a research bureau, the Centre enjoys the special independence of a catalyst. My old student dictionary (dated 1936) says that
catalysis is the 'acceleration of a reaction produced by a substance, called the
catalyst, which may be recovered practically unchanged at the end of the reaction'. The reaction we have in mind results from bringing together (a) an issue
of economic policy that is currently being discussed and debated in Europe and
(b) the relevant theoretical and empirical findings of serious economic research
in universities, think-tanks and research bureaux. Acceleration is desirable because it is better that reaction occurs before minds are made up and decisions
taken, not after. We hope that the Cournot Centre can be recovered practically
unchanged and used again and again.

Notice that 'policy debate' is not exactly what we are trying to promote. To
have a policy debate, you need not only knowledge and understanding, but also
preferences, desires, values and goals. The trouble is that, in practice, the debat-
ers often have only those things, and they invent or adopt only those 'findings'
that are convenient. The Cournot Centre hopes to inject the findings of serious
research at an early stage.

It is important to realize that this is not easy or straightforward. The analytical issues that underlie economic policy choices are usually complex.
Economics is not an experimental science. The available data are scarce, and
may not be exactly the relevant ones. Interpretations are therefore uncertain.
Different studies, by uncommitted economists, may give different results.
When those controversies exist, it is our hope that the Centre's conferences
will discuss them. Live debate at that fundamental level is exactly what we
are after.

This particular conference is unique to the Series. Here the contribution and
continued relevance of the Centre's namesake, Augustin Cournot, is debated
and elaborated. While this has the advantage of avoiding questions of short-term
applicability, it is less evident what impact the subject may have on decision-

making processes or policy issues. Nevertheless, the subject has great relevance to the Centre's work.

Augustin Cournot's pluridisciplinary vision and approach are reflected in the Centre's activities. We all know Cournot's role in the development of mathematical modelling, industrial economics and game theory in the field of economics. It is less known, however, that Cournot's interests and contributions extended also to the fields of philosophy, history – in particular the history of philosophy – and, more generally, to the social sciences. Although it took sometimes several decades after his death for economists to begin to take notice of his knowledge and intuitions, Cournot has provided immeasurable inspiration to his successors the world over. Emphasizing the theoretical, economic and mathematical lineage from Cournot to the Centre focuses and highlights its work, inscribing the Centre's activities as part of Augustin Cournot's legacy.

I used the words 'serious research' a moment ago. That sort of phrase is sometimes used to exclude unwelcome ideas, especially unfashionable ones. The Cournot Centre does not intend to impose narrow requirements of orthodoxy, but it does hope to impose high standards of attention to logic and respect for facts. It is because those standards are not always observed in debates about policy that an institution like the Cournot Centre has a role to play.

The complete works of Antoine Augustin Cournot

Published under the direction of André Robinet, in collaboration with J. Vrin and the Centre National de la Recherche Scientifique (CNRS, France), with introductions and notes by the editors.

I   *Exposition de la théorie des chances et des probabilités* (1843), Bernard Bru (ed.) (1984), *Œuvres complètes*, Paris: Vrin.

II   *Essai sur les fondements de nos connaissances et sur les caractères de la critique philosophique* (1851), Jean-Claude Pariente (ed.) (1975), *Œuvres complètes*, Paris: Vrin.

III   *Traité de l'enchaînement des idées fondamentales dans les sciences et dans l'histoire* (1861), Nelly Bruyère (ed.) (1982), *Œuvres complètes*, Paris: Vrin.

IV   *Considérations sur la marche des idées et des événements dans les temps modernes* (1872), André Robinet (ed.) (1973), *Œuvres complètes*, Paris: Vrin.

V   *Matérialisme, vitalisme, rationalisme* (1875), Claire Salomon-Bayet (ed.) (1979), *Œuvres complètes*, Paris: Vrin.

VI-1   *Traité élémentaire de la théorie des fonctions et du calcul infinitésimal* (1841), Pierre Dugac (ed.) (1984), *Œuvres complètes*, Paris: Vrin.

VI-2   *De l'origine et des limites de la correspondance entre l'algèbre et la géométrie* (1847), Nelly Bruyère (ed.) (1989), *Œuvres complètes*, Paris: Vrin.

VII   *Des Institutions d'instruction publique en France* (1864), Angèle Kremer-Marietti (ed.) (1977), *Œuvres complètes*, Paris: Vrin.

VIII   *Recherches sur les principes mathématiques de la théorie des richesses* (1838), Gérard Jorland (ed.) (1980), *Œuvres complètes*, Paris: Vrin.

IX   *Principes de la théorie des richesses* (1863), Gérard Jorland (ed.) (1981), *Œuvres complètes*, Paris: Vrin.

X   *Revue sommaire des doctrines économiques* (1877), Gérard Jorland (ed.) (1982), *Œuvres complètes*, Paris: Vrin.

XI   *Pièces diverses et correspondance*, Bernard Bru and Thierry Martin (eds), in preparation.

ENGLISH TRANSLATIONS OF COURNOT'S WORKS

Cournot, A.A. (1897) [1838], *Researches into the Mathematical Principles of the Theory of Wealth* [*Recherches sur les principes mathématiques de la théorie des richesses*], translated by N.T. Bacon with a Bibliography of Mathematical Economics by I. Fisher, New York: Macmillan.

Cournot, A.A. (1956) [1851], *An Essay on the Foundations of our Knowledge* [*Essai sur les fondements de nos connaissances et sur les caractères de la critique philosophique*], translated by M.H. Moore, New York: The Liberal Arts Press.

EDITOR'S NOTE

With the exception of the two works cited above, all quotations from Cournot's writings are our translations.

Chronological biography of Antoine Augustin Cournot

28 August 1801	Birth in Gray (Haute-Saône); son of Claude-Agapit Cournot, merchant, descended from a long line of farmers
1809–16	Educated at the Collège des Jésuites in Gray
1820	Admitted to the Collège royal de Besançon for studies in mathematics
1821	Enters the École Normale Supérieure; the school is closed by the authorities one year later
1822	Undertakes undergraduate studies at the Sorbonne, particularly enjoying his courses with Lacroix and Hachette, and becoming friends with Dirichlet. Thanks to Hachette, has the opportunity to meet Ampère, Laplace and Lagrange. Regularly attends lectures at the Académie des Sciences, notably those of Poisson, Biot, Arago, Gay-Lussac, Poinsot, Berthollet, Legendre, Fourier et Cauchy
1823	Obtains a Bachelor's degree in science
1827	Obtains a Bachelor's degree in law
1823–33	Works as private tutor to the son of Marshal Gouvion-Saint-Cyr, whose memoirs he helps write

17 and 24 February 1829	Defends doctoral thesis
July 1834–October 1835	Holds the Chair of Mechanics and Analysis at the Faculté des sciences de Lyon
October 1835–September 1838	Rector of the Academy of Grenoble and Professor of Mathematics at the Faculté des sciences
1836	Succeeds Ampère as Matter's assistant at the Inspection générale, in the post of Interim Inspector General
10 September 1838	Marries Colombe-Antoinette Petitguyot, with whom he has a son
September 1838–September 1854	Inspector General of Education
1839–43	Following Poisson, president of the jury overseeing France's highest level of competitive examinations for teachers of mathematics
1848	Appointed to the Commission for Superior Studies
22 August 1854	Appointed Rector of the Académie de Dijon
May 1862	Retires from his post as Rector of the Académie de Dijon. Moves to Paris
1877	Death; buried 2 April at the Montparnasse cemetery, Paris

x 20

Book Title:

Introduction

Thierry Martin and Jean-Philippe Touffut

> If a symbolic date were to be chosen for the birth of mathematical economics, our profession, in rare unanimous agreement, would select 1838, the year in which Augustin Cournot published his *Recherches sur les principes mathématiques de la théorie des richesses.*
>
> Gerard Debreu (1984, p. 267)

Economics has secured the posterity of Augustin Cournot's works, but there was a large temporal gap between their application and their original publication. Cournot's role in applying mathematics to the social sciences is an exceptional, and perhaps unique, contribution. Clearly ahead of his time, the nineteenth-century French mathematician found almost no interlocutors. The engineer–economists, for whom he wrote, had no need for his abstract and general approach, and the theoreticians simply ignored him. It was not until Walras, Jevons, Marshall or Pareto that Cournot found attentive readers who were eager to further his work. It is without a doubt Irving Fisher who introduced Cournot to economists in his 1898 commentary on the English translation of *Recherches sur les principes mathématiques de la théorie des richesses*, exactly 60 years after its original publication in French. In the second half of the twentieth century, the triumph of game theory consecrated Cournot's market theories, which were nonetheless marked by the ambiguities inherent in such a time lag. Finally, in 2008, Cournot's name will appear for the first time on the list of authors on secondary school biology syllabi in France.

Cournot's works have had such a vast influence on the social sciences that it would be futile to try to separate that which he would have recognized as a continuation of his work from that which he would have rejected. In and of itself, the question is of little interest, given that Cournot remained remarkably detached from his writings. The question gains pertinence, however, when one considers the contribution that his works have made to founding a normative discourse, a discourse that Cournot did not participate in. The aim of the conference proceedings presented in this book, however, is neither to legitimate one particular approach to research born from his works, nor to prove his paternity to developments born of his intuitions. The aim is above all to pay homage to

1

Cournot's originality and modernity in the area of social mathematics, and more precisely in the field of economics.

The specificity of Augustin Cournot's work does not reside in his use of mathematics to describe the properties of social phenomena. During his life, Cournot only made irregular contributions to the 'theory of wealth', and the very nature of the subjects of the moral sciences, as they were called at the time, invites quantification. He was, however, the first to construct a mathematical model enabling those subjects to be treated analytically. In *Recherches sur les principes mathématiques de la théorie des richesses* (1838) (published in English as *Researches into the Mathematical Principles of the Theory of Wealth* in 1897), he set out to establish that 'the solution of the general questions which arise from the theory of wealth, depends essentially not on elementary algebra, but on that branch of analysis which comprises arbitrary functions' (p. 4). Cournot undertook this task 'from a purely abstract standpoint, without reference to proposed applications' (p. 5). While Cournot is certainly not the Galileo of economics, we must recognize that, just as the founder of classical physics broke with his predecessors, not by applying mathematical instruments to physical reality, but by upholding the mathematization of its phenomena as an inescapable methodological principle, Cournot's approach initiated the mathematical modelling of social phenomena.

At the same time, he indicated the fundamental orientation of its relation to mathematics. He was not concerned with producing new results in that discipline, as a scientist seeking to invent or discover new theorems would be, or with applying them to a particular object, as an engineer would be, so much as with considering, in a theoretical and reflexive manner, the applicability of mathematics to phenomena, in other words with exploring its conditions and limits. Cournot was profoundly convinced of the intelligibility of mathematics. This was not prompted by mysticism or naïve Pythagorism on Cournot's part, first because he never reduced mathematics to the quantitative dimension, and second because he was clearly aware of the diversity of the subjects and methods that makes mathematics so rich.

The mechanism of knowledge is essentially a process of ordering. This may be limited to a distribution of objects into distinct categories according to various principles of classification, placing the objects in their reciprocal exteriority. This represents a first level of organization, necessary but not sufficient for the intelligibility of these objects, for it is no more than descriptive. We take a further step forward when we seek to clarify the relations of dependence and subordination between ideas, and between phenomena, on the basis of their constituent properties. Not only is such an order constructed logically; it is also, according to Cournot, *rational*, in the sense that we can use it to explain things. Not that this rational order can mysteriously reveal to us the very essence of things (assuming that this term actually means anything), but by identifying the multiplicity of relations by which objects are linked, it reveals the different ways and degrees to which they are interdependent. What Cournot called the 'fundamental ideas of mathematics' play a decisive role in this ordering: concepts such as number, distance, volume and so on, on which the mathematical sciences rely. In *Essai sur les fondements de nos connaissances et sur les caractères de la critique philosophique* (1851), he specified that it 'is to be noted that many of these ideas, in spite of their high degree of generality and abstraction, are only particular forms and, as it were, concrete species of ideas still more abstract and general' (1956 [1851], p. 233), such as combination, order, symmetry, inclusion, exclusion and so on.

Because of their high degree of generality, these 'even more abstract' ideas reach beyond the field of mathematics. They also form the basis of logic, and thus constitute the foundation of the formal sciences, which are characterized by their independence from any specific content or empirical determination. Cournot could not express himself in these exact terms, but this is the very conception that he proposed by invoking a 'theory of order and form'. Moreover, it is precisely because of their independence, and therefore their formal character, that mathematical ideas are so fertile. These fundamental mathematical ideas designate formal, general relations between symbols, which can then be applied to the study of the relations between phenomena.

What is true for natural phenomena is equally valid for economic and social events. This is a first consequence of the above argument. The formal and symbolic character of mathematical ideas liberates them from any specific empirical content, so that they are capable of describing the diverse forms of relations between elements in any domain. Cournot actually applied this thesis, before formulating it explicitly, as early as 1838, in *Recherches*.

This does not mean, however, that the various mathematical sciences can be successfully applied indiscriminately to each domain of objects, or, to put it more clearly, to each of the different disciplines they study. We know that Cournot attached particular importance to two main branches of mathematics: infinitesimal calculus on the one hand, and probability calculus and statistics on the other. Two questions then arise. First, how did Cournot himself envisage the fertility of these instruments when applied to the investigation of social phenomena? Second, and more broadly, what has been the legacy of Cournot's development of these instruments in the field of economics? More specifically, what remains, today, of the impetus given by Cournot to the mathematical modelling of the economy?

One may wonder whether fundamental mathematical ideas are pure intellectual constructions enabling a set of operations to be performed on the symbols that they both connect and designate, thanks to which we can then identify and classify the relations between phenomena, or whether these ideas are discovered by the mathematician, rather than invented, because they stem from the very 'nature of things' and are somehow 'realized' by phenomenal relations. Whatever Cournot's position on this point, he believed that fundamental mathematical ideas formally designate general relations of order that *correspond* to the general relations that link phenomena to each other, and thus bring intelligibility. 'The mind', he wrote in 1872 in *Considérations sur la marche des idées et des événements dans les temps modernes*, 'discovers mathematical truths through its own powers, and considers them as necessary truths: after which, in fact much later, the observer proves that the truths thus discovered do indeed explain and govern natural events' (1973, p. 415–16).

Finally, the central motivation driving Cournot's epistemological reflection is the desire to elucidate the significance and scope that can be attached to the applications of mathematics. He stressed this problem repeatedly: whereas mathematicians easily agree about the methods that should be used to obtain a result, they differ about the way that we should interpret its application to experience. Above all, Cournot devoted himself to forestalling the risk of confusion between an artificial process and a property of the object under study, or of the mistaken projection onto the object of characteristics inherent to the conceptual instrument used and the way it is implemented. Here, Cournot displayed an epistemological perceptiveness, the continuations and echoes of which we shall seek to discern in contemporary thought.

Our aim is not historiographical. We do not seek to reproduce Cournot's thought as faithfully as possible for its own sake by comparing the diverse interpretations to which it has given rise, but instead to assess the relevance of his heritage, and therefore his topicality, on the epistemological, methodological and doctrinal levels. There is nothing self-evident about this heritage. When *Recherches* was published in 1838, it went almost completely unnoticed. Cournot's later economic writings, *Principes de la théorie des richesses* (1863) and *Revue sommaire des doctrines économiques* (1877), stripped of the mathematical apparatus, did not meet with any warmer reception. Yet in the early 1940s, his contributions to economic theory were widely recognized and discussed. To what can we attribute this tardy recognition? What do we retain, today, from Cournot's economic work? And, more broadly, how does it improve our conception of the relation between mathematics and experience?

These are the questions we shall be addressing in this work, in which economists, mathematicians, philosophers and statisticians have been invited to measure the legacy of Cournot's work in the twenty-first century. The probabilistic approach lies at the heart of Cournot's thought, not only because, as a mathematician, he wrote a treaty devoted to this branch of the discipline, *Exposition de la théorie des chances et des probabilités* (1843), but also because his epistemology is founded on the assertion that the relation of the theoretical hypotheses that constitute scientific knowledge to empirical reality can only be affirmed probabilistically, philosophical reflection then serving to evaluate, in each case, the strength of that probability. Thus, it was as a probabilistic philosopher that Cournot investigated the relation of probability theory to experience and the status of the mathematical concept of probability.

To start with, Jean Magnan de Bornier recalls the essential contributions of Cournot's work to the discipline of economics that took shape in the twentieth century. He describes how attitudes towards them were modified and enhanced by subsequent developments in economics, paying particular attention to the theory of markets, Cournot's analysis of taxation and the key concepts of marginal cost and elasticity. He underlines the historical importance, for the constitution of mathematical economics, of Cournot's pioneering work on modelling, even if this latter was of limited extension, showing both its fertility and its limits. The destiny of *Recherches* is of particular interest to Jean Magnan de Bornier, first within the life and work of Cournot himself, who appeared to be curiously unconcerned about the future of a work of whose originality he was nevertheless well aware, and then within the later developments of the science of economics, mainly in the context of marginalist theory and then, more recently, in that of game theory, where Cournot's position has been redefined.

For his part, Thierry Martin shows that Cournot's representation is structured by a double distinction, first between mathematical and philosophical probabilities, and second between objective and subjective probabilities. Cournot's originality here was to make explicit this duality in the meaning of mathematical probability, not in order to reject it by favouring one interpretation to the detriment of the other, but to accept it as two forms of the probabilistic approach, depending on the way it is applied to things. The difficulty resides in determining how to attribute an objective meaning to mathematical probability when this latter cannot be reduced to a frequentist premise. This is addressed by two major theses of Cournot's epistemology: his objectivist representation of chance on the one hand, and the principle of physical impossibility, the forerunner of what contemporary probabilists call 'Cournot's principle', on the other. As this same epistemological concern governs Cournot's exposition of statistics, Martin goes on to re-examine the primacy that Cournot accorded to differential calculus in the analysis of economic equilibrium, refuting the idea that this bears witness to Cournot's resistance to the use of statistics in the field of economics.

As Bernard Walliser shows, if we can regard Cournot as the initiator of mathematical modelling in economics, it is in the sense that he used the mathematical instrument to consider economic phenomena. His epistemological reflection is not deployed in the form of a theory of models. Thus, to put Cournot's heritage to the test, Bernard Walliser defines six essential functions of modelling and uses them to form the basis of a general epistemology of models as they are constructed today. He then subjects their products to a critical examination with the aim of bringing to light their strengths and limits, and their respective capacities for explaining natural or social phenomena. His analysis highlights the diversity in forms of modelling according to the theoretical principles by which they are governed and the empirical domains to which they refer, according to the formalisms they employ and the social roles they fulfil, and according to the operational and educational mechanisms they bring into play. Over and above these differences, however, and thanks to the operational power and formal simplicity of the mathematical instrument used, models provide access to results that a literary account could hardly, if at all, reach. In Walliser's words, they enable 'reasoning to be pursued through other means'. Nevertheless, every model needs to be completed by reflexive analysis, with the aim of interpreting the results obtained.

Glenn Shafer takes as his subject 'Cournot's principle', according to which an event of very low or zero probability will not occur. This principle, employed particularly by French and Russian probabilists during the first half of the twentieth century, makes it possible to give a clear empirical content to applications of probability calculus. Shafer shows that it was precisely the neglect of this principle that obscured the practical significance of probabilities, and in particular their application to the hypothesis of efficient markets. The principle can in fact be incorporated into game theory, where it signifies that no strategy exists by which the bettor can multiply his stake by an infinite factor without risking bankruptcy. He starts by describing the ways in which the principle was mobilized both before and after Cournot made it explicit, first in the form of the moral certainty so dear to eighteenth-century probabilists (notably Bernoulli and Buffon), and later by Chuprov, Markov and, in the French tradition, Borel, Lévy and Fréchet. This leads the author to recall the debates between probabilists in Europe and the USA over the significance of probabilities, and the role played by Cournot's principle in Kolmogorov's axiomatization of probability. After presenting the principles of probabilistic game theory, and explaining how it provided probability calculus with a richer foundation than the theory of measurement, in keeping with the analysis of Shafer and Vovk (2001), he shows how Cournot's principle can, in this context, be applied to market prices to obtain a weaker, and therefore more realistic, hypothesis of market efficiency than the classic hypothesis, according to which price variations are a function of new information.

Robert Aumann's text is the reproduction of his 2005 Prize Lecture, a version of which was presented at the Cournot Centre's conference. The lecture, which explains his contribution to economic theory, and particularly to non-cooperative game theory, pays direct homage to the works of Cournot. In discerning the equilibrium that is today associated with John Nash, Cournot laid the mathematical foundations for the analysis of non-cooperative games more than a century before the topic was systematically examined.

In his contribution, Robert Solow explores Augustin Cournot's macroeconomic intuitions and the degree to which his works heralded the theoretical current of which the author was to be one of the founding fathers. Solow's re-reading of *Recherches* leads him to a mixed review: Cournot's great intuitions are sometimes marred by simplifications that modern economists see as errors. Solow, however, shows how much the latter owe to Cournot in their understanding of themes as diverse as variations in social income, the profits of international trade, duopolies, oligopolies and forms of competition.

Alain Desrosières presents two strong ideas from Cournot's probabilistic and statistical epistemology, and describes how fertile they proved to be in the twentieth century: first, his distinction between the objective and subjective meanings of probabilities, and second, his discussion of the interpretation of 'cuts', in other words, the distribution of a population of objects into distinct statistical categories. Both of these ideas raise the question of the way we interpret the results of mathematical analysis. We cannot neglect this interpretation, Cournot argued, without exposing ourselves to areas of ambiguity or obscurity; mathematical analysis makes it possible to denounce such areas in advance. Alain Desrosières puts particular emphasis on the construction of statistical nomenclatures, stressing that this presupposes active intervention on the part of the statistician to define a space of equivalence, thanks to which objects become comparable, beyond their particularities, and so lend themselves to categorization and statistical treatment. As we are in the domain of the social sciences, the operation of quantification, differentiated from that of measurement, does not encounter an object already constituted and offered up to the operation of measuring; it must construct its object, which does not pre-exist the analysis. By means of three examples – probabilistic risk assessment, the evaluation and interpretation of macroeconomic aggregates, and the evaluation of public management – Alain Desrosières examines the epistemological and sociological conditions of the translation through which the convention of equivalence, which makes quantification possible, is established. His analysis is bent to the task of showing how, during the second half of the twentieth century, the social uses of probability and statistics helped to provide a *practical* solution to the epistemological difficulties raised by the enterprise of quantifying social phenomena by defining equivalence conventions that enable us to 'compare the incomparable'.

REFERENCES

Debreu, G. (1984), 'Economic Theory in the Mathematical Mode', *American Economic Review*, **74** (3), Nashville, TN: American Economic Association, pp. 267–78.
Shafer, G. and V. Vovk (2001), *Probability and Finance: It's Only a Game!*, New York: Wiley.

1. Cournot as economist: 200 years of relevance

Jean Magnan de Bornier

Augustin Cournot (1801–77) was a singular figure of the nineteenth century: mathematician, economist and philosopher, senior civil servant in education, he produced a considerable body of work covering numerous fields. In this chapter, we shall deal only with Cournot's special place in economics: having published *Recherches sur les principes mathématiques de la théorie des richesses* ([1838], 1980) – published in English as *Researches into the Mathematical Principles of Wealth* (1897) – at a relatively early age, he then devoted himself to other disciplines, only returning to economics towards the end of his life, essentially to reaffirm his earlier positions.

The few pages that follow present the most important elements that an economist can learn from *Recherches*[1] and briefly describe the mixed fortunes of his ideas since their first publication.

A SIGNIFICANT ECONOMIC LEGACY

A simple enumeration of the concepts Cournot introduced into political economics, still in its infancy in the 1830s, gives a good idea of how much the discipline owes to him today. Some of these innovations are striking and are prominent in any evocation, however superficial, of Cournot's legacy. Others are more obscure, having not received the necessary subsequent development, not been understood, or quite simply not been given a name.

In retrospect, Cournot's first work on economics, *Recherches*, was like a thunderbolt, despite the fact that it was largely ignored during the 50 years following its publication.

THE USE OF MATHEMATICS

One of the most important advances made by Cournot was to show how political economics could benefit from the power of mathematical reasoning. Cournot's main educational background was in mathematics. Indeed, he had been the favourite student of Poisson, who saw him as a future innovator in this domain – a prediction that was not confirmed. Cournot, however, did propose and employ a well-balanced approach to the necessary mathematization of economic reasoning.

While accepting that certain authors, such as Adam Smith and Jean-Baptiste Say, did very well without mathematical tools, Cournot observed that others, including Ricardo,

> when treating the most abstract questions, or when seeking great accuracy, have not been able to avoid algebra, and have only disguised it under arithmetical calculations of tiresome length. Any one who understands algebraic notation, reads at a glance in an equation results reached arithmetically only with great labour and pains. (Cournot, 1897 [1838], p. 4)[2]

Cournot sought to position himself on the same level of rigour as Ricardo, while applying the appropriate tools to the task, that is to say 'this branch of analysis whose object is arbitrary functions, which are only constrained to satisfy certain conditions' (ibid., p. 4).

The mathematics involved is simple – 'the first notions of differential and integral calculus' – but Cournot acknowledged that his readers would be neither novices, out of their depth with this abstract approach, nor true mathematicians, 'professional geometricians'. In fact, Cournot intended his work for a very specific category:

> But there is a large class of men, and thanks to a famous school, especially in France, who, after thorough mathematical training, have directed their attention to applications of those sciences which particularly interest society. Theories of the wealth of the community must attract their attention. (Cournot, 1897 [1838], p. 4)

Cournot was referring to what were later called 'engineer–economists', a category, still very much alive today, to which he did not belong, but to which he felt close. Yet the mathematical economics of Cournot is fundamentally different from that of the engineer–economists: although it springs from the same technicality in mathematical formalization, it does not tackle the themes that interest the latter, such as the establishment of canal toll houses that Jules Dupuit, the epitome of the engineer–economist, studied not long after the publication of Cournot's *Recherches*; Cournot remained essentially a pure theorist, conscious of the mistakes that could stem from an overhasty application of theory. Indeed, he believed that theory should renounce all normative pretensions.

That Cournot wrote for a specific category of reader is a contingent fact that is now, and has been for a long time, of no more than historical interest. Advances in economic modelling have made of Cournot's mathematical economics a relevant and valid science, becoming more easily accessible in the process;

conversely, the non-formalized versions of the theory of markets that Cournot saw fit to propose (Cournot, [1863] 1981; [1877] 1982) now appear to us of little interest. That modelling has now become commonplace, however, should not detract from the fact that Cournot was profoundly innovative in using it. Indeed, he handled this technique with totally new depth and precision (in the world of economic thought, at least). Despite the power of the mathematical tool, of which he was well aware, Cournot did not believe that all economic problems could be modelled, as testified by the doubts he expressed concerning the interdependence of markets.[3]

THE ANALYSIS OF MONOPOLY AND COMPETITION

One of Cournot's greatest successes is to have provided, for the first time, a complete – by which we do not mean exhaustive – theory of *market forms*: monopoly, which we do not need to define; oligopoly, where a small number of sellers compete with each other; and 'indefinite' competition, where there is a large number of suppliers. All three linked together in Cournot's analysis as different instances of a single law expressing itself in different economic environments.

Modern economic theory takes a different approach; it identifies a few elementary 'market structures', of which not only the hypotheses, but also the modes of functioning, are different. Despite their differences, these structures – monopoly, oligopoly, pure and perfect competition or monopolistic competition, just to cite the most classic cases – can be compared in terms of performance, essential for satisfying the normative inclinations of modern economic analysis. One of the fundamental discontinuities between these approaches is that pure and perfect competition is a situation in which economic agents are assumed to be incapable of manipulating prices; they are 'price-takers', while oligopolistic firms and monopolies are considered to have the power to set the price(s) in their market(s). Despite certain shared characteristics, there is then a different theory (and sometimes several) for each market structure, and no unitary theory.

The theory of markets proposed by Cournot, several decades before the analysis of market structures emerged, was, on the contrary, a unitary theory, in which we can move from one structure to another without changing the framework, the optimization mechanism; only the number of suppliers gradually changes.

Moreover, the theory is founded on a limited number of hypotheses:

- Maximization of profit: each producer seeks maximum profit.
- Residual demand: to this end, each producer manipulates the market price, assuming that his competitors, if there are any, leave him a constant share of consumer demand.

It is this second hypothesis that really characterizes Cournot's theory, and it is thus useful to describe clearly its meaning and consequences.

In the case of two competitors (duopoly), Cournot proposed an analysis of the market whereby each producer establishes his production plan in the belief that it will not prompt the competitor to modify his plans. The producer can therefore consider his competitor's observed policy to be stable, and the demand that his competitor does not meet can only be met by the producer's own supply. He considers himself as the 'owner' of this share of the demand (the residual demand) for the same reason that the monopolist is the 'owner' of all the demand in his market. The analysis of duopoly therefore boils down to the analysis of the policies adopted by two small monopolies. When Cournot examined duopoly, he had already presented his theory of monopoly, and it only remained for him to apply it to this particular case. This theory made it possible to specify what the market equilibrium would be; in modern jargon, this is, of course, a 'Cournot equilibrium'.

There is no reason why this analysis should stop at two firms: the reasoning can be extended to an ever greater number of firms and continue to give solid and intuitively satisfying results. For a large number of competitors, we could speak of 'unlimited competition',[4] whereas modern theory refers to this market state as 'pure and perfect competition' (PPC), with the addition, it is true, of some extra hypotheses. What is remarkable is that Cournot, with only these two hypotheses, formulated the condition of fundamental equilibrium for this market, that is, equality between price and marginal cost, long before the theorists of PPC. What might, however, in retrospect, appear to be a *tour de force* was only achieved by Cournot at the price of an implausible representation of market mechanisms. In fact, the hypothesis of *residual demand*, which is indispensable here, while being credible up to a certain point in the case of small number oligopolies, is hardly tenable in the context of small economic agents. For example, it is difficult to imagine a producer representing a market share of one ten-thousandth acting as though he were a small monopoly in the belief that he could fix the price on this market.

Another notable difference between the two approaches is that Cournot's analysis starts with a monopoly and then gradually increases the number of players on the market. Closely connected with Cournot's hypotheses, this method of exposition has the advantage of sticking relatively closely to what we can imagine to be the real historical development of markets, starting with a monopoly situation, followed by the entry of more and more competitors, attracted by competitive forces, until it becomes impossible for new arrivals to make a profit by entering a market saturated by abundant supply.

Thus, despite the elegance of its architecture and its consistency with observable modes of market development, Cournot's theory of markets has not been adopted as standard theory by modern economists, who prefer to use other hypotheses, a little more reasonable than those of Cournot, but still far from realistic, to describe competitive markets. In reality, the central hypothesis of PPC is the polar opposite of Cournot's hypothesis that each agent fixes his production while at the same time manipulating the market price. This is the hypothesis of agents as 'price-takers', resulting in an object, the 'market', which may be easy for the economist to study, but which is fundamentally unacceptable, because the price is assumed to fix itself 'on its own', without the intervention of any agent.

Cournot's theory of markets does, however, constitute the generally recognized basis for the study of situations outside of PPC, what is now called 'imperfect competition'. But this study, analysing many cases not included in Cournot's initial programme, is of a conceptual and formal complexity far beyond whatever could have been imagined in 1838.

THE ECONOMIC ANALYSIS OF TAXATION

Alongside the theory of markets, Cournot touched on many other questions, though without exploring them in as much detail, and defined and used instruments and concepts without really building them into a systematic theory. Some of these are now central to modern economic science.

One example of a question explored only too briefly is that of *tax incidence*. By devoting a chapter of *Recherches* to 'the influence of taxation on commodities produced under a monopoly' (Cournot, 1897 [1838], p.67), Cournot sought to show that the question of taxation could be approached in a rational manner. He was not, of course, the first economist to concern himself with this issue. Taxation is a favourite theme of economists: the search for a tax system that contributes to the common good can be traced back at least as far as Vauban and Boisguilbert, and was a central interest of the physiocrats.

Once again, however, Cournot's method was innovative. His aim was to *evaluate* the practical solutions as accurately as possible; it is here, indeed, that Cournot came closest to the engineer–economists and the idea of *social engineering*. It is also here that his preoccupation with the general interest was most evident. He expressed a concern for the output – the efficiency – of the tax from a social point of view, and no longer simply from the point of view of fiscal administration.

Within the context of monopoly, Cournot's analysis takes the form of a comparison between two main systems: tax being levied either on the monopolist's income or on his sales. In the latter case, he examined three different modalities: the tax could be a fixed sum per unit sold, a percentage of sales or a deduction in kind proportional to the quantity sold.

How can we judge whether one tax is better or worse than another? Cournot did not pass judgement on the *amount* of the tax, apparently considering that the justification for this lay outside the realm of pure logic in which he sought to operate, but only on the fiscal technique. This is an important question, because

> [e]ven though this tax does not affect consumers it may be nevertheless very prejudicial to public interests … because the part withdrawn by the tax from the income of the producer is ordinarily employed in a manner less advantageous for the increase of the annual product, the national wealth, and the comfort of the people, than if it had remained at the disposal of the producer himself. (Cournot, 1897 [1838], pp. 68–9)

We can see that, for Cournot, growth is one of the fundamental concerns – or at least constraints – of taxation, a viewpoint that has obviously lost none of its relevance.

ESSENTIAL CONCEPTS OF ECONOMIC ANALYSIS

Among the concepts that Cournot either defined or helped to define, we can include *price elasticity* and *marginal cost*. These concepts are considered indispensable in economics, and they are also widely used outside the strictly scientific context.[5]

Price Elasticity

Cournot may not have actually defined price elasticity, but he gave us all the tools needed to do so in the chapter devoted to the law of demand, or '*loi du débit*'. This is a decreasing function of price, and certain hypotheses can be applied to it:

> Suppose that when the price becomes $p + \Delta p$, the annual consumption (…) becomes $D - \Delta D$. According as
>
> $$\frac{\Delta D}{\Delta p} < \frac{D}{p} \text{ or } \frac{\Delta D}{\Delta p} > \frac{D}{p},^6$$
>
> the increase in price, Δp, will increase or diminish the product $pF(p)$; and, consequently, it will be known whether the two values p and $p + \Delta p$ (assuming Δp to be a small fraction of p) fall above or below the value which makes the product under consideration a maximum. (Cournot, 1897 [1838], pp. 53–4)

Clearly, the alternative proposed by Cournot can be written:

$$\frac{\Delta D}{\Delta p} \frac{p}{D} < \text{or} > 1$$

which is nothing other than the proposition: 'price elasticity is smaller or larger than 1'. Even if Cournot's general remarks on this subject are not really clear, the tool remains relevant.

Marginal Cost

Marginal cost plays an important role in *Recherches*. This 'differential coefficient', which Cournot referred to poetically as $\varphi'(D)$,

> ... is capable of increasing or decreasing as D increases, according to the nature of the producing forces and of the articles produced.
>
> For what are properly called *manufactured articles*, it is generally the case that the cost becomes proportionally less as production increases, or, in other words, when D increases $\varphi'(D)$ is a decreasing function. This comes from better organization of the work, from discounts on the price of raw materials for large purchases, and finally from the reduction of what is known to producers as *general expense*. It may happen, however, even in exploiting products of this nature, that when the exploitation is carried beyond certain limits, it induces higher prices for raw materials and labour, to the point where $\varphi'(D)$ again begins to increase with D. (Cournot, 1897 [1838], pp. 59–60)

This constitutes a complete presentation of the theory of decreasing costs, resulting from both *increasing returns* and favourable trading conditions. The U-shaped cost curve, which modern economists consider to be the standard case, is portrayed as a likely prospect, but not inevitable. In these few sentences – admirably clear, but all too brief – Cournot provided a masterly précis of the theory of costs. But who was ever going to pay enough attention to these ideas, which, although extremely novel, were presented as obvious facts, and which involved a *differential coefficient* that did not even have a name! This differential coefficient is the marginal cost, and in all likelihood, if he had pushed the concept a little, simply by giving it a name,[7] Cournot could have considerably accelerated the 'discovery', or rather the systematization, of marginalism, which actually took place in the 1870s thanks to Jevons, Menger and Walras. With Cournot, it is clear that having new ideas and being able to promote them are two very different talents.

Cournot, however, went even further, the analysis of manufactured products being just one part of his exposition:

> Whenever it is a question of working agricultural lands, of mines, or of quarries, *i.e.* of what is essentially real estate, the function $\varphi'(D)$ increases with D ; and, as we shall soon see, it is in consequence of this fact alone that farms, mines and quarries yield a net revenue to their owners, long before all has been extracted from the soil which it is physically able to produce, and notwithstanding the great subdivision of these properties, which causes between producers a competition which can be considered as unlimited. On the contrary, investments made under the condition that as

D increases φ'(*D*) decreases, can only yield a net income or a *rent* in the case of a monopoly properly so-called, or of competition sufficiently limited to allow the effects of a monopoly collectively maintained to be still perceptible. (Ibid., p. 60)

As in Ricardo's analysis, diminishing returns (or more accurately, here, increasing unit costs) produce the economic or farm rent. Without explicitly recognizing that Ricardo's analysis preceded his own,[8] Cournot showed that he accepted the reasoning while at the same time situating it within a more general context. It is clear on reading this text that the theory of rent is not regarded as a specificity of the factor of production 'land', nor of any given order of succession in land exploitation; it is the application to particular circumstances of a more general law that could, after all, apply equally well in industrial sectors; this is not far off Marshall's 'quasi-rent'.[9]

By contrasting the behaviour of costs in the 'primary' sector with that of industry, Cournot indicated the importance of the interaction between the conditions of production and the conditions of competition in a market. It is this interaction that makes this branch of economics such a rich domain.

THE UNCERTAIN DESTINY OF COURNOT'S ECONOMIC WORKS

Little-known and Poorly Received Theories

For several decades after its publication, the exceptional achievement of *Recherches* was almost completely overlooked in French intellectual life. Cournot pursued his career as a senior civil servant: Professor of Calculus at Lyon University in 1834, then Rector of the Academy of Grenoble and Professor in the Faculty of Sciences in 1835. In 1836, he was appointed Inspector General of Education, then, from 1854 to 1861, Rector of the Academy of Dijon. He was not a professional economist, but he remained an active thinker and writer; his interest covered all fields of knowledge, with the philosophy of sciences and especially of probabilities becoming his major preoccupations (Martin, 1994, 1995).

Thus, after 1838, political economy was no longer one of Cournot's prime concerns; not only did he not publish any other work on economics until 1863, but neither does he appear to have made any effort to spread his ideas, be it among the general public – which is quite understandable, given the nature of *Recherches* – or among the very people to whom his work was addressed, the engineer–economists. Cournot behaved as if the accuracy and relevance of his treatise were sure to be recognized sooner or later (as indeed they were, although it certainly took a long time!). He did not undertake any promotion of his ideas, or participate in the debates on the organization of society held by socialists (either 'utopian' or 'scientific'), philosophers, economists, public law specialists and so on; nor did he seek to form a school, an essential basis for the diffusion of new theories. Although it is not easy to explain this attitude, the idea that Cournot had lost interest in the discipline is implausible; that he considered *Recherches* to be a fully realized work, complete and unable to be improved upon, is equally unlikely; his professional career left him little time to pursue his economic research, but this alone cannot explain his apparent disinterest. In his last years, however, Cournot did return to economic theory in two works that present elements of *Recherches*, particularly the main conclusions of the theory of markets in a non-mathematical form.

Recherches took a long time to attract the attention of the intellectual world. A review of the book appeared in the *Canadian Journal of Industry, Science and Art* in 1857 (Cherriman, 1857); it was probably not widely read in France, and we have no evidence that Cournot knew about it. Fauveau (1867) published a short article essentially concerned, not with Cournot's theory itself, but with the difficulties involved in reading (or understanding) the mathematical signs. On publication of *Principes de la théorie des richesses* (Cournot, [1863] 1981), Cournot's second work devoted to economics, Fontenay wrote a critique of it (de Fontenay, 1863), but it was only in 1883, six years after Cournot's death, that the first serious analysis of *Recherches* appeared in France. This was a fundamental examination, written by the most eminent French mathematician of the time, Joseph Bertrand. In fact, Bertrand's primary object (1883) was to criticize Walras's *Théorie mathématique de la richesse sociale* (*Mathematical Theory of Social Wealth*), more current and much more actively promoted by its author; Bertrand judged it appropriate to comment on Cournot's work at the same time. Unconvinced by the application of mathematics to the human sciences, Bertrand was hardly complimentary. Although the criticisms he levelled at Cournot were not nearly as severe as those he aimed at Walras, it is his criticism of the former that has gone down in history; today we speak of 'Bertrand's model' as an alternative to Cournot's model of oligopoly.[10]

Translations were also a long time coming; the first of them, an Italian translation of *Recherches*, was published in 1878, a year after Cournot's death. The first English translation appeared in 1897, and there was no German translation until 1924. Eventually, however, Cournot's economic work did reach a wider public thanks to advances in the discipline, especially the marginalist revolution of the 1870s and the appearance of a new generation of economists convinced of the usefulness of the mathematization[11] of economics.

Debates started up about some of his propositions, in particular the theory of markets. Although the theory of monopoly was widely accepted, the theory of competition met with opposition. From the 1880s on, Francis Edgeworth was the fiercest critic of Cournot – especially of his model of duopoly and oligopoly.

Edgeworth[12] exerted a lasting influence in this domain, both in the intellectual landscape of Britain and, to a lesser degree, in that of the USA (see Edgeworth, 1881, 1889, 1897).

Thus, after languishing in the wilderness of obscurity during the mid-nineteenth century, Cournot's economic theories underwent a period of criticism and rejection at the beginning of the twentieth century. The most glaring defects in the theory of markets were brought to light and considered reason enough to reject the whole body of work (Magnan de Bornier, 2000). To a greater or lesser degree, the many works on imperfect competition that appeared during the late 1920s and the 1930s – a very fertile period in economic theory – all relegated the Cournotian approach to the category of errors of the past (Robinson, 1969; Chamberlin, 1933).

French economists took very little part in these debates of the first half of the twentieth century, of which they seem to have been largely unaware. At best, they considered Cournot more as a precursor to the mathematical economics of their time – the approach founded by Walras and Pareto – rather than a modern economist whose ideas might have some relevance.[13] Among mathematical economists, he was appreciated as a theorist of probability and statistics rather than an economist.

GAME THEORY AND THE COURNOTIAN REVIVAL

In 1950, John Nash described a mathematical solution to the problem of equilibrium in non-cooperative games, a solution that came to be known as the *Nash equilibrium*. This discovery revolutionized game theory, at the time barely inchoate, and has remained a 'concept of solution' of prime importance up to the present day. It is now present in many forms and in many areas of economics, the other social sciences, biology and even computing.

It did not take long for researchers to discover, at the beginning of the 1950s, that the equilibrium defined by Cournot in his theory of markets, essentially in the case of oligopolies, is technically a Nash equilibrium, certain authors going as far as to call it the 'Cournot–Nash equilibrium'. Cournot's work regained a legitimacy that could only be strengthened by his anticipation of an important mathematical discovery by more than a century. What had been treated as naïve and incoherent by the economic theory of the 1930s and 1940s now appeared in a completely different light.

For economists, the advantages presented by the new paradigm of game theory were many and varied, but one of the most important was that it enabled them to represent the *strategies* of economic agents, and more precisely, in the case of complicated markets like oligopolies, to tackle the problem of *strategic interactions*.

The concept of strategic interactions revolves around the fact that each agent defines his strategy in relation to what he believes are (or could be) the strategies of his competitors, and also in relation to the way in which the agent believes he can influence the strategy or actions of his competitors through his own choice of strategy. Together, these two factors generate a very high level of complexity.

Although Cournot's solution to the problem of oligopoly can effectively be regarded as a first formulation of Nash equilibrium, it does not follow, as has too often been supposed, that he recognized or sensed the concept of strategic interactions.[14] On the contrary, his hypothesis of *residual demand*, which he himself considered as more of an obvious fact than a hypothesis, is simply the negation of all strategic interaction. It is only by perceiving the excessive simplification of this hypothesis, by rejecting Cournot's approach, that his successors[15] have gradually developed this idea of interaction. Cournot can only be said to be the originator of this paradigm in the sense that the inadequacies of his model of competition have prompted his successors to recognize the importance of interactions. The renewal of interest in Cournot's economic thought among professional economists since the 1950s is therefore ambiguous; it is largely deserved, but probably for reasons other than those most often envisaged.

The case of Cournot as an inventor in the field of economics is most particular, if not unique. Clearly far ahead of his time, Cournot had almost no interlocutors: the engineer–economists for whom he wrote and who could understand him had no real need for his over-abstract and generalizing approach, and the others, not being able to understand him, preferred to ignore him.

It was not until the arrival of Walras, Jevons, Marshall, Pareto and Irving Fisher (only Walras actually had any contact with him) that Cournot had any true readers and continuators – but they were not interlocutors.

In the twentieth century, it was not until the triumph of game theory that Cournot's theory of markets was taken seriously, and not without the ambiguities inevitably created by such a temporal gap.[16]

NOTES

1. Cournot's position on foreign trade – his reserve with regards to free trade – will not be treated here.
2. One of Ricardo's such methods is the famous example of trade on wine and cloth between Portugal and Great Britain, which illustrates the general principle of comparative advantage, a principle that Ricardo does not really demonstrate. This clearly illustrates the need for a more abstract method for obtaining truly general results.
3. Here he gives his opinion on the subject, 'But this would surpass the powers of mathematical analysis and of our practical methods of calculation, even if the values of all the constants could be assigned to them numerically', (Cournot, 1897 [1838], p. 127).

4. This is the term used by Cournot, and the title of Chapter 8 of *Recherches*.
5. These concepts, for example, are used daily by trade authorities such as the European Commission or the *Conseil de la Concurrence* in France.
6. This is how the equation appeared in Cournot's original work of 1838. The English translation of 1897 contained a misprint.
7. Cournot prefers using 'expenses' to 'costs', and could have spoken of 'additional expenses'.
8. Cournot broached the same subject in *Principes*, 'this famous theory of rents, for which Ricardo is respected', but considers that it is 'an economic fact so simple as to pass almost unnoticed'. He certainly intends to show that Ricardo is wrong to insist on differences of fertility as a major determining factor of rents when what is essential is the differential in the *expense of production* (Cournot [1863] 1981, pp. 75–80).
9. In *Principes*: 'One must have recourse to a more general explanation, one in which Ricardo's explanation fits as a corollary, or as a particular case' (Cournot [1863] 1981, p. 78).
10. This is in fact a misunderstanding, the history of which can be found in Magnan de Bornier (1992).
11. Sometimes, this meant much less mathematization than found in Cournot; such was the case of Alfred Marshall and Clément Colson. These two authors, who wished to limit themselves to a minimum of formalization, are nonetheless true successors to Cournot.
12. Who, it must be remembered, taught at Oxford and held the Drummond chair at All Souls College.
13. The worst case being an economist who knew and described Cournot's theory of markets entirely from the perspective of Edgeworth, Cournot's fiercest critic.
14. For more on this, see Leonard (1994) and Magnan de Bornier (2000).
15. Bowley (1924), Frisch (1933) and von Stackelberg (1934) were the first to have modified or extended the hypothesis of residual demand. They can thus be seen as the first true pioneers of the strategic interaction pardigm.
16. Robert Leonard (1994) has provided valuable developments on this subject.

REFERENCES

Bertrand, J. (1883), 'Théorie Mathématique de la Richesse Sociale, par L. Walras; Recherches sur les Principes Mathématiques de la Théorie des Richesses, par A. Cournot', *Journal des Savants*, September, 499–508.

Bowley, A.L. (1924), *Mathematical Groundwork of Economics*, Oxford: Oxford University Press.

Chamberlin, E.H. (1933), *The Theory of Monopolistic Competition*, Cambridge, MA: Harvard University Press. French translation: Chamberlin, E.H. (1954), *La théorie de la concurrence monopolistique*, Paris: PUF.

Cherriman, J.B. (1857), 'Recherches sur les Principes Mathématiques de la Théorie des Richesses, par Augustin Cournot', *Canadian Journal of Industry, Science and Art*, 185–94.

Cournot, A.A. (1838), *Recherches sur les principes mathématiques de la théorie des richesses*, reprinted in G. Jorland (ed.) (1980), *Œuvres complètes*, Tome VIII, Paris: Vrin.

Cournot, A.A. (1863), *Principes de la théorie des richesses*, reprinted in G. Jorland (ed.) (1981), *Œuvres complètes*, Tome VIII, Paris: Vrin.

Cournot, A.A. (1877), *Revue sommaire des doctrines économiques*, reprinted in G. Jorland (ed.) (1982), *Œuvres complètes*, Tome X, Paris: Vrin.

Cournot, A.A. (1897) [1838], *Researches into the Mathematical Principles of the Theory of Wealth* [*Recherches sur les principes mathématiques de la théorie des richesses*], translated by N.T. Bacon with a Bibliography of Mathematical Economics by I. Fisher, New York: Macmillan.

Fontenay, R. de (1863), 'Principes de la Théorie des Richesses par M. Cournot', *Journal des Economistes*, 231–51.

Edgeworth, F.Y. (1881), *Mathematical Psychics. An Essay on the Application of Mathematics to the Moral Sciences*, London: C. Kegan Paul.

Edgeworth, F.Y. (1889), 'Points at which Mathematical Reasoning is applicable to Political Economy' (Opening Address to the British Association, section F, Economic science and statistics), *Nature*, 496–509.

Edgeworth, F.Y. (1897), 'La Teoria Pura del Monopolio', French translation in G. Jorland (ed.) (1980), *A. A. Cournot: Œuvres complètes*, Tome VIII, Paris: Vrin.

Fauveau, P.-G. (1867), 'Considérations mathématiques sur la théorie de la valeur', *Journal des Economistes*, 31–40.

Frisch, R. (1933), 'Monopole – Polypole – la notion de force dans l'économie', *Nationalekonomisk Tidsskrift*, **LXXI**, 241–59.

Leonard, R.J. (1994), 'Reading Cournot, Reading Nash: the Creation and Stabilisation of the Nash Equilibrium', *The Economic Journal*, **104** (424), 492–511.

Magnan de Bornier, J. (1992), 'The "Cournot–Bertrand Debate": A Historical Perspective', *History of Political Economy*, **24** (3), 623–56.

Magnan de Bornier, J. (2000), 'Cournot avant Nash: grandeur et limites d'un modèle unitaire de la concurrence', *Cahiers d'Économie Politique*, **37**, 101–25.

Martin, T. (1994), 'La valeur objective du calcul des probabilités selon Cournot', *Mathématiques et Sciences Humaines*, **127**, 5–17.

Martin, T. (1995), 'Probabilités et philosophie des mathématiques chez Cournot', *Revue d'Histoire des Mathématiques*, **1**, 111–38.

Robinson, J. (1969), *The Economics of Imperfect Competition*, London: Macmillan.

Stackelberg, H. von (1934), *Marktform und Gleichgewicht*, Vienna and Berlin: Springer.

2. Cournot's probabilistic epistemology

Thierry Martin

INTRODUCTION

One of the most immediately striking features of Cournot's work is its wide diversity. Although *Recherches sur les principes mathématiques de la théorie des richesses* (1838) falls within the domain of economics, a field to which he returned in *Principes de la théorie des richesses* (1863) and *Revue sommaire des doctrines économiques* (1877), Cournot's publications were first and foremost those of a mathematician, including his 1847 work, *De l'origine et des limites de la correspondance entre l'algèbre et la géométrie*, numerous scientific articles and reports published between 1825 and 1831,[1] and his treatises on infinitesimal calculus (1841) and probability calculus (1843). His work is also that of a philosopher eager to subject all contemporary scientific knowledge to critical investigation, an approach he adopted in *Essai sur les fondements de nos connnaissances et sur les caractères de la critique philosophique* (1851) and *Traité de l'enchaînement des idées fondamentales dans les sciences et dans l'histoire* (1861), to which he added a historical dimension in *Considérations sur la marche des idées et des événements dans les temps modernes* (1872) and which he summed up in *Matérialisme, vitalisme, rationalisme. Études sur l'emploi des données de la science en philosophie* in 1875. Finally (although this aspect of his work is not relevant to our present purposes), Cournot held the position of Rector of the Academy of Dijon and displayed an enduring interest in questions of education, embodied in his work *Des Institutions d'instruction publique en France* (1864).

This diversity raises the twin questions of the unity and internal coherence of Cournot's work. This issue is of more particular interest to a historian of thought specializing in the nineteenth century, and we shall not attempt to tackle it *per se*, in all its different aspects, in this chapter. What does interest us is the way that Cournot's mathematical work is inextricably linked to his philosophical project. Even when his concerns are of a clearly mathematical nature, they are always accompanied by an epistemological reflection on the meaning and scope of mathematical concepts, on the unity of the mathematical field, its foundations and its relations with other fields of knowledge. The main purpose of this epistemological reflection is to discover the order and sequence of ideas, whether logical or historical. In this way, Cournot's mathematical works on the one hand, and his philosophical reflection and historical analyses on the other, are closely interconnected.

This orientation is not specific to the philosophy of mathematics: according to Cournot, it tackles the central question animating philosophy in its application to the different sciences. If scientists cannot hope to determine the essential nature of things, a task left to the speculations of metaphysicians, they must do their utmost to identify and define the relations that exist between phenomena and that explain the effects of their interactions. The difficulty then lies in determining whether the order and rational connections perceived by the scientist correspond to the real linking of the phenomena themselves. 'Does the human mind', asked Cournot in *Matérialisme* ([1875] 1979, p. 199[2]), 'resemble the flat mirror or the cylindrical mirror? Is it constituted in such a way as to apprehend the relations of things as they are, without altering them in some essential way?'[3] The approach Cournot adopted to study this question consisted, not in a Kantian-style return to the source of knowledge, seeking therein the *a priori* conditions of the possibility of all knowledge within the powers of the knowing subject, but rather, in the tradition of Auguste Comte,[4] in concentrating on the products of knowledge, examining, in both their internal constitution and history, the results of the diversified activity of scientists. Cournot's solution was of a probabilistic character. It involved calculating the probability that the relations through which phenomena become intelligible to us are not purely artificial constructions, but correspond to real phenomenal relations. Such is the subject of what would now be called Cournot's epistemology, and which he himself referred to as 'the critical philosophy which probes the foundations of knowledge, judges the representative value of our ideas, and distinguishes between the constitution of the outside world and the configuration of the mirror that reflects it' ([1872] 1973, vol. 2, p. 101). Here, therefore, probabilities occupy a singular position to the extent that, as a mathematical discipline, probability calculus is one of the subjects of epistemological reflection, and yet Cournotian epistemology is, at the same time, dominated by a probabilistic perspective.

The question we wish to explore here is how Cournot's probabilistic epistemology can still instruct us and help us in our reflections today. This is not, therefore, a purely historical question, but it does call for a reconstruction of Cournot's probabilistic thinking, with which the economist, more focused on his analysis of monopoly and market equilibrium, may not be familiar. We therefore propose to outline briefly the guiding principles of Cournot's probabilistic epistemology and to consider how it may relate to his economic thinking, hoping, in the process, to shed light on our original question of the internal coherence of his thought.

THE DUALITY OF THE CONCEPT OF PROBABILITY

The lasting interest of Cournot's probabilistic thinking lies in the reflexive and epistemological character of the analysis he brought to bear on the theory of probabilities and its applicability. Here, more than anywhere else, the question of the correspondence between theory and reality raises problems, not only because probability is not an observable, but also because the answer to this question itself cannot be more than probable (compare Borel, 1939, p. 5). This reflection concerns the significance that we should attach to the concept of probability and to the results obtained from probability calculus. The question is whether probability applies to the events themselves or to the judgements we make about those events. This question has faced us ever since the inception of probability theory,[5] and it has been left open by the axiomatic theory of Kolmogorov, the standard form of probability calculus used today.

For Cournot, however, it was not just a question of determining the significance that should be attached to applications of probability calculus, but of deciding whether or not the application itself was possible. Today, this question may seem surprising, such are the number and variety of uses of probability calculus in the different scientific disciplines, but it was expressed in a radical fashion by d'Alembert in 1767 who, drawing a distinction between what is mathematically valid and what is physically valid, accepted the rigour of mathematical theory, but questioned its applicability; it was again the subject of heated debate among mathematicians and philosophers at the beginning of the nineteenth century.

This explains why Cournot, having laid down the elements of the theory of probabilities, immediately added that we should ask ourselves whether 'this theory is no more than a mental exercise, a curious speculation, or if, on the contrary, it concerns important and very general laws, governing the real world' ([1843] 1984, p. 53).

The choice seems clear, but in fact this phrase covers two separate questions, that of the applicability of the theory and, in the case of a positive answer, that of the significance of its applications. Cournot treated these two questions simultaneously by showing under what conditions the concept of probability can measure a phenomenal reality and, consequently, under what conditions the theory of probabilities possesses an 'objective value', as he put it (1956 [1851] pp. 50–52); the question must be asked concerning the principles in order to found, and so establish beyond doubt, the theory's legitimate claim to the status of a positive science.[6]

In Cournot's terms, the question is therefore to determine whether we can attach an objective significance to the theory of probabilities, or if we must limit ourselves to a subjective interpretation.[7] In this, Cournot launched a subject of reflection, suggested by the work of Bernoulli and roughly outlined by d'Alembert, which is still alive today, and which was to lie at the heart of the debate over the interpretation of probabilities that stirred mathematicians and philosophers during the first half of the twentieth century.

The question is of decisive importance as it involves both a representation of reality and a representation of rational knowledge. On the one hand, affirming that probability has an objective significance means admitting the effective existence of random phenomena, and therefore opposing the hypothesis of complete and universal determinism.[8] On the other hand, depending on the significance attached to the results of calculus, rational knowledge will either be considered as adequate to the task of accounting for reality, or simply as the tool that enables us to construct our representation of it.

On this point, Cournot's thought is fertile on two accounts: philosophically, because of the coherence and refinement of the answer he provided to the above question, and historically, because he was one of the first to confront this question explicitly and for its own sake. From a historical perspective, Cournot was responding to attacks on the legitimacy of the theory of probabilities and its applicability. The fiercest of the nineteenth-century critics, though not the only, was Auguste Comte, who denounced numerical probability as a 'directly irrational and even sophistic' concept, adding that it was founded on a 'radically false' philosophical conception.[9] For Cournot, this was therefore a question of defending the scientific nature of probability calculus and its applicability, particularly in the social domain, against its detractors, whether philosophers, such as Bordas-Desmoulin[10] and Royer-Collard, or mathematicians, such as Poinsot,[11] and giving it a rational foundation, as mentioned above.[12]

The originality of Cournot's approach lay in his rejection of the alternative between objective and subjective interpretations of probability, recognizing the 'double meaning' to which the concept of mathematical probability is open, 'which sometimes pertains to a certain measurement of our knowledge, and sometimes to a measurement of the possibility of things, independently of the knowledge we have of them' ([1843] 1984, Preface, p. 4); the same approach was adopted in the twentieth century, independently of Cournot, by Rudolph Carnap (see Carnap, 1945, 1950). For Cournot, it was not a question of choosing one or the other representation, but of ascribing the conditions and limits of the applicability of the calculus, and therefore of differentiating between the situations in which probability can possess an objective significance and those where it can only be subjectively valid.

We should note that attributing a subjective significance to probability did not lead Cournot to define it as a 'degree of confidence', as the proponents of a 'subjectivist' interpretation, such as Bruno de Finetti and Frank Ramsey, were later to do. When Cournot attributed a subjective significance to probability, he was not considering it as a psychological concept, but simply as the expression of a lack of knowledge: even if the occurrence of a future event is rigorously determined, one can do no more than estimate its probability if one does not know all the causes and conditions that govern this realization. The idea that probability could in this way result from a lack of knowledge presents no problems; it was a common representation throughout the eighteenth century,[13] dominating what has sometimes been called the 'classic interpretation' (Daston, 1988) of probability calculus, running from Pascal through to Poisson and Cournot, and conceiving of probability as an instrument to guide the actions of reasonable men confronted with situations of uncertainty.

It is, on the other hand, much more problematical to establish that probability can effectively measure the possibility of occurrence of an event, or its 'chance', as Cournot called it; it is precisely this point that makes it possible to show that probability is not only a representation made by the subject, varying according to the subject's degree of knowledge, but the measurement of an effective reality. With this in mind, Cournot's analysis introduces a double distinction: the one between mathematical and philosophical probability on the one hand, and the one between the objective and subjective significances of mathematical probability on the other.

MATHEMATICAL PROBABILITY AND PHILOSOPHICAL PROBABILITY

Cournot considers mathematical probability classically as an extension of combinatorial mathematics, probability being defined as the ratio of the number of favourable cases to the number of possible cases, or, within the context of continuous probabilities, as the 'ratio of the range of chances favourable to an event to the total range of chances' ([1843] 1984, p. 29).[14] Mathematical probability is thus open to exact numerical measurement and calculation operations.

This distinguishes mathematical probability from what are called philosophical probabilities, which characterize all the judgements that cannot be formally demonstrated, primarily those by which we attempt to account for reality with the help of explanatory hypotheses. These latter are supported by inductions and analogies, which may have sufficient probative force to impose themselves on rational judgement, but without being able to establish absolute certainty. It is impossible to measure precisely the intensity of this probative force. We certainly possess criteria allowing us to confirm the conformity of a given representation with the phenomenon it describes, but they cannot be expressed numerically.

Chief among these criteria are: (1) the power of the hypothesis in question to bring to light the order of the sequence and generation of phenomena; (2) the simplicity of the hypothesis; and (3) its explanatory fertility.

Nevertheless, although the fact that a hypothesis can be used to establish the order of a set of phenomena may reveal the theoretical interest of that hypothesis, it is insufficient to guarantee its explanatory validity, even less its correspondence with reality. Indeed, far from providing the answer, it actually raises the question. In fact, we can imagine the relations of sequence and inter-dependence between phenomena according to various principles of organization. The need for the ordered arrangement of our knowledge that brings to light the relations established between our representations stems first from the solidarity that unites thought and language in both the expression and the construction of our knowledge. This point was particularly emphasized by Cournot (1956 [1851], ch. 14), although from a different standpoint to that later adopted by Bergson: articulate language is characterized by two fundamental properties, linearity and discontinuity, which make it necessary for us to order our ideas to achieve clarity and intelligibility in their organization and to restore the continuity of our thought and the multidirectional orientation in the relations between ideas, which makes them so rich. Here, we are dealing with what Cournot called the *logical order*, subject to the constraints imposed by language and responding to a pedagogical requirement. It is highly possible, however, that such an organization of knowledge will not correspond to the actual relations that build up between phenomena and that determine their properties. In other words, knowing means more than just arranging our representations of phenomena according to a given classificatory principle, chosen on the grounds of its simplicity and fertility. It is also, and above all, a matter of bringing to light the relations of dependence and subordination that exist between ideas, because of their contents, and between phenomena, because of their natural properties. We should, therefore, differentiate between fundamental ideas and subordinate ideas, the latter being explained in terms of their dependence on the former. Likewise, in the order of phenomena we should differentiate between the determinant and the determined. Alongside the logical order, we must therefore seek to attain what Cournot calls the *rational order*, that is to say, the order that succeeds in accounting for these relations of dependence between ideas, and at the same time between phenomena, which enables us to conceive their generation. The whole difficulty then resides in being able to identify this *rational order* that organizes phenomenal relations. This is exactly the task that probabilistic epistemology – or the 'philosophical critique' – must tackle, a task clearly described by Cournot in the field of mathematical knowledge when he defined the aim of the philosophy of mathematics. He wrote that this latter consists

> essentially in discerning the rational order of dependence of as many abstract truths as the sagacity of inventive minds has successively and laboriously discovered, often by very roundabout means. It also consists in preferring one concatenation of propositions to another (although the latter is just as impeccable from the point of view of logic, or sometimes even more convenient logically), because it satisfies better the condition of exhibiting this order and these connections, just as they fol-

low from the nature of things, independently of the means that we have of demonstrating and knowing the truth. (1956 [1851], pp. 475–6; see also [1847] 1989, pp. 366–7)[15]

As this involves phenomenal knowledge, the simplicity of the explanatory hypothesis and its *a posteriori* fruitfulness serve to estimate the probability that the theoretical construction created to explain a set of phenomena corresponds to the rational order.

The simplicity of the hypothesis is of no more than informative value, however: it cannot prove categorically that the hypothesis is realistic, not only because it is sometimes found wanting,[16] but also because the hypothesis that the phenomenon obeys a law that can be simply formulated is itself only probable. Most importantly, moreover, the simplicity of a hypothesis can have several different meanings. The simplicity of the theoretical explanation should not be confused with the simplicity of the mathematical formula that expresses that explanatory principle; this simplicity of the mathematical formula can itself be characterized in different ways: should we judge the simplicity of a hypothesis by the number of coefficients involved in the formula or by their degree? This is why the simplicity of the hypothesis is informative rather than decisive, and in fact intervenes in a negative fashion. Thus, recalling that it is always possible to construct a mathematical law connecting several numerical values, and even, as Leibniz had already demonstrated, that there exists an infinite number of such laws, Cournot specifies, not that the possibility of writing a simple law is sufficient for that law to be considered expressive of the phenomenal relation it describes, but that if

> the mathematical law introduced to show the relation between the observed numbers were to become increasingly complex, it would become less and less probable, in the absence of any other indication, that the succession of these numbers is not the result of chance. (1956 [1851], pp. 54–5)[17]

It is, however, impossible to give a numerical formulation to this reduction in probability, or, consequently, to the relative simplicity of the law.

Likewise, the probability of the hypothesis increases when it can account for phenomena for which it had not originally been envisaged, or even phenomena that were unknown when the hypothesis was formulated. The probability of the hypothesis increases significantly if, in addition to its simplicity, 'facts acquired by observation after the hypothesis has been formulated, as well as those facts which served as the basis for its construction, are unified by it, and especially if facts predicted on the basis of the hypothesis are strikingly confirmed by later observations ...' (ibid., p. 62). It is, however, equally impossible to give a numerical value to the degree of probability that this subsequent confirmation bestows on the hypothesis.

Consequently, philosophical probability is both qualitative and subjective. Mathematical probability differs in being both quantitative and capable, under certain conditions, of objective significance.

THE OBJECTIVE VALUE OF THE CONCEPT OF MATHEMATICAL PROBABILITY

To support his assertion that the concept of mathematical probability can have an objective significance, Cournot established the possibility of a correspondence between the planes of the concept and the phenomena by means of two arguments. First, he showed that, contrary to the traditional representation,[18] chance is more than just a subjective illusion resulting from our ignorance of the causes of phenomena: it corresponds to a real situation. In other words, he developed an objectivist conception of chance, positing the existence of random – or 'fortuitous', to use Cournot's term – events, the possibility of whose existence can then be measured probabilistically. Second, and reciprocally, he showed that the concept of mathematical probability could, under certain circumstances, be capable of measuring the physical possibility of fortuitous events, which is established by the principle of physical impossibility. We shall now explore these two arguments briefly.[19]

The Objective Reality of Chance

Cournot defined chance as the accidental meeting of two independent causal series: 'Events brought about by the combination or conjunction of other events which belong to independent series are called *fortuitous* events, or the results of *chance*' (1956 [1851], p. 41).[20]

This representation has often been misconstrued, because it has been interpreted naïvely. To avoid twisting Cournot's thought, we must bear in mind the following points:

1. The distribution of causal relations in linear series has no realistic meaning; for Cournot, it was no more than a useful representation to help him expound his thoughts. He described these linear series as 'groups of concurrent lines, by means of which the *imagination pictures*[21] the bonds which connect events' (ibid., p. 40).
2. The source of the event's fortuitousness lies in the independence of its causes. This serves to ensure the variability of one series when the other series is given. For Cournot, there was no question of absolute independence, such that the two series of phenomena would have no relation with each other, however slender. From the moment that causal series intersect,

they are in relation, even if only spatially and temporally. According to Cournot, however, the independence of two series obtains so long as the events belonging to one of them, or the properties defining those events, are not the product of events belonging to the other series or of their properties. Causal series are independent from each other from the moment that we cannot explain the coincidence of properties defining an event by means of a set of causes necessarily connected with each other, so that we are obliged to identify causes of diverse origins to account for it. Cournot gave a striking historical illustration: the simultaneous death, on 14 June 1800, of two generals of the French Empire, Kléber and Desaix, in totally unrelated circumstances:

> when the two great brothers-in-arms, Desaix and Kléber, fell on the same day, indeed almost at the same moment, one on the field of battle at Marengo, the other, at the hand of a fanatic, in the city of Cairo, there certainly was no connection between the maneuvers of the armies on the plains of Piedmont and the causes which, on the same day, led the assassin to attempt his work. Furthermore, there was no connection between these diverse causes and the circumstances of previous campaigns along the Rhine which had led those interested in the glory of our arms to link together the names of Desaix and Kléber'. (Ibid., p. 42)

This example may be anecdotal, but it highlights the central element of Cournot's doctrine. Chance is not the result of an absence of cause, which would be absurd, but of the absence of solidarity between the different causes that combine to produce an event. A fortuitous event is therefore caused, but not necessary: it is impossible to account fully for its occurrence by invoking a law that could exhaust the whole contents. This means that we cannot account for the event without also taking into consideration the irreducible elements of the system of laws governing the phenomena, the initial data that we observe but cannot deduce. In Cournot's terms, this complementarity between the necessity of law and observed data is expressed by the distinction between law and fact, between theoretical knowledge and historical knowledge – two distinct but complementary modalities of scientific knowledge.

Cournot illustrated this relation between the concepts of chance and theoretical knowledge in Point 304 of *Essai* (pp. 439–41) with an example borrowed from the field of natural phenomena: a comet passing through a planetary system, into which it introduces an accidental disturbance. Such a system, including the periodic return of comets as recorded by astronomical observations, fully respects the postulate of determinism in the sense that it is always possible to calculate all the reciprocal effects that the different constituent bodies have on each other; it is therefore possible to determine the position of a given planet at any given moment, past or future. Cournot added, however, that 'the accuracy of the applications that we may make of the theory to future phenomena will rest upon the hypothesis that no unforeseen event [such as the passage of a hitherto unknown comet] will occur to disturb the condition of the system' (ibid., p. 440). Admittedly,

> if we were to know perfectly the present state of the whole universe, and not only that of the bodies which make up our planetary system, we should be in a position to predict theoretically a similar occasion or to affirm that one has not occurred. But … grounds would still remain for considering the planetary system as forming a separate system in the universe, a system having its own theory; and events whose sequence is determined by the laws and by the particular organization of the system should not be confused with accidental and adventitious disturbances whose causes lie outside of this system. These are those irregular and fortuitous external influences which must be regarded as becoming a part of knowledge under the heading of historical data, in contrast with that which is for us the regular result of the permanent laws and of the nature of the system. (Ibid., pp. 440–41)

This representation has three important consequences.

1. Already, as we saw above, affirming the objective reality of fortuitous situations has the consequence of rendering chance and determinism compatible. We must therefore conceive, not so much of islets of fortuitousness dotting, as it were, the sea of determinism, but rather of degrees of fortuitousness, and consequently of different modes of solidarity between phenomena. Thus, wrote Cournot, 'Natural phenomena, being linked to one another, form a network all the parts of which are connected with one another, but neither in the same manner nor to the same degree' (ibid., p. 97). Thus, contrary to the Laplacian assertion of complete, universal determinism, which leaves open the hope of an absolute triumph of mechanics, we must envisage a multiplicity of modes for explaining phenomena and the complexity of their relations.
2. The fortuitousness of an event does not entail its unpredictability. Precise knowledge of the causes of an event and the parameters involved in its occurrence may enable us to predict the event, but, from the moment that these causes and parameters are not necessarily connected in a relation of reciprocal dependence, they do not eliminate its fortuitousness. The applicability of probability calculus is thereby justified, at least in principle.
3. Neither does the fortuitousness of an event entail its scarcity. There is nothing exceptional about fortuitous situations. Generally, however, we only pay attention to chance events when we feel there is something singular and remarkable about them. History has recalled the coincidence in the deaths of Desaix and Kléber, and forgotten all the others who died tragically, but anonymously, on the same day. Moreover, the commonplace

nature of fortuitous situations holds true for all fields of reality, whether they are natural or human. This is why Cournot, while pointing out the limits to the mechanical explanation of phenomena, emphasized at the same time the vast scope of application of probability calculus:

> Given the present state of our knowledge, we cannot, and we may boldly announce that we never shall be able to, explain the actions of intelligent and moral living beings by the mechanics of geometricians. It is not, therefore, by way of geometry or mechanics that these actions fall within the domain of numbers; but they are placed in that domain, insofar as the concepts of combination and luck, cause and chance, are superior in the order of abstractions to geometry and mechanics, and apply to the facts of living nature, to those of the intellectual world and of the moral world, as they do to the phenomena produced by the movements of inert matter. ([1843] 1984, p. 61)

The Principle of Physical Impossibility

Cournot called on the concept of the physically impossible event to support his theory of chance. Examples include trying to balance a cone on its tip, or applying a force exactly through the centre of a sphere so that its translation is not accompanied by any rotary movement. Such events are characterized not by the fact that the probability of their occurrence is very low, their conditions of production being so difficult to obtain, but more radically by the fact that they only have one chance in favour of their realization as opposed to an infinite number of chances against it. According to Cournot, the consequence of this disproportion is that such an event cannot occur within a finite number of tests, and therefore within the conditions of experience. Inversely, we could consider as physically certain an event whose contrary is physically impossible, in other words 'an event whose mathematical probability deviates from unity by no assignable fraction, no matter how small. Such an event, however, must not be confused with that which brings together absolutely all the combinations or all the chances in its favor, and hence is certain, in the mathematical sense of that term' (1956 [1851], p. 47).

As a consequence, the concept of the physically impossible event plays a particularly important role in our conception of the applicability of probability calculus, for it enables us to make the transition from mathematical probability to physical reality, and therefore from the conceptual plane to the plane of reality, in so far as it relates a mathematical determination – the ratio of one positive chance to an infinity of negative chances – and a physical reality – the non-existence of the event. Such a concept, Cournot wrote, therefore confers an 'objective and phenomenal value' to the theory of probabilities ([1843] 1984, p. 58).

The recognition of the objective value of probability, however, suffers from two limitations. First, it concerns only infinitely small probabilities, and second, it is valid only negatively, since the principle of physical impossibility entails the non-existence of the event. To obtain a more general and more positive result, Cournot used Bernoulli's theorem, arguing that as the number of tests increases, it is the probability of a perceptible divergence between frequencies and probabilities that tends to become physically impossible. At the limit, that is to say under the hypothesis of an infinite number of tests, the probability of a divergence between probabilities and frequencies becomes infinitely small, so that it becomes physically impossible 'for the two ratios to differ from each other by any fraction, however small' (ibid., p. 59). To put it another way, the possibility of a significant divergence between frequencies and probabilities can be considered negligible, and the mathematical probability, here defined as the limit of frequencies, measures the physical possibility of the event: 'The mathematical probability is no longer simply an abstract ratio, stemming from our mental viewpoint, but the expression of a ratio supported by the very nature of things and evinced by observation' (ibid.).

As we can see, the concept of the physically impossible event relies on the application of a principle of negligible probability. Cournot was not the first to make use of such a principle. Jacob Bernoulli had already defined the 'morally impossible' event as the opposite of the 'morally certain' event, defining the latter as follows: 'Something is morally certain if its probability is so close to certainty that the shortfall is imperceptible' ([1713] 1987, p. 213). Buffon had asserted that an event whose probability is lower than one in 10 000 'should be considered void, and any fear or hope that lies below ten thousand, should not influence us or occupy our hearts or heads even for one moment' ([1777] 1977, p. 38). Cournot, however, gave the concept a rigorous expression (although it raises several difficulties) by requiring that the one and only chance in favour of the event's occurrence should be opposed by the infinity of chances against it. Why, indeed, should it be impossible to balance a cone, assumed to be perfectly homogeneous, on its tip? 'Among the infinite number of directions that chance must randomly bring about', Cournot replied, 'only one is compatible with equilibrium: it is as if one had to lay one's hand by chance on the one white ball mixed in, not with a million, not with a thousand million or many thousands of millions, but with an infinity of black balls' ([1872] 1973, vol. 3, pp. 182–3).[22]

We shall not discuss the legitimacy of this principle here, but it should be noted that the attribution of an objective value of mathematical probability is only possible under strict restrictive conditions, namely that it is applied to a fortuitous event, and therefore to an event produced by a combination of independent causes. Whenever this condition cannot be satisfied, the determination of the probability will have only a subjective value.

STATISTICS AND ECONOMICS

The analysis presented above nevertheless raises a problem. When he turned his attention to statistics, Cournot gave it a field of application as extensive as the one he attributed to probability calculus. In effect, he affirmed that 'phenomena that occur in the celestial spaces ... can be submitted to the rules and investigations of statistics, like atmospheric agitations, disturbances of the animal economy, and like the most complex events that arise, in the state of society, out of the friction between individuals and peoples' ([1843] 1984, p. 125).

Yet the role he gave to economic and social events in *Exposition* was limited, only touching on demography, insurance theory and legal statistics. Furthermore, in his treatment of these subjects, he insisted on the difficulties of statistical processing. This suggests that there is a conflict between Cournot's epistemological position and its effective implementation. He affirmed the general heuristic power of statistics, whose aim is the 'investigation of the causes governing phenomena of the physical or social order' (ibid., p. 138), but at the same time he manifested 'resistance' (Ménard, 1977) to the application of statistics to economic phenomena.

When we take into account the project motivating Cournot and the historical context in which he worked, however, this problem disappears.

On the one hand, as Yves Breton (1987) observed, the application of statistical instruments to the field of economics remained tentative and provoked fierce controversy among liberal economists during the first half of the nineteenth century. In particular, Breton pointed out that the application of probabilities to economic phenomena was restricted to demographic questions, the calculation of life annuities and insurance theory. On this point, Cournot's work was conventional.

On the other hand, Cournot envisaged the fruitful use of economic statistics as early as 1838 with *Recherches*. Of course, when it comes to explaining the way several interdependent variables tend towards a state of equilibrium, we can understand why Cournot resorted to the mechanical model and the theory of functions, but that in no way excludes the possibility of attributing a role to statistical analysis. Thus, in chapter 4 of *Recherches*, which studies the relation between price and demand, statistics comes into play as the instrument by which the empirical formula of the law of demand can be constructed. In fact, Cournot explained, this law depends on a large number of economic and social factors of different natures: 'on the kind of utility of the article, on the nature of the services it can render or the enjoyments it can procure, on the habits and customs of the people, on the average wealth, and on the scale on which wealth is distributed' (1897 [1838], p. 47). Consequently, it cannot be constructed algebraically, he continued, any more than 'the law of mortality, and all the laws whose determination enters into the field of statistics, or what is called social arithmetic'. It is therefore up to observation to provide 'the means of drawing up between proper limits a table of the corresponding values of D and p' (*idem*). Here, D denotes yearly demand, a function of the price p, thanks to which we can then construct the 'empirical formula' by which the demand curve can be represented. Cournot was doubtless aware that such an undertaking was vulnerable to obstacles that could jeopardize its realization, 'on account of the difficulty of obtaining observations of sufficient number and accuracy, and also on account of the progressive variations which the law of demand must undergo in a country which has not yet reached a practically stationary condition ...' (ibid., p. 48). Be that as it may, Cournot did not oppose the formal and analytical approaches to the use of the statistical instrument. On the contrary, he considered them to be complementary. Analysis, he explained, 'by showing what determinate relations exist between unknown quantities, ... reduces these unknown quantities to the smallest possible number, and guides the observer to the best observations for discovering their values. It reduces and coördinates statistical documents ; and it diminishes the labour of statisticians at the same time that it throws light on them' (ibid., pp. 48–9). To illustrate this complementarity, he gave the example of a survey on mortality in Duvillard's 1806 work. If it is not possible to attribute *a priori* an algebraic form to the law of mortality, nor the form of the age distribution function in a stationary population, Duvillard succeeded in showing how these two functions are linked by a simple algebraic relation. He did it so well, observed Cournot, that when enough statistical observations have been made to enable a table of mortality to be drawn up, it will be possible to deduce the law of population age distribution without any need to make further observations. Cournot later returned to this comparison between the law of mortality and the law of demand in *Principes*, again recognizing that it would be 'a long time before we will be able to construct and confidently use [empirical tables], because of the difficulty in obtaining exact and conclusive documents in a great enough number to compensate for accidental irregularities' ([1863] 1981, p. 67).

Finally, and most importantly, Cournot's analysis of statistics in *Exposition* shares the same epistemological and critical orientation as his analysis of probabilities. There is no expression of distrust or principled resistance as regards the fruitfulness of statistics; on the contrary, Cournot showed a clear desire to explore the conditions and difficulties of application of the theory, with a view to guaranteeing its scientific foundation and exposing any inept or unjustifiable claims. This critical approach was expressed particularly strongly in *Exposition*. Analysing the birth of statistics as an independent discipline during the nineteenth century, Michel Armatte (1991) has shown how, during the first half of that century, two very different conceptions struggled for dominance, one of them descriptive and empirical, born out of the German tradition, the other mathematical and closely connected with the theory of probabilities. It is in this context that Cournot's position can best be understood.[23] Thus, when he denounced what he considered 'exuberant' developments in statistics, his aim was to 'warn against untimely and inappropriate applications that could discredit it for a time' ([1843] 1984, p. 123) and to promote mathematical statistics over and above a simple accumulation of numerical data.

Once again, the aim of this analysis of the epistemological status and applications of statistics is to differentiate between 'the constitution of the external world and the configuration of the mirror that reflects it' (Cournot, [1872] 1973, p. 101): to distinguish, in other words, within the statistical results, between what is due to the phenomena themselves and what results from the intervention of the informed subject and the instruments she uses. Cournot wrote that the statistician must 'as far as possible, by rational discussion, isolate the immediate data of observation from the modifications that affect those data and that are simply due to the observer's point of view and the means of observation available to him' ([1843] 1984, p. 125). Here Cournot came up against a particular difficulty arising out of the need to define the classifications of the population under study and the criteria governing those classifications. Both the criteria and the separation into distinct categories – into 'sections', as Cournot put it – involve a 'conjectural judgement, itself founded on probabilities, but on probabilities that cannot be reduced to an enumeration of chances, and the discussion of which does not strictly belong to the doctrine of mathematical probabilities' (ibid., p. 132), in other words philosophical probabilities.

Thus Cournot did not in any way question the capacity of statistics to contribute to the intelligibility of economic and social phenomena; on the contrary, he sought to determine their conditions of validity. Such an undertaking is essential, because if statistical results are not subjected to an interpretation[24] that gives them meaning, if they are considered independently of the methods that made them feasible, they risk being abandoned to arbitrariness and to the incomprehension of their users. So it is with the comparative analysis needed to determine the 'sections':

> Ordinarily, these tests conducted by the experimenter leave no traces; the public only knows the result that appeared to deserve presentation; consequently, someone with no knowledge of the work of testing which has brought this result to the fore will have absolutely no fixed rule for wagering on whether or not the result is attributable to the anomalies of chance.' (Ibid., p. 130)

CONCLUSION

In this analysis, we have been able to verify that Cournot's approach to scientific knowledge, in general, and mathematical knowledge, in particular, is never exclusively technical. It always includes a reflexive and critical dimension that examines the epistemological status and practical function of the theory. Cournot was constantly motivated by the desire to determine the conditions for coherence between theory and reality.

This is also the best way to consider the orientation guiding Cournot's reflections on probability and statistics. By stressing the need for epistemological questioning of the possible interpretations of the probabilistic approach, and by admitting their potential plurality, Cournot paved the way for the decisive debates that were to mark the development of probability calculus and the philosophy of probabilities during the twentieth century, debates whose echoes still resonate today.

At the same time, looking back over the birth of probability calculus, in a chapter devoted to the seventeenth-century 'revolution in mathematics', Cournot saw in it the seeds of a renewal of logic and philosophy, revitalized by the theory of probabilities, a renewal of which he was one of the most enthusiastic advocates:

> The theory of mathematical probability, of which Pascal and Fermat laid the foundations, contained more than just the rational principles of statistics, a science yet to be born when these fine geniuses were alive: by the unexpected precision it gave to the hitherto confused ideas of chance and probability, it established or should have established true principles of criticism of all kinds; it opened or should have opened to logicians the only way out of the circle in which logic had been enclosed since the time of the Stagirite. ([1872] 1973, p. 184)

NOTES

1. These are listed in Martin (2005), and will appear in Tome XI of the *Œuvres complètes*, edited by Bernard Bru and Thierry Martin, to be published by Vrin.
2. All the page references to Cournot's works are taken from the *Œuvres complètes* published by Vrin, under the editorship of André Robinet, with the exception of the English translation of *Recherches* by N.T. Bacon (1897) and *Essai* by M.H. Moore (1956).
3. For a more detailed analysis of this expression, see Claire Salomon-Bayet (1978), who studies its application to Cournot's biological philosophy.
4. A. Comte ([1830–42] 1975, p. 32).
5. It is implied in the approach of Jacques Bernoulli who, in *Ars conjectandi* (1713), defined probability as a degree of certainty, but sought at the same time to give it objective significance by means of the theorem named after him.
6. The mathematical sciences are both pure and positive, inasmuch as they concern 'exact truths that reason is capable of discovering without the help of experience and which can nevertheless always be confirmed by experience, within the limits of approximation that experience allows', ([1847] 1989, p. 355, and 1956 [1851], p. 471).
7. 'It is … from the language of metaphysicians', Cournot acknowledged, 'that I have borrowed, without compunction, the two epithets objective and subjective, which I needed in order to make a radical distinction between the two meanings of the term probability to which the combinations of calculus are applied' ([1843] 1984, Preface, p. 5). It may be desirable, as Norbert Meusnier and Michel Armatte in particular have argued, to replace these polysemous terms, sources of potential confusion, by those of ontic and epistemic probability. Here,

however, I will keep to the terms used by Cournot himself, even if I may have to specify the exact significance when the need arises.

8. In reply to Laplace ([1814] 1986, pp. 32–3), who affirmed that an 'intelligence which, for a given moment in time, knows all the forces by which nature is animated and the respective situation of its constituent beings, if, moreover, it is wide enough to subject these data to analysis, would embrace in the same formula the movements of the largest bodies in the universe and those of the lightest atoms', so well that the calculus of probabilities constitutes 'the most felicitous supplement to the ignorance and weakness of the human mind' (ibid., p. 206), Cournot argued that chance would continue to exist for this fictional intelligence, of which the prerogative is not that it can dispense with calculus, but that it performs it faultlessly (Cournot, [1843] 1984, pp. 59–61); for this, it is sufficient to admit a relative independence between phenomena and between the laws governing them.

9. Comte, *Cours de philosophie positive*, 27th lesson ([1835] 1975, p. 435). Auguste Comte repeated his criticism, applying it to social phenomena in the 49th lesson ([1839] 1975, pp. 168–9): 'Can anyone imagine a more radically irrational conception than that which consists in giving to the whole of social science, as a philosophical basis or a main means of final elaboration, a so-called mathematical theory in which, generally taking signs for ideas, following the usual character of purely metaphysical speculations, one strives to subject to calculation the necessarily sophistic concept of numerical probability, which leads directly to the adoption of our real ignorance as the natural measure of the degree of plausibility of our diverse opinions?'.

10. Seeking to apply probability calculus to natural and social phenomena 'always leads to false or illusory results', wrote J.-B. Bordas-Desmoulin. This project, he continued, 'is one of the greatest extravagances ever to spring into the human mind' (1843, p. 419).

11. The application of probability calculus to the social domain is, in his eyes, 'a sort of aberration of the mind, a false application of science that can only discredit this latter' (Poinsot, 1836, p. 399).

12. Such an undertaking makes it possible to dissociate the theory of probabilities from the sensualist philosophy with which certain thinkers, notably Lacroix (1816), felt that it must necessarily be linked. Right from his first article on probability, Cournot was motivated by the project of establishing the independence of the theory of probabilities with regard to any one philosophical orientation, particularly sensualism (Cournot, [1828] 2005).

13. See for example Bernoulli ([1713] 1987, p. 14–16), or Laplace ([1814] 1986, p. 34).

14. According to the historian Oscar B. Sheynin (1976, p. 153), this was the first *explicit* definition of geometric probability.

15. To illustrate this distinction between the logical order and the rational order, Cournot showed that one can, in keeping with a logical order, deduce Thales's theorem from that of Pythagoras, but that the rational order requires one to operate the other way round, because Thales's theorem contains the reason of Pythagoras' theorem ([1847] 1989, pp. 172–87).

16. 'It is not enough for a hypothesis to possess more simplicity: for, how many times have we not surprised nature following a path which does not appear to us to be the simplest of all!' wrote Cournot ([1872] 1973, p. 100).

17. Cournot returned to this idea in *Considérations*, affirming, in the text following the passage quoted in the previous note, that a hypothesis is only admissible to the extent that improvements in the observation and calculations 'lead, in the opposite hypothesis, to increasing complications, so that it is clearly demonstrated that it leads us astray' ([1872] 1973, p. 100).

18. For example, Voltaire ([1764] 1867, vol. 1, p. 166): 'What we call *chance* can only be the unknown cause of a known effect'; d'Holbach ([1770] 1990, p. 98): 'We attribute to chance all those effects whose connection with their causes is not seen. Thus, we use the word *chance* to cover our ignorance of those natural causes which produce visible effects through means that we cannot envisage, or in whose manner of action we cannot perceive an order or system of actions similar to our own'; or Laplace ([1776] 1891, p. 145): 'We consider something as being the result of chance when it offers nothing singular to our eyes, or when it indicates a design but we do not know the causes that have produced it. Chance in itself therefore has no

reality: it is no more than a suitable term for designating our ignorance of the way in which the different parts of a phenomenon coordinate with each other and with the rest of Nature'.

19. See Martin (1996) for more detailed explanations.
20. In *Traité*, Cournot later defined chance more accurately as 'a meeting between events that are rationally independent of each other' ([1861] 1981, p. 62).
21. Our italics.
22. It is interesting to note that this principle of physical impossibility was re-interpreted, under the name of 'Cournot's principle', in various forms in the twentieth century by M. Fréchet in 1949, for example, or O. Anderson (1949, 1963), and discussed by Maurice Boudot in 1972. It also constitutes Borel's 'single law of chance' (1914, 1939, 1950), illustrated by the 'typewriting monkeys' metaphor, and the root of the interpretation of probability as a measurement of frequency proposed by Lévy (1925, p. 30; see Bru, 1999), although these authors do not use the actual expression 'Cournot's principle'. For more detailed analysis of this principle, see Shafer and Vovk (2001), and the contribution by Glenn Shafer (Chapter 4) in this volume.
23. 'For statistics to deserve the name of science', wrote Cournot ([1843] 1984, pp. 124–5), 'it must not consist in a simple compilation of facts and figures: it must have its theory, rules and principles. Now, this theory applies to events of a physical and natural order, as it does to those of a social and political order.'
24. This point is explored by Alain Desrosières in his contribution to the present volume (Chapter 7).

REFERENCES

D'Alembert, Jean (1767), *Doutes et questions sur le calcul des probabilités*, reprinted (1821), *Œuvres*, vol. I, Paris: Belin.

Anderson, Oskar (1949), 'Die Begründung des Gesetzes der grossen Zahlen und die Umkehrung des Theorems von Bernoulli', *Dialectica*, **3** (9/10), 65–77.

Anderson, Oskar (1963), *Probleme der statistischen Methodenlehre in den Sozialwissenschaften*, Würzburg: Physica Verlag.

Armatte, Michel (1991), 'Une discipline dans tous ses états: La statistique à travers ses traités (1800–1914)', *Revue de synthèse*, April–June, **CXII** (2), 161–206.

Bernoulli, Jacob (1713), *Ars conjectandi*, part IV translated from Latin into French by Norbert Meusnier, printed (1987), *Jacques Bernoulli et l'Ars Conjectandi*, Rouen: IREM.

Bordas-Desmoulin, Jean-Baptiste (1843), *Le cartésianisme ou la véritable rénovation des sciences*, Paris: J. Hetzel.

Borel, Émile (1914), *Le hasard*, Paris: Félix Alcan.

Borel, Émile (1939), *Valeur pratique et philosophie des probabilités*, Paris: PUF.

Borel, Émile (1950), *Probabilité et certitude*, Paris: Gauthiers-Villars.

Boudot, Maurice (1972), *Logique inductive et probabilité*, Paris: A. Colin.

Breton, Yves (1987), 'Les économistes libéraux français et la statistique. Débat et controverses 1800–1914', *Journal de la société de statistique de Paris*, no. 2, 79–99.

Bru, Bernard (1999), 'Borel, Lévy, Neyman, Pearson et les autres', *Matapli*, **60**, 51–60.

Buffon, Georges-Louis Leclerc de (1777), *Essai d'arithmétique morale*, reprinted in Jacques-Louis Binet and Jacques Roger (1977), *Un autre Buffon*, Paris: Hermann, pp. 32–91.

Carnap, Rudolf (1945), 'The two concepts of probability', *Philosophy and Phenomenological Research*, **5**, 513–32.

Carnap, Rudolf (1950), *Logical Foundations of Probability*, Chicago, IL: The University of Chicago Press.

Comte, Auguste (1830–42), *Cours de philosophie positive*, reprinted (1975), Paris: Hermann.

Cournot, Antoine Augustin (1828), 'De la théorie des probabilités considérée comme la matière d'un enseignement', *Le Lycée*, Tome II, pp. 243–54; republished in the online review *Journ@l électronique d'histoire des probabilités et des statistiques*, www.jehps.net, **1/2**, 2005, *Œuvres complètes*.

Cournot, Antoine Augustin (1838), *Recherches sur les principes mathématiques de la théorie des richesses*, reprinted in Gérard Jorland (ed.) (1980), *Œuvres complètes*, Tome VIII, Paris: Vrin.

Cournot, Antoine-Augustin (1841), *Traité élémentaire de la théorie des fonctions et du calcul infinitésimal*, reprinted in Pierre Dugac (ed.) (1984), *Œuvres complètes*, Tome VI, vol. I, Paris: Vrin.

Cournot, Antoine Augustin (1843), *Exposition de la théorie des chances et des probabilités*, reprinted in Bernard Bru (ed.) (1984), *Œuvres complètes*, Tome I, Paris: Vrin.

Cournot, Antoine-Augustin (1847), *De l'origine et des limites de la correspondance entre l'algèbre et la géométrie*, reprinted in Nelly Bruyère (ed.) (1989), *Œuvres complètes*, Tome VI-2, Paris: Vrin.

Cournot, Antoine Augustin (1851), *Essai sur les fondements de nos connaissances et sur les caractères de la critique philosophique*, reprinted in Jean-Claude Pariente (ed.) (1975), *Œuvres complètes*, Tome II, Paris: Vrin.

Cournot, Antoine Augustin (1861), *Traité de l'enchaînement des idées fondamentales dans les sciences et dans l'histoire*, reprinted in Nelly Bruyère (ed.) (1982), *Œuvres complètes*, Tome III, Paris: Vrin.

Cournot, Antoine Augustin (1863), *Principes de la théorie des richesses*, reprinted in Gérard Jorland (ed.) (1981), *Œuvres complètes*, Tome VIII, Paris: Vrin.

Cournot, Antoine Augustin (1864), *Des Institutions d'instruction publique en France*, reprinted in Angèle Kremer-Marietti (ed.) (1977), *Œuvres complètes*, Tome VII, Paris: Vrin.

Cournot, Antoine Augustin (1872), *Considérations sur la marche des idées et des événements dans les temps modernes*, reprinted in André Robinet (ed.) (1973), *Œuvres complètes*, Tome IV, Paris: Vrin.

Cournot, Antoine Augustin (1875), *Matérialisme, vitalisme, rationalisme. Études sur l'emploi des données de la science en philosophie*, reprinted in Claire Salomon-Bayet (ed.) (1979), *Œuvres complètes*, Tome V, Paris: Vrin.

Cournot, Antoine Augustin (1897) [1838], *Researches into the Mathematical Principles of the Theory of Wealth* [*Recherches sur les principes mathématiques de la théorie des richessess*], translated by N.T. Bacon with a Bibliography of Mathematical Economics by I. Fisher, New York: Macmillan.

Cournot, Antoine Augustin (1956) [1851], *An Essay on the Foundations of our Knowledge* [*Essai sur les fondements de nos connaissances et sur les caractères de la critique philosophique*], translated by M.H. Moore, New York: The Liberal Arts Press.

Daston, Lorraine J. (1988), *Classical Probability in the Enlightenment*, Princeton, NJ: Princeton University Press.

Duvillard de Durand, Emmanuel (1806), *Analyse et Tableaux de l'influence de la petite vérole sur la mortalité à chaque âge, et de celle qu'un préservatif tel que la vaccine peut avoir sur la population et la longévité*, Paris: Imprimerie impériale.

Fréchet, Maurice (1949), 'Rapport général sur les travaux de la section de calcul des probabilités', *XVIII congrès international de philosophie des sciences*, Actualités scientifiques et industrielles, no. 1146, Paris: Hermann, 1951, pp. 3–21; *Les mathématiques et le concret*, Paris: PUF, 1955, pp. 205–30.

d'Holbach, Paul Henri (1770), *Système de la nature, ou des lois du monde physique et du monde moral*, reprinted in J. Boulad-Ayoub (ed.) (1990), Paris: Fayard, coll. Corpus.

Lacroix, Sylvestre-François (1816), *Traité élémentaire du calcul des probabilités*, Paris: Courcier.

Laplace, Pierre-Simon (1776), 'Recherche sur l'intégration des équations différentielles aux différences finies, et sur leur usage dans la théorie des hasards', reprinted in Pierre-Simon Laplace (1891), *Œuvres Complètes*, Tome VIII, pp. 69–197.

Laplace, Pierre-Simon (1814), *Essai philosophique sur les probabilités*, reprinted (1986) Paris: Christian Bourgeois.

Lévy, Paul (1925), *Calcul des probabilités*, Paris: Gauthier-Villars.

Martin, Thierry (1996), *Probabilités et critique philosophique selon Cournot*, Paris, Vrin, coll. 'Mathesis'.

Martin, Thierry (2005), *Nouvelle bibliographie cournotienne*, Besançon: Presses universitaires de Franche-Comté; available online at http://presses-ufc.univ-fcomte.fr.

Ménard, Claude (1977), 'Trois formes de résistance aux statistiques: Say, Cournot, Walras', *Pour une histoire de la statistique*, INSEE, Paris, Economica, pp. 417–30; rev. 2nd edn, trans.: 'Three forms of resistance to statistics: Say, Cournot, Walras', *History of Political Economy*, Durham, **12**, 1980 (4), 524–41.

Poinsot, Louis (1836), 'Discussion de la "Note sur le calcul des probabilités" de Poisson', *Comptes rendus hebdomadaires des séances de l'Académie des Sciences*, 2, pp. 399–400.

Salomon-Bayet, Claire (1978), 'A. A. Cournot ou la règle de l'anamorphose', in *Études pour le centenaire de la mort de A. Cournot*, J. Brun and A. Robinet (eds), Paris: Vrin and Economica, pp. 91–105.

Shafer, Glenn and Vladimir Vovk (2001), *Probability and Finance: It's Only a Game*, New York: Wiley.

Sheynin, Oscar B. (1976), 'P.-S. Laplace's Work in Probability', *Archive for History of Exact Sciences*, **16** (2), 137–87.

Voltaire (1764), *Dictionnaire philosophique*, article 'Atomes'; reprinted in É. de la Bedollière and G. Avenel (eds) (1867), *Œuvres complètes*, Paris: Aux bureaux du siècle, vol. I, p. 166.

3.   The functions of economic models[1]

Bernard Walliser

INTRODUCTION

In his *Recherches sur les principes mathématiques de la théorie des richesses* ([1838] 1980), Antoine Augustin Cournot established himself as a forerunner in the construction of mathematicized economic models. He is known primarily for his models of monopoly and duopoly in partial equilibrium, but he extended his aim to models of markets and international trade. His mathematical tools, however, were restricted to differential calculus, which had already proved itself in mechanics, without including his own contributions on probabilities. Consequently, he initiated a movement of modelling which, first revived by the Marginalists and Walras, really started to blossom in the mid-twentieth century.

In his *Essai sur les fondements de la connaissance et sur les caractères de la critique philosophique* (1851), Cournot developed his epistemological ideas about the production of scientific knowledge. Although he investigated the mathematization of the real, he did not speak of models, but of theories for expressing abstract mechanisms on a generic level, and laws for expressing empirical regularities on a more specific level. As far as the economic and social sciences are concerned, he certainly introduced innovations, but he drew his examples exclusively from existing knowledge in the physical and biological sciences. From this perspective, his contribution was less innovative in that he did no more than extend reflections already proposed by his contemporaries.

The present chapter does not, therefore, aim to describe the implicit or explicit epistemology of Cournot's models, an epistemology that cannot be described as any more than embryonic (Martin, 1996). Our aim is to present a general epistemology of models in their modern incarnation (see Israël, 1996; Morgan and Morrison, 1999; Bouleau, 1999; Grenier *et al.*, 2002; Nouvel, 2002; Armatte and Dahan Dalmenico, 2004), based on the six fundamental functions they fulfil. It is only when we come to deal with each of these functions in turn that we shall examine the way in which Cournot himself envisaged them.[2] For each function, we start by examining the main strengths and weaknesses of models, their relevance in the natural and social sciences and, finally, the fundamental mechanisms they bring into play.

THE ICONIC FUNCTION

A model is a set of statements expressed in formal language, making possible the *symbolization* of a natural or artificial system. It is in this sense that we talk of 'capturing' a phenomenon in a model, in other words subsuming it into a condensed form. A model is then judged on its *expressiveness*, in other words its ability to convey faithfully the salient characteristics of the system in question.

A model provides a more precise representation than natural language, through the use of concepts that are more accurate and relations that are more clear-cut. On the one hand, concepts are expressed by values measured on explicit formal scales and split up in the event of multiple connotations. Thus a utility function can be ordinal or cardinal, and if it initially expresses both the estimation of sure gains and risk aversion, then these two interpretations can be disconnected from each other. Relations, on the other hand, are expressed by means of equations with variable levels of specification and can often be broken down into more basic relations. Thus a consumption function can be expressed in a generic, parametric or specific form and might be decomposable into consumption related to future income and an expectation function of future income based on past income.

A model can slip into simplistic formalism, however, if it mobilizes desubstantialized concepts and purely abstract relations. On the one hand, the formal structure adopted for a given magnitude may prove to be too demanding, or incapable of expressing certain phenomena. Thus an agent's knowledge is difficult to sum up in a homogeneous, quantitative magnitude, and the appearance of new knowledge is even more inexpressible, unless we assume that it is potentially already there. On the other hand, relations may suffer from too much rigidity between magnitudes, or from the absence of relevant magnitudes. Thus a production function treats labour as a factor that intervenes mechanically, overlooking the many cultural phenomena connected with work practices.

Compared to the other social sciences, economics has obvious advantages pertaining to formalization: economic variables appear in a 'naturally' quantitative form (prices and quantities of goods); likewise, the basic economic structures appear to be 'spontaneously' formalizable (for example, an agent's order of preferences over goods). Compared to the hard sciences, on the contrary, economics remains handicapped by its informal dimension: certain concepts appear to resist, at least for the time being, any formal expression (for example, a decision maker's emotions); likewise, certain sets of relations are hard to express in classic mathematical structures (relations of power between transactors).

Here, the central problem is that of the *interpretation* of a model, in other words the correspondence between the model and a concrete system, real or imaginary. Different forms of interpretation can be considered, but they all share the same idea of 'laws of correspondence', which connect the magnitudes of the model with the properties of the system represented. These interpretations can also possess different degrees of depth, from the simple literary 'reading' of the model's relations to the evocation of underlying principles. For example, the random events present in models are sometimes interpreted as expressing an intrinsic indetermination in the system, sometimes as shortcomings in the specification of the model, and sometimes as errors in the measurement of magnitudes.

In general, all models are open to multiple interpretations, in so far as the formalization does not exhaust the literary discourse. Nevertheless, a 'standard' interpretation may impose itself, with reference to a more general paradigm encompassing the model. The first danger here – under-interpretation – consists in assuming that the formal model speaks for itself without any need for further comment (the meaning given to the equality between supply and demand in a market). Over-interpretation, on the other hand, occurs when an exclusive interpretation is imposed as if it were self-evident (equilibrium interpreted as a harmonic state of the system under consideration).

Cournot considered that the mathematical language is a language that, once the mathematical concepts have been duly interpreted, facilitates the statement of facts, enables concise laws to be formulated and forestalls vague argumentation. He stressed the fact that this language can be expressed at a high level of generality, making it extremely suitable for the expression of theory. For Cournot, those skilled in mathematical analysis know that its object is not simply to calculate numbers, but that it is also employed to find the relations between magnitudes which cannot be expressed in numbers ... (*Recherches*, Preface).

He upheld that mathematics, although constructed by the human mind, applies perfectly to the real world, independently of the laws that govern our intelligence (Cournot, 1956 [1851], pp. 234–5). He introduced a probabilistic dimension to the content of models, the probability that characterizes chance and measures physical possibility, here considered to assume an objective form and to be empirically measurable (ibid., p. 48). More precisely, 'Events brought about by the combination or conjunction of other events which belong to independent series are called *fortuitous* events, or the results of *chance*' (ibid., p. 41).

THE SYLLOGISTIC FUNCTION

A model is a conceptual object, structured and self-enclosed, which permits, or at least favours, the *simulation* of a system. In this sense, one can 'run a model', in the same way one runs a motor, or even a table. A model is then judged on its *tractability*, in other words its capacity to allow original or even surprising conclusions to be derived from its hypotheses.

A model allows for rigorous demonstration moving from explicit hypotheses to systematic consequences. On the one hand, the hypotheses are exhaustive and progressively unveiled and can be treated simultaneously in large numbers. Thus the hypothesis of perfect information (and, later, that of common knowledge) has been gradually updated and its ultimate consequences, associated with other hypotheses, duly made explicit. On the other hand, the consequences are precise and controlled, although residual errors can subsist for a certain time and often turn out to be unpredictable and even counter-intuitive. Thus, if the value of information for a decision maker can be precisely defined and calculated, surprising cases of negative value, observed in game theory, are duly recorded.

A model, however, can slip into a pure formal interaction between abstract hypotheses and unreal consequences. On the one hand, if the 'technical' hypotheses are often *ad hoc*, the 'substantial' hypotheses are endlessly refined. Thus, in game theory, the chief virtue of the 'trembling-hand' hypothesis, often interpreted as expressing errors in the implementation of actions, is that it introduces random events into the choice of actions; likewise, the main purpose of ultra-sophisticated hypotheses about players' beliefs is to characterize eductively the equilibrium notion. On the other hand, the consequences are not always obtained 'constructively' and are rarely univocal. Thus market equilibria are defined without describing any clear process by which they may be attained, and they most often turn out to be multiple without any realistic selection criteria being proposed.

Compared with the other social sciences, economics appears to be a much more structured discipline. It introduces nested levels of organization interacting by means of two-way relations (individual behaviours versus collective phenomena). It makes explicit clear chains of influence between more or less observable magnitudes (the effect of an agent's mental states on his actions). It suffers, however, from a deficit of intelligibility compared to the natural sciences. A daunting obstacle is raised by the particular complexity and instability of the economic system (heterogeneous agents, tangled interactions). It also introduces concepts that are hard to implement, because of the difficulties of calculability encountered by the modeller – and even more so by the actors (perfect Bayesian equilibrium).

Here, the central problem is that of the *explanation* of a phenomenon, in other words, if we adopt Hempel's viewpoint, its derivation from general laws and specific conditions. Different types of explanation are always available, such as explanation by causes or explanation by reasons. There are also different levels of explanation, such as explanation by implicit structures or explanation by underlying mechanisms. For example, economic cycles can be explained by classic structural conditions (cyclical or random exogenous shocks, second-order delays or non-linearities) or by more detailed generative processes.

It is usually possible to provide multiple explanations for an observed phenomenon. It may even be possible to propose a 'minimal' explanation, in the sense that it uses a minimum of explanatory factors and proposes simple mechanisms for their conjunction. The risk of under-explanation consists in simply describing a statistical correspondence between magnitudes without presenting any underlying mechanism (quantitative theory of money). The risk of over-explanation derives from the superposing of several different explanatory factors, without giving any account of the hierarchy into which they are ordered (model of the firm).

Cournot highlighted, as the driving force behind research, the quest for the 'reason of things', admittedly constrained, but always evolving (Cournot, 1956 [1851], p. 18). Explaining phenomena means apprehending the general relations through which they are articulated synchronically and linked together diachronically, according to interdependent or independent sequences of influence (ibid., pp. 33–5). For Cournot, '[g]eneralizations which are fruitful because they reveal in a single general principle the rationale of a great many particular truths, the connections and common origins of which had not previously been seen, are found in all the sciences' (ibid., p. 24).

He particularly emphasized explanation through the realization of fortuitous combinations (chance), through mutual reactions (causes) or through an internal finality (design). He believed that these modes of explanation are the same in all the sciences, although their relative importance changes as we gradually move from the physical to the social. Thus, he affirmed that 'the notions ... cause and of fortune ... apply to phenomena in the domain of living things as to those that produce the forces which activate inorganic matter ; to the reflective acts of free beings as to the inescapable determinations of appetite and of instinct' (ibid., p. 50).

THE EMPIRICAL FUNCTION

A model is a schematic representation of an existing system, which lends itself to easy *validation* in the face of empirical data. In this sense, we can 'test a model' in the same way we test new materials or genetically modified organisms. A model is then judged on its *veridicality*, in other words its capacity to apprehend the observable properties of the system under consideration.

A model can be subjected to systematic validation in relation to 'stylized facts', through a top-down (projective) approach or, more rarely, a bottom-up (inductive) approach. Using the projective approach, on the one hand, one can derive testable consequences from the model, between observable magnitudes.

These consequences can then be subjected to simple validation tests. Thus an investment function is derived from an investment optimization model and can be subjected to classic tests. The inductive approach, on the other hand, allows for the treatment of a large number of data, to which other classic techniques are applied with the aim of getting a model to emerge. Thus the relation between the performance and the size of companies is drawn from a large body of empirical knowledge, through the medium of data analysis methods.

A model cannot lead to crucial tests, however, for the projective approach is inconclusive and the inductive approach is often blind. On the one hand, the validation of a stochastic model relies on conventional criteria, and its possible refutation tells us little about its actual weaknesses, because of the Duhem–Quine problem. Thus a random model of the labour market can never be strictly refuted by the data, and if it turns out to be implausible, it gives no indication of the particular hypotheses that should be called into question. On the other hand, the structuring of data requires a preliminary model, many of the hypotheses of which are not tested. Thus the formalization of the money market entails *a priori* hypotheses about the composition of money and the determinants of supply and demand, as well as their postulated exogeneity.

Here again, economics has comparative advantages over the other social sciences. It possesses a great number of historical data, especially of a financial nature (real-time data). It conducts systematic laboratory experimentation, under the auspices of cognitive psychology and, more recently, neuro-economics (the theory of decision under uncertainty). Compared with the practices of the hard sciences, on the other hand, it remains disadvantaged. Economic phenomena are subject to disruptive factors that are more numerous and of comparable significance (information or transaction costs in exchanges). It also has more difficulty in moving from the laboratory to the real world, causing it to attach more importance to purely historical data (the econometric analysis of the causes of unemployment).

Here, the central problem is that of the *idealization* of the model, in the sense that it is only valid under certain aspects and within certain contexts. We can consider various types of idealization: isolation from the context, expressed in hypotheses of exogeneity, stability and negligibility; internal stylization, which leads to structural, analytic and parametric approximations. We can also consider different degrees of idealization, if we may say that 'all models are ideal, but some are more ideal than others'. For example, we can consider that a competitive market is realized under the usual conditions (the market for glass), under potential circumstances that may, at a stretch, be realizable (the labour market) or under virtual circumstances that are, in practice, inaccessible (the market for time).

Various idealized representations of the same system are generally proposed, making more or less sophisticated approximations on one or another of its dimensions. An idealization, like any caricature, is successful if it reduces the system to its essential features with regard to the intended use of the model. The first risk, under-idealization, consists in constructing a model with a number of superfluous details (the urban model in geographical economics). The second, over-idealization, leads to the construction of a model about which one can only conclude that 'any similarity to reality is purely coincidental' (Becker's crime model).

Cournot introduced the concept of abstraction, close to that of idealization, defining it as the analysis to which sensibility is subjected by the force of intelligence, and which finds expression both in taxonomies and theoretical principles. He made a distinction between artificial (or logical) abstraction, which is a pure construction by the modeller, adapted to his needs, and rational abstraction, which expresses, in a refined form, the relations inherent in the facts. In his words, '[w]hen a study is made of the laws according to which wealth is produced, distributed, and consumed, it is discovered that they may be theoretically established in a simple enough manner, if we abstract them from certain accessory circumstances which complicate them ... ' (Cournot, 1956 [1851], p. 229).

In keeping with the epistemology of his time, he favoured the inductive approach based on observations, particularly focusing on the observations of our senses, perpetually disrupted by various filters (external environment, instruments, illusions). He introduced a probabilistic dimension into the appreciation of models, probability (expressing the degree of verisimilitude of the model for the modeller) here being subjective, although it can be strengthened as the result of debate among the scientists. For Cournot, '[t]he judgment that reason gives as to the intrinsic value ... of the theory is a probable judgment. The probability of this judgment depends upon two things: First, on the simplicity of the theoretical formulation, and, second, on the number of facts ... which the theory connects' (ibid., p. 61).

THE HEURISTIC FUNCTION

A model is a modular and evolving artefact that contributes to a progressive *crystallization* of knowledge into a seamless whole. This view is expressed in the action of 'tinkering with a model' as one might tinker with an artistic work or craft product. A model is then judged on its *fertility*, in other words its capacity to engender a new generation of models of recognized significance.

A model serves as a support to the imagination in the context of discovery and as a support to legitimation in the context of proof. On the one hand, it facilitates analogical transfer between two disciplines and opens up the possibility of reusing the same formal structures within the same discipline. Thus the ideas of selection and mutation have been incorporated into evolutionary game theory, and the formal structure associated with them has proved to be isomorphic to that resulting from a process of reinforcement learning. On the other hand, it facilitates the resolution of logical paradoxes (vicious logical circularity or infinite regression), theoretical paradoxes (counter-intuitive consequences) or empirical paradoxes (predictions contrary to experience). Thus the meta-optimization paradox, Condorcet's paradox and Allais's paradox have all stimulated the construction of models aiming precisely to resolve them.

Modellization, however, may lead to an anarchic profusion of models, disparate in the context of discovery, trivial in the context of proof. On the one hand, the models may not prevent haphazard or flat analogies and can sometimes be reduced to formalized common sense. Thus the diffusion of knowledge has been likened to the simple diffusion of a material item and its acquisition by an agent to the simple acquisition of this item. On the other hand, the models may provide transparent explanations, in the sense that the conclusions are already present in the hypotheses, or *ad hoc* explanations, in the sense that the hypotheses only concern the phenomenon under consideration. Thus agents' preferences embrace ever more heterogeneous arguments, from the preferences of others (to account for envy) through to social norms (to account for obedience to those norms).

Nevertheless, economics appears to be more unified than the other social sciences. It possesses a common ontology (game theory as a unifying matrix) and a common methodology (mathematics as a federative language). With regard to the other social sciences, the discipline of economics appears both as an importer (the concept of reputation) and exporter, at the risk of a certain 'imperialism' (the rational model of behaviour). With regard to the homogeneous development of the hard sciences, however, economics remains very dispersed. It is still animated by currents that diverge in both their views (neoclassicism versus institutionalism) and their methods (formal approach versus historical approach). It benefits from deliberate borrowing from the hard sciences (evolutionary microeconomics), but it also suffers from more involuntary imports, close to entryism (the statistical physics view of diffusion).

Here, the central problem is that of the *cumulativity* of knowledge, which first requires commensurability between models, and then their relative positioning in terms of complementarity and substitutability. Diverse forms of cumulativity can be envisaged: the structuralist analysis of models in the form of conceptual lattices, the genetic analysis of models in the form of conceptual trees. We can also distinguish between different degrees of depth in cumulativity: widening of the domain of validity, weakening of the analytic form, rooting in founding principles. Thus models of choice under uncertainty have been gradually generalized by widening their field to include animals, by adopting formalisms that extend the structure of expected utility and by supplying axioms justifying these extended criteria.

The cumulativity of models can manifest itself in different typologies and lines of evolution, and often leads to networks of models derived from one seminal model (the models of Hotelling, Spence, Akerlof, Rubinstein and so on). The most striking form of cumulativity corresponds to successive waves of weakening of the hypotheses of models, when this weakening becomes formally realizable and leads to original consequences (bounded rationality, endogenous preferences). The risk of under-cumulativity consists in a 'Balkanization' of knowledge, as if inspired by the saying 'may a hundred models bloom' (evolutionary models). The risk of over-cumulativity consists in the hegemony of one research programme expressing a doctrinaire approach (general equilibrium).

Cournot affirmed that phenomena can be classified into categories of objects (or phenomena) that are more or less subordinate to each other, and characterized by different concepts, principles and methods. He singled out fertile generalizations, which lead to the inclusion of hitherto unsuspected fields, but also 'sterile generalizations', which only integrate very marginal domains (Cournot, 1956 [1851], pp. 22–4). In a more diachronic fashion, he observed that 'ideas that we call new, because they throw new light on the objects of our knowledge, have their periods of fruitfulness and their periods of sterility and exhaustion' (ibid., p. 233).

He upheld that scientific discovery does not obey psychological or social laws that can be made explicit, but he believed, nevertheless, that the scientist is fundamentally guided by an idea of world harmony. The idea of simplicity, in particular, even if its definition is a delicate affair, appeared to him to be a regulating idea, to the extent that that which is the most simple is also the most probable. He spoke of '[t]his indefinable premonition ... by which the mathematician is put on the trail of his theorems and the physicist on the track of a physical law, to the degree that it appears to them that the suggested theorem or the law satisfies the conditions of generality and simplicity and symmetry which contribute to the perfection of order in all things ...' (ibid., p. 103).

THE PRAGMATIC FUNCTION

A model is a powerful conceptual tool enabling the efficient *adaptation* of actors to their context of action. It is in this sense that we speak of 'using a model', as we might use any tool of investigation. A model is then judged on its *operationality*, in other words its capacity to meet certain demands of its potential users.

A model can shed light on the economic context of choices through clear, well-focused forecasts and simple, applicable instructions. On the one hand, it is capable of providing answers under all circumstances and qualifying them by means of contrasting future trajectories. Thus the effects of the reduction in working hours are forecast for all combinations of environmental conditions and may be presented, for example, in a variety of 'rosy' or 'grey' scenarios. On the other hand, it promotes guiding operating principles and serves as the language of reference for experts. Thus public economic calculation is based on the calculable concept of surplus and enables the problem of the evaluation of public projects to be considered within a common framework upon which agreements and conflicts can be articulated.

A model can lend itself to magical use because of uncertain and unstable forecasts and superficial and fragile instructions. On the one hand, forecasts are rarely accompanied by margins of error and often manifest a 'Panurge effect' of imitation between forecasters. Thus forecasts of oil prices, which often turn out to be far removed from reality, are very similar between different forecasters, who share not only a common culture, but also a preference for being wrong together rather than right alone. On the other hand, instructions are based on non-causal structures and underestimate the strategic conditions of their application. Thus monetary policy is based on a demand for money that expresses simple regularities in behaviour, which may be sensitive to the policy itself (the Lucas problem).

Here, economics displays great originality compared with the social sciences. Apart from the representation of the system on which one wishes to act, it explicitly modellizes the means that can be mobilized by the decision maker and the norms being pursued (efficiency/fairness), which leads, at least in some particular cases, to the very direct implementation of instructions (financial engineering). The level of practical application in economics, however, is much lower than in the hard sciences. Not only are the decision makers more dispersed and with multiform objectives (transport economics), but they also have much more indirect relations with the experts (the expert's schizophrenia between the advice he gives and his real beliefs, the cannibalism of the decision maker who only chooses to adopt certain disparate elements of the instructions).

Here, the central concept is that of the *contextualization* of a model, in the sense of the adaptation of the model to a certain external demand. There are various types of context to which one might wish to adapt the model: classes of environment, types of policy or categories of norm (traffic forecasts). There are also different depths of adaptation of the model to the context: marginal modifications of the model, finite shocks to the model, comparison of rival models (macroeconomic forecasts). For example, models of a financial market can give rise to numerous variants, resolved analytically or by numerical simulation ('computational economics').

The contextualization of the model may take several directions and test the model's robustness, in other words the sensitivity of its consequences to the hypotheses adopted. The 'principle of continuity of approximation', proposed by Herbert Simon (1963), affirms precisely that close hypotheses must lead to close consequences. The first danger, that of under-contextualization, results from the reluctance to apply a model to a problem that nevertheless falls within its field of application because of prejudices about its value (calculable micro-economic model). The second danger, over-contextualization, results from the blind application of a general model to a problem, without looking too closely into the specific characteristics of the situation in question (economic calculation applied to developing countries by the International Monetary Fund).

Cournot, in keeping with the ideas of Bacon, was fascinated by the parallelism between ideas of a natural order and those of an artificial order, between the government of the physical world and the government of states (Cournot, 1956 [1851], pp. 233–4). He underlined the complementarity between the capacities for knowledge and the capacities for action, and considered that moral ideas, compared with scientific ideas, undergo a parallel process of crystallization from experience and idealization for operative purposes. More fundamentally, he affirmed that, 'since, in matters pertaining to knowledge, man has faculties which are much superior to those of animals, he is for that reason called to a higher destiny and should perform acts of a higher sort' (ibid., p. 252).

He was no less aware of the fact that moving from theory to governmental applications represents a huge step (*Recherches*, Preface). From a counterfactual perspective, he distinguished between 'intrapolative' inductions, close to the proven field of study, and extrapolative inductions, which depart from this field and become more and more random, although they cannot be simply probabilized. He affirmed that '[r]ules are established [and] limits are set up so that the conscientious evaluation of an expert, an arbiter, a jury, a judge, or an administrator is kept within more or less narrow bounds. Evaluation rebels at analysis and consequently breaks loose from rigorous control' (ibid., p. 302).

THE RHETORICAL FUNCTION

A model is a convenient and economical medium for the *transmission* of knowledge between the actors concerned. This involves 'selling a model' in much the same way as one promotes any material or intellectual product. A model is then judged on its *performativity*, in other words its capacity to convince the milieus concerned to adopt it and, in turn, to diffuse it.

A model facilitates the communication of knowledge to and among both specialists and the public. On the one hand, it constitutes an object of reference between scientists and a pedagogical tool for students. Every economist, whether a novice or well qualified, immediately knows what we are talking about when we evoke the 'cobweb' model in the market for pork or the Rubinstein model of bargaining. On the other hand, a model favours the impregnation of technical concepts in the form of images and an assimilation of partial mechanisms in the form of 'mental maps'. Thus the media, or even the public, have internalized, relatively faithfully, the concepts of 'marginal cost' or 'value added', or again the 'polluter pays' principle.

A model, however, is also an instrument of power in the hands of scientists, used against their colleagues or in the face of opinion. On the one hand, it displays the primacy of formalized works within the profession and raises entry barriers against students. Thus the use of formalisms for theoretical or statistical purposes is widespread in the economic journals and plays the role of essential scales or imposed figures for the students. On the other hand, it cannot prevent the diffusion of fuzzy concepts or ill-defined mechanisms, repeated in loops. Thus, and not without weakening or even distorting them, the media have seized on such concepts as 'financial bubbles', 'sustainable development' or 'precautionary principle'.

Economics has particular collaborative relations with the other social sciences, because of its specific characteristics. Although it exports, in 'literary' terms, certain evocative concepts (symbolic capital, social oligopoly), it exerts a more ambivalent influence of attraction and repulsion (game theory). It enjoys calmer relations of dialogue with the hard sciences, even if it is obliged to study original phenomena because of the intentionality of the actors. It may import certain images for didactic purposes (the concept of hysteresis), but it is also the object of specific phenomena of self-fulfilling expectations, operating on endogenous magnitudes (increase in the price of sugar) or on the relations between magnitudes (the influence of sunspots on prices).

Here, the central problem is that of the *popularization* of models, in other words their transmission in a didactic form. Various supports are used to favour this popularization, from literary narrations to visual elements, such as bar charts, graphs or diagrams. There are also different depths of popularization, with an increasing risk of 'ideological' discourse creeping into the interstices of knowledge: well-targeted approximations, strained interpretations, groundless explanations. For example, game theory draws on various anecdotes (the prisoner's dilemma, the battle of the sexes) that are supposed to summarize exemplary configurations of strategic interactions.

One and the same model may be the object of several different attempts at popularization, more or less well endorsed by the constructors of the model. Among them, some are officially recognized and labelled in current and even academic discourse (the Keynesian multiplier concept). The first danger, under-popularization, consists in the abandonment of a model by its constructor, giving free rein to any subsequent interpretation (multiple readings of Coase's model). The second danger, over-popularization, consists in misusing a model that is claimed to say more than it actually does (improper interpretations of Arrow's theorem).

Cournot stressed that 'ideas', which have been gradually crystallized out of perceptions through the work of the mind, must again be supported in return by 'images', which call on the senses (Cournot, 1956 [1851], pp. 165–6). He observed that for any given idea, it is not necessarily the same images that have the most impact on each individual, and he drew an analogy by comparing the position of someone blind from birth with a sighted person (ibid., pp. 166–7). In his words, 'hypothetical conceptions are not introduced as ideas but as images, and introduced because the human mind finds it necessary to graft ideas onto images' (ibid., p. 180).

He insisted on the need to guard against the misuse of formalism and to offer the public models that are at the same time simple and robust, expressing clear, applicable messages. The most important objective of calculation is not to achieve a high degree of precision so much as a sufficient degree of approximation to make its result significant. According to Cournot, 'an illusory precision has been effected in calculations or in certain details of experiments. This apparent precision is inconvenient not so much because it involves useless exertion and work, as because it gives the mind a wrong idea of the result obtained' (ibid., p. 303).

CONCLUSION

As can be seen from the above, the concept of a model is a category with very disparate contents and rather blurred boundaries, which might explain why it has not yet become the subject of a specific epistemology. A model is a multifactorial object that incorporates wide-ranging components, from the theoretical principles that inspire it to the empirical data that support it, from the mathematical languages it uses to the social demands to which it responds. A model is also a plurifunctional object, fulfilling various roles involving the formal expression of a phenomenon, its gradual empirical validation or its use for operative or teaching purposes.

Cournot, however, felt that the mathematical expression of principles and laws of nature harbours potentialities reaching far beyond what a simple literary discourse could pretend to achieve. He did not hesitate to apply to economics the methods he had seen at work in the physical and biological sciences, taking simplifying hypotheses and deriving from them consequences that, without always being testable, could at least be subjected to independent assessment. He was motivated by a rationalist vision while remaining aware of the limits of reason, without, for all that, lapsing into the relativism that he felt to be inappropriate.

In brief, a model can fundamentally be analysed as a conceptual object that enables reasoning to be pursued through other means. It is usually seen as being non-necessary, in the sense that a literary 'narrative' can express the same ideas, but sufficient, in the sense that it brings relevant, independent knowledge. It is more surely seen as being non-sufficient in so far as that its theses need to be constantly reinterpreted, but necessary to the extent that it allows operations that are inaccessible and complementary to the literary narrative.

NOTES

1. I would like to thank Thierry Martin and André Orléan for their constructive criticism of this chapter.
2. Subsequent references to Cournot refer to sections of the Essay of 1851, unless otherwise specified.

REFERENCES

Armatte, Michel and Amy Dahan Dalmenico (2004), 'Modèles et modélisations, 1950–2000: Nouvelles pratiques, nouveaux enjeux', *Revue d'Histoire des Sciences*, **57** (2), 245–305.
Bouleau, Nicolas (1999), *Philosophie des mathématiques et de la modélisation*, Paris: L'Harmattan.
Cournot, Antoine Augustin (1838), *Recherches sur les principes mathématiques de la théorie des richesses*, reprinted in Gérard Jorland (ed.) (1980), *Œuvres complètes*, Tome VIII, Paris: Vrin.
Cournot, Antoine Augustin (1956) [1851], *An Essay on the Foundations of our Knowledge [Essai sur les fondements de nos connaissances et sur les caractères de la critique philosophique]*, translated by M.H. Moore, New York: The Liberal Arts Press.
Grenier, Jean-Yves, Claude Grignon and Pierre-Michel Menger (eds) (2002), *Le modèle et le récit*, Paris: Editions de la Maison des Sciences de l'Homme.
Israël, Giorgio (1996), *La mathématisation du réel: Essai sur la modélisation mathématique*, Paris: Seuil.
Martin, Thierry (1996), *Probabilités et critique philosophique selon Cournot*, Paris: Vrin.
Morgan, Mary and Margaret Morrison (eds) (1999), *Models as Mediators: Perspectives on natural and social science*, Cambridge: Cambridge University Press.
Nouvel, Pascal (ed.) (2002), *Enquête sur le concept de modèle*, Paris: Presses Universitaires de France.
Simon, Herbert (1963), 'Problems of Methodology: Discussion', *American Economic Review*, **53** (1), 229–31.

B 16   G 12
C 70   G 14

4.   From Cournot's principle to market efficiency[1]

Glenn Shafer

INTRODUCTION

Cournot's principle says that an event of small or zero probability singled out in advance will not happen. From the turn of the twentieth century through the 1950s, many mathematicians, including Chuprov, Borel, Fréchet, Lévy and Kolmogorov, saw this principle as fundamental to the application and meaning of probability.[2] In their view, a probability model gains empirical content only when it rules out an event by assigning it small or zero probability.

In the 1960s, when probability theory was gaining in importance in economics, and especially finance, Cournot's principle was no longer so widely accepted. In fact, the principle had almost disappeared with those who had espoused it in the first half of the twentieth century. In this chapter, I argue that its disappearance entailed a loss of clarity in the interpretation of probability, which accounts in part for the high level of confusion in initial formulations of the efficient-markets hypothesis.

The game-theoretic framework for probability (Shafer and Vovk, 2001) revives Cournot's principle in a form directly relevant to markets. In this framework, Cournot's principle is equivalent to saying that a strategy for placing bets without risking bankruptcy will not multiply the bettor's capital by a large or infinite factor. It can therefore be applied directly to strategies for exploiting market prices without assuming the existence of meaningful probability distributions related to these prices.

The claim that an investor cannot make a lot of money using public information is part of the efficient-markets hypothesis as it was formalized in the 1980s (LeRoy, 1989). But this efficient-markets hypothesis also says that market prices are discounted expected values with respect to a probability distribution that changes only in accordance with relevant information. This bundling of ideas has enabled scholars to talk past each other. Some (for example Malkiel, 2003) claim the efficient-markets hypothesis is vindicated when strategies for making money fail. Others (for example Shiller, 2003) claim it is refuted by any evidence that price changes are not always based on information.

The game-theoretic framework allows us to unbundle the efficient-markets hypothesis in a useful way. This unbundling is encouraged by the framework's success in dealing with classical probability. The framework accommodates both the case where an investor or a bettor may buy any variable at its expected value with respect to a specified probability distribution, as in classical probability theory, and the case where only some variables are priced and offered for sale, as in the incomplete markets in which real investors participate. In the case where all variables are priced, the framework reduces to classical probability, but many classical results extend to the case where only limited prices are given.

As it turns out, the game-theoretic form of Cournot's principle, applied directly to market prices, implies several stylized facts commonly associated with the existence of a whole probability distribution for future value, including the $\sqrt{dt}$ scaling of price changes (Vovk and Shafer, 2003a) and CAPM-type relations between the realized average return for a particular security and that of the market (Vovk and Shafer, 2002). To the extent that they are confirmed by data, these stylized facts can count as demonstrations of the usefulness of that part of the efficient-markets hypothesis represented by Cournot's principle, but this will not, by itself, provide any support for the quite separate hypothesis that price changes are usually or always based on information.

The following sections review the rise and fall of Cournot's principle in classical probability (section 1); its new form in game-theoretic probability (section 2); and its potential in this new form for probability, economics and finance theory (section 3).

1.   THE RISE AND FALL OF COURNOT'S PRINCIPLE

This section traces Cournot's principle from its inception in Jacob Bernoulli's discussion of moral certainty in the early eighteenth century to its disappearance in Joseph Doob's reformulation of mathematical probability theory in the 1950s.

The section is organized along conceptual as well as chronological lines. In section 1.1, I trace the relatively uncontroversial concept of moral certainty from the seventeenth to the twentieth century. In section 1.2, I trace the development of a more controversial idea – that Cournot's principle is the only bridge from a probability model to the world; this idea first emerged in Cournot's analysis of moral certainty, and it was best articulated by Paul Lévy in the 1920s. In section 1.3, I distinguish between the strong form of Cournot's principle, which asserts that a particular event of very small probability will not happen on a particular trial, and the weak form, which asserts merely that events of small probability happen rarely on repeated trials. Then I turn to the history of the opposition; in section 1.4 I acknowledge the indifference of British mathematicians and statisticians, and in section 1.5 the more explicit opposition of German philosophers. Finally, in section 1.6, I explain how Doob's mathematical framework for stochastic processes contributed to the disappearance of Cournot's principle after the Second World War.

Section 1 draws heavily on recent papers with Vladimir Vovk on the historical context of Andrei Kolmogorov's contributions to the foundations of probability (Shafer and Vovk, 2005, 2006; Vovk and Shafer, 2003b).

1.1 Moral Certainty

An event with very small probability is *morally impossible*; it will not happen. Equivalently, an event with very high probability is *morally certain*; it will happen. This principle was first formulated within mathematical probability by Jacob Bernoulli. In his *Ars conjectandi*, published posthumously in 1713, Bernoulli proved that in a sufficiently long sequence of independent trials of an event, there is a very high probability that the frequency with which the event happens will be close to its probability. Bernoulli explained that we can treat the very high probability as moral certainty and so use the frequency of the event as an estimate of its probability. Beginning with Poisson (Bru, 2002; Poisson, 1837; Stigler, 1986), this conclusion was called the law of large numbers. (Only later, mostly in the last 50 years, was 'the law of large numbers' used to designate Bernoulli's theorem itself and its generalizations, which are purely mathematical statements.)

Probabilistic moral certainty was widely discussed in the eighteenth century. In the 1760s, Jean d'Alembert muddled matters by questioning whether the prototypical event of very small probability, a long run of many happenings of an event as likely to fail as happen on each trial, is possible at all. A run of 100 may be metaphysically possible, he felt, but physically impossible. It has never happened and never will (d'Alembert, 1761, 1767; Daston, 1979). In 1777, George-Louis Buffon argued that the distinction between moral and physical certainty was one of degree. An event with probability 9999/10 000 is morally certain; an event with much greater probability, such as the rising of the sun, is physically certain (Buffon, 1777; Loveland, 2001).

Augustin Cournot, a mathematician now remembered as an economist and a philosopher of science (Martin, 1996, 1998), gave the discussion a nineteenth-century cast in his 1843 treatise on probability (Cournot, [1843] 1984). Because he was familiar with geometric probability, Cournot could talk about probabilities that are vanishingly small. He brought physics to the foreground. It may be mathematically possible, he argued, for a heavy cone to stand in equilibrium on its vertex, but it is physically impossible. The event's probability is vanishingly small. Similarly, it is physically impossible for the frequency of an event in a long sequence of trials to differ substantially from the event's probability (Cournot, [1843] 1984, pp. 57 and 107).

In the second half of the nineteenth century, the principle that an event with a vanishingly small probability will not happen took on a real role in physics, most saliently in Ludwig Boltzmann's statistical understanding of the second law of thermodynamics. As Boltzmann explained in the 1870s, dissipative processes are irreversible, because the probability of a state with entropy far from the maximum is vanishingly small (von Plato, 1994, p. 80; Seneta, 1997). Also notable was Henri Poincaré's use of the principle. Poincaré's recurrence theorem, published in 1890 (Poincaré, 1890; von Plato, 1994), says that an isolated mechanical system confined to a bounded region of its phase space will eventually return arbitrarily close to its initial state, provided only that this initial state is not exceptional. Within any region of finite volume, the states for which the recurrence does not hold are exceptional inasmuch as they are contained in subregions whose total volume is arbitrarily small.

At the turn of the twentieth century, it was a commonplace among statisticians that one must decide what level of probability will count as practical certainty in order to apply probability theory. We find this stated explicitly in 1901, for example, in the articles by Georg Bohlmann and Ladislaus von Bortkiewicz in the section on probability in the *Encyklopädie der mathematischen Wissenschaften* (von Bortkiewicz, 1901, p. 825; Bohlmann, 1901, p. 861).

Aleksandr Chuprov, Professor of Statistics at Saint Petersburg Polytechnical Institute, was the champion of Cournot's principle in Russia. He called it Cournot's lemma (Chuprov, [1910] 1959, p. 167) and declared it a basic principle of the logic of the probable (Sheynin, 1996, pp. 95–6). Andrei Markov, also at Saint Petersburg, learned about mathematical statistics from Chuprov (Ondar, 1981), and we hear an echo of Cournot's principle in Markov's textbook, published in German in 1912:

> The closer the probability of an event is to one, the more reason we have to expect the event to happen and not to expect its opposite to happen.
>
> In practical questions, we are forced to regard as certain events whose probability comes more or less close to one, and to regard as impossible events whose probability is small.
>
> Consequently, one of the most important tasks of probability theory is to identify those events whose probabilities come close to one or zero. (Markov, 1912, p. 12)

The importance of Cournot's principle was also emphasized in the early twentieth century by Émile Borel. According to Borel, a result of the probability calculus deserves to be called objective when its probability becomes so great as to be practically the same as certainty (Borel, [1906] 1972, [1909] 1965, 1914, [1930] 1991). Borel gave a more refined and demanding scale of practical certainty than Buffon's. A probability of 10^{-6}, he suggested, is negligible at the human scale, a probability of 10^{-15} at the terrestrial scale, and a probability of 10^{-50} at the cosmic scale (Borel, [1939] 1991, pp. 6–7).

1.2   Probability's Only Bridge to the World

Saying that an event of very small or vanishingly small probability will not happen is one thing. Saying that probability theory gains empirical meaning only by ruling out the happening of such events is another. Cournot may have been the first to make this second assertion:

> *The physically impossible event is therefore the one that has infinitely small probability,* and only this remark gives substance – objective and phenomenal value – to the theory of mathematical probability. (Cournot, [1843] 1984, p. 78)

Cournot's wording reflects the influence of Immanuel Kant; 'objective and phenomenal' refers to Kant's distinction between the noumenon, or thing-in-itself, and the phenomenon, or object of experience (Daston, 1994).

Paul Lévy, a French mathematician who began writing on probability in the 1920s, stands out for the clarity of his articulation of the thesis that Cournot's principle is the only way of connecting a probabilistic theory with the world outside mathematics. In a note published in 1922, Lévy's teacher Jacques Hadamard explained that probability is based on two basic notions: the notion of perfectly equivalent (equally likely) events and the notion of a very unlikely event (Hadamard, 1922, p. 289). In his *Calcul des probabilités*, published in 1925, Lévy emphasized the different roles of these two notions. The notion of equally likely events, Lévy explained, suffices as a foundation for the mathematics of probability, but so long as we base our reasoning only on this notion, our probabilities are merely subjective. It is the notion of a very unlikely event that permits the results of the mathematical theory to take on practical significance (Lévy, 1925, pp. 21, 34; see also Lévy, [1937] 1954, p. 3). Combining the notion of a very unlikely event with Bernoulli's theorem, we obtain the notion of the objective probability of an event, a physical constant that is measured by relative frequency. Objective probability, in Lévy's view, is entirely analogous to length and weight, other physical constants whose empirical meaning is also defined by methods established for measuring them to a reasonable approximation (Lévy, 1925, pp. 29–30).

Lévy's views were widely shared in France. Starting in the 1940s, Borel called Cournot's principle first 'the fundamental law of chance' (*la loi fondamentale du hasard*) (Borel, 1941) and then 'the only law of chance' (*la loi unique du hasard*) (Borel, [1943] 1962, [1950] 1963). The latter phrase was taken up by Robert Fortet (Le Lionnais, [1948] 1971).

Neither Lévy nor Borel used the name 'Cournot's principle', which was coined by Maurice Fréchet in 1949. Fréchet's inspiration was Oskar Anderson, who had talked about the *Cournotsche Lemma* ('Cournot's lemma') and the *Cournotsche Brücke* ('Cournot's bridge') (Anderson, 1935, 1949). Anderson was following his teacher Chuprov in the use of 'lemma'. Fréchet felt that 'lemma', like 'theorem', should be reserved for purely mathematical results and so suggested 'principe de Cournot' ('Cournot's principle'). Fréchet's coinage was used in the 1950s in French, German and English (de Finetti, 1951; Richter, 1954, 1956; von Hirsch, 1954).

1.3   Weak and Strong Forms of the Principle

Fréchet distinguished between strong and weak forms of Cournot's principle (Fréchet, 1951; Martin, 2003, p. 6). The strong form refers to an event of small or zero probability that we single out in advance of a single trial: it says the event will not happen on that trial. The weak form says that an event with very small probability will happen very rarely in repeated trials. Some authors, including Lévy, Borel and Kolmogorov, adopted the strong principle. Others, including Chuprov and Fréchet himself, preferred the weak principle.

The strong principle combines with Bernoulli's theorem to produce the unequivocal conclusion that an event's probability will be approximated by its frequency in a particular, sufficiently long, sequence of independent trials. The weak principle combines with Bernoulli's theorem to produce the conclusion that an event's probability will *usually* be approximated by its frequency in a sufficiently long sequence of independent trials, a general principle that has the weak principle as a special case. This was pointed out by Castelnuovo in his 1919 textbook (p. 108). Castelnuovo called the general principle 'the empirical law of chance' (*la legge empirica del caso*):

> In a series of trials repeated a large number of times under identical conditions, each of the possible events happens with a (relative) frequency that gradually equals its probability. The approximation usually improves with the number of trials. (Castelnuovo, [1919] 1948, p. 3)

Although the special case where the probability is close to zero is sufficient to imply the general principle, Castelnuovo thought it pedagogically preferable to begin his introduction to the meaning of probability by enunciating the general principle, which accords with the popular identification of probability with frequency. His approach was influential at the time. Maurice Fréchet and Maurice Halbwachs adopted it in their 1924 textbook (Fréchet and Halbwachs, 1924). It brought Fréchet to the same understanding of objective probability as Lévy: it is a physical constant that is measured by relative frequency (Fréchet, 1937–8, p. 5 of Book 1; Fréchet, 1938, pp. 45–6).

The weak point of Castelnuovo and Fréchet's position lies in the modesty of their conclusion: they conclude only that an event's probability is usually approximated by its frequency. When we estimate a probability from an observed frequency, we are taking a further step: we are assuming that what usually happens has happened in the particular case. This step requires the strong form of Cournot's principle. According to Kolmogorov (Kolmogorov, [1956] 1965, p. 240), it is a reasonable step only if 'we have some reason for assuming' that the position of the particular case among other potential ones 'is a regular one, that is, that it has no special features'. Kolmogorov and his contemporaries considered the absence of special features that would enable one to single out particular trials essential to any application of probability theory to the world. Richard von Mises formalized this absence in terms of rules for selecting subsequences from infinite sequences of trials (von Mises, 1919, 1928, 1931), but Kolmogorov did not consider such infinitary principles relevant to applications (Shafer and Vovk, 2005, section A.2). A finitary principle, one applicable to a single trial, is needed, and this is Cournot's principle.

1.4 British Practicality

For Borel, Lévy and Kolmogorov, probability theory was a mathematical object, and there was a puzzle about how to relate it to the world. Cournot's principle solved this puzzle in a way that minimized the importance of the distinction between subjective and objective meanings of probability. For Borel and Lévy, probabilities begin as subjective but become objective when they are sufficiently close to zero or one and we adopt Cournot's principle. Kolmogorov, faithful to Soviet ideology, avoided any hint of subjectivism but still recognized the role of Cournot's principle in relating the mathematical formalism of probability to the world of frequencies.

The British saw quite a different picture in the late nineteenth century (Porter, 1986, p. 74 ff.). There was little mathematical work on probability in Britain in this period, and in any case the British were not likely to puzzle over how to relate abstractions to the world. They saw probability, to the extent that it was of any use at all, as a way of directly describing something in the world, either belief or frequency, which led them to quarrel. Many, including Augustus De Morgan, William Stanley Jevons and Francis Edgeworth, said belief (De Morgan, [1838] 1981; Edgeworth, 1887, 1996; Jevons, 1874). A few, the most influential being John Venn (1888), said frequency. R.A. Fisher and Harold Jeffreys carried the debate into the twentieth century (Fisher, 1922, 1925; Howie, 2002). Neither side had any need for Cournot's principle, and some participants in the debate saw no use even for Bernoulli's theorem (Daston, 1994; Ellis, 1849).

British authors did sometimes discuss the classical puzzles about very unlikely events. Could a pair of dice come up sixes a thousand times running? Could Shakespeare's plays be produced by drawing random letters from a bag? But they resolved these questions by reminding their readers that rare is not the same as impossible. As Venn put it (1888, p. 349), 'A common mistake is to assume that a very unlikely thing will not happen at all.' In the period before the Second World War, I have yet to find, however, a British discussion of the French and Russian viewpoint on Cournot's principle.

With the work of Francis Galton in the 1880s and then Karl Pearson in the 1890s (Aldrich, 2003; Porter, 2004; Stigler, 1986), the British began to take a leading role in the application and development of statistics, while remaining less interested in the classical theory of probability. One aspect of this development was the emergence of principles of statistical testing. For those on the continent who subscribed to Cournot's principle, no additional principles were needed to justify rejecting a probabilistic hypothesis that gives small probability to an event one singles out in advance and then observes to happen (Bru, 1999). But in the British tradition, the problem of testing 'significance' came to be seen as something separate from the meaning of probability itself (Fisher, [1925] 1958; Martin-Löf, 1970).

1.5 German Philosophy

In contrast with Britain, Germany did see a substantial amount of mathematical work in probability during the first decades of the twentieth century, much of it published in German by Scandinavians and Eastern Europeans. But the Germans were already pioneering the division of labour, to which we are now accustomed, between mathematicians who prove theorems about probability and philosophers (including philosophically minded logicians, statisticians and scientists) who analyse the meaning of probability. German philosophers did not give Cournot's principle a central role.

The Germans, like the British, argued vigorously at the end of the nineteenth and beginning of the twentieth century about whether probability is subjective or objective. Karl Friedrich Stumpf is remembered as one of the most articulate proponents of subjectivism (Stumpf, 1892), while Johannes von Kries was the most influential objectivist (von Kries, [1886] 1927).

Von Kries was the most cogent and influential of all the German philosophers who discussed probability in the late nineteenth century. In his *Principien der Wahrscheinlichkeitsrechnung*, which first appeared in 1886, von Kries rejected the philosophy of Laplace and the mathematicians who followed him. As von Kries pointed out, Laplace and his followers started with a subjective concept of probability, but then used observations to validate claims about objective probabilities. They seemed to think that objective probabilities exist and can be the subject of reasoning by Bayes's theorem whenever observations are numerous. This nonsensical law of large numbers, von Kries thought, was the result of combining Bernoulli's theorem with d'Alembert's mistaken belief that small probabilities can be neglected.

Von Kries believed that objective probabilities sometimes exist, but only under conditions where equally likely cases can legitimately be identified. Two conditions, he thought, are needed.

- Each case is produced by equally many of the possible arrangements of the circumstances, and this remains true when we look back in time to earlier circumstances that led to the current ones. In this sense, the relative sizes of the cases are natural.
- Nothing besides these circumstances affects our expectation about the cases. In this sense, the *Spielräume*[3] are *insensitive*.

Von Kries's 'principle of the *Spielräume*' was that objective probabilities can be calculated from equally likely cases when these conditions are satisfied. He considered this principle analogous to Kant's principle that everything that exists has a cause. Kant thought that we cannot reason at all without the principle of cause and effect. Von Kries thought that we cannot reason about objective probabilities without the principle of the *Spielräume*.

Even when an event has an objective probability, von Kries saw no legitimacy in the law of large numbers. Bernoulli's theorem is valid, he thought, but it tells us only that a large deviation of an event's frequency from its probability is just as unlikely as some other unlikely event, say a long run of successes. What will actually happen is another matter. This disagreement between Cournot and von Kries can be seen as a quibble about words. Do we say that an event will not happen (Cournot), or do we say merely that it is as unlikely as some other event we do not expect to happen (von Kries)? Either way, we proceed as if it will not happen. But the quibbling has its reasons. Cournot wanted to make a definite prediction, because this provides a bridge from probability theory to the world of phenomena – the real world, as those who have not studied Kant would say. Von Kries thought he had a different way of connecting probability theory with phenomena.

Von Kries's critique of moral certainty and the law of large numbers was widely accepted in Germany (Kamlah, 1983). In an influential textbook on probability, Emmanuel Czuber named Bernoulli, d'Alembert, Buffon and De Morgan as advocates of moral certainty and declared them all wrong; the concept of moral certainty, he said, violates the fundamental insight that an event of ever so small a probability can still happen (Cournot, [1843] 1984, p. 15). This thought was echoed by the philosopher Alexius Meinong (1915, p. 591).

This wariness about ruling out the happening of events whose probability is merely very small did not prevent acceptance of the idea that zero probability represents impossibility. Beginning with Wiman's work on continued fractions in 1900, mathematicians writing in German had worked on showing that various sets have measure zero, and everyone understood that the point was to show that these sets are impossible (Bernstein, 1912, p. 419). This suggests a great gulf between zero probability and merely small probability. One does not sense such a gulf in the writings of Borel and his French colleagues; for them, the vanishingly small was merely an idealization of the very small.

Von Kries's principle of the *Spielräume* did not endure, for no one knew how to use it. But his project of providing a Kantian justification for the uniform distribution of probabilities remained alive in German philosophy in the first decades of the twentieth century (Meinong, 1915; Reichenbach, 1916). John Maynard Keynes (1921) introduced it into the English literature, where it continues to echo, to the extent that today's probabilists, when asked about the philosophical grounding of the classical theory of probability, are more likely to think about arguments for a uniform distribution of probabilities than about Cournot's principle.

1.6   The Fracture

The destruction wrought in the 1930s and 1940s by Hitler and Stalin and then by the Second World War disrupted or destroyed individuals, families and nations. It also fractured intellectual traditions. In the case of probability theory, mathematical and philosophical traditions that had thrived in Western Europe gave way to new currents of thought, often centred in the Soviet Union and the USA. The mathematical leadership of Paris gave way to Moscow, where philosophical discourse could be dangerous, and to the USA, where it was often despised. The philosophical traditions of mathematicians in continental Europe faded away as English became the dominant language of the philosophy of science, now more heavily influenced by German-speaking philosophers who had escaped from Central Europe than by mathematicians of any other language. Cournot's principle was one victim of this fracture.

In his *Grundbegriffe der Wahrscheinlichkeitsrechnung*, published in 1933, Kolmogorov had articulated a frequentist interpretation of probability that relied on Cournot's principle. He had stated two principles for interpreting probability: Principle A said that probabilities were approximated by frequencies on repeated trials; and Principle B was the strong form of Cournot's principle, which applies to a single trial. The axiomatization of probability in the *Grundbegriffe*, though it added little to earlier formulations by Fréchet and others (Shafer and Vovk, 2006), was widely acknowledged after the Second World War as the definitive mathematical foundation for probability. For a short moment, it appeared that Kolmogorov's prestige might carry Cournot's principle into the new age as well.

Harald Cramér repeated Kolmogorov's two principles in his influential *Mathematical Methods in Statistics*, written during the war and published in English in 1946. Hans Richter's 1956 probability textbook, from which West Germans learned the new approach to mathematical probability, also recognized the *Cournotsche Prinzip* as the foundation for applications. But such philosophizing fell out of favour among the new generation of mathematicians. Although Kolmogorov's student, Yuri Prokhorov, kept it alive in the Soviet encyclopaedias (Prokhorov and Sevast'yanov, 1987), there was no mention of Cournot's principle in Boris Gnedenko's Курс теории вероятностей, published in 1950, or in Michel Loève's *Probability Theory*, published in 1955, and I have not seen it in any textbook for mathematical probability after Richter's.

In addition to taking the French probabilists seriously, Kolmogorov also showed interest in debates on the foundations of statistics taking place in the West after the war (Kolmogorov, [1948] 1998). But even with his immense mathematical prestige, he took care to make his philosophical comments brief and incidental to the mathematical theory, and his Soviet colleagues usually dared less (Anonymous, 1954; Kolmogorov, [1954] 1998; Kotz, 1965; Lorentz, 2002; Sheynin, 1996). The Moscow probabilists became known and admired abroad as formalists, who showed the rest of the world how mathematical probability could dispense with worries about meaning. This formal spirit took hold even in France, with the rise of Bourbaki, a band of mathematical reformers who often looked askance at the generation of mathematicians represented by Fréchet and Lévy and at probability theory itself (Brissaud, 2002; Bru, 2002).

In the USA, a pivotal role was played by the mathematician Joseph Doob, who extended Kolmogorov's formalism to accommodate continuous stochastic processes. An experiment with a random outcome is represented in Kolmogorov's formalism by its set E of possible outcomes, together with a set $\Im$ of subsets of E (the σ-algebra) and a real-valued function P on $\Im$. For each $A \in \Im$, $P(A)$ is the probability of A, which is supposed to approximate the frequency with which the outcome falls in A in repeated trials. In a seminal paper on continuous Markov processes, published in 1931 (Kolmogorov, [1931] 1992), Kolmogorov had used this framework to discuss transition probabilities – the probabilities for a stochastic process's value $y_{t'}$ at time t' conditional on its value y_t, where $t < t'$. This use of the framework lies within the boundaries of Kolmogorov's Principle A (frequency on repeated trials), at least if we have the means of repeatedly starting the process at any particular value y, for Kolmogorov's frequentism required only that the experiment be susceptible of repetition, not that it actually be repeated. But Kolmogorov never showed how to use his framework to describe probabilities for the entire time series or trajectory $y = \{y_t\}_{0 \leq t < \infty}$. He did not, that is to say, define a useful σ-algebra $\Im$ for the case where E consists of possible trajectories.[4] This left a mathematical challenge and also a philosophical question, for in many cases it is unrealistic to talk about repeating an entire time series. One thinks, for example, of the daily Dow Jones average from 1896 to the present; we may want to think that this sequence of numbers is random, but the experiment cannot be repeated.[5]

Doob is celebrated for having met the mathematical challenge; he introduced the concept of a *filtration*, a sequence $\{\mathfrak{I}_t\}$ of σ-algebras that grows with time, reflecting the growth of knowledge as values of the time series previously lying in the future are observed, and he generalized Kolmogorov's concept of conditional expectation of one variable given another to the concept of expectation given each of the $\mathfrak{I}_t$. But what of the philosophical problem? If a time series cannot be repeated, then we cannot interpret the probability for a property of the time series as the frequency with which that property occurs. So how do we interpret it? One answer is found in the history I have been recounting. Kolmogorov did not really need both Principle A (the frequency interpretation) and Principle B (Cournot's principle), because Principle A can be derived from Principle B when there are repeated trials (Bernoulli's theorem). All he needed was Cournot's principle, and this is available even when there is only a single trial. It tells us that the meaning of the probability measure P lies in the prediction that a property to which P assigns very small probability will not happen. This is, in fact, how we test a hypothesized probability measure for a stochastic process.

Had he been a colleague of Paul Lévy's, living in a Paris unravaged by Hitler, Doob might have settled on this solution, but he was an American, a pragmatist living in a far different world from that of Lévy or Kolmogorov. Having himself worked as a statistician, Doob believed that the application of mathematical theory could be left to the practitioner. As he told von Mises in a debate at Dartmouth College in 1940, a practitioner must use 'a judicious mixture of experiments with reason founded on theory and experience' (Doob, 1941, p. 209). There is no use in a philosopher telling the practitioner how to use the mathematician's formalism.

Doob's attitude did not prevent philosophers from talking about probability, but as I have already mentioned, English-language philosophy of probability after the Second World War was dominated by traditions that had developed in the English and German languages. The German scholars Rudolf Carnap, Hans Reichenbach and Richard von Mises all settled in the USA on the eve of the Second World War and published treatises on probability in English that did not mention Cournot's principle (Carnap, 1950; Reichenbach, 1949; von Mises, [1928] 1957).

Because of mathematicians' emphasis on the formal character of Kolmogorov's axioms, the one consensus that emerged in English-language philosophy of probability in the postwar years was that probability calculus has many interpretations. This idea was first articulated by Ernst Nagel in 1939 with respect to the new measure-theoretic formalism. Nagel listed nine interpretations, including multiple versions of the traditional rivals in the English and German traditions – belief and frequency (Nagel, 1939, pp. 40–41).

In this environment, where Cournot's principle was fading away, the one person who bothered to articulate a case against the principle was the subjectivist

Bruno de Finetti. De Finetti participated in the 1949 Paris conference where Fréchet coined the term (and he may have been the first to use it in English), when he deplored 'the so-called principle of Cournot' (de Finetti, 1951). He did not really disagree with the statement that one should act as if an event with a very small probability would not happen, but took the principle as a tautology, a consequence of the subjective definition of probability, not a principle standing outside probability theory and relating it to the world (de Finetti, 1955, p. 235; Dawid, 2004).

The one prominent postwar philosopher who might have been expected to champion Cournot's principle was Karl Popper, who taught that all scientific theories make contact with reality by providing opportunities for falsification. Cournot's principle tells us how to find such an opportunity in a probability model: single out an event of very small probability and see if it happens. Popper was sympathetic to Cournot's principle; this is already clear in his celebrated *Logik der Forschung*, published in 1935 (Popper, [1935] 1959, section 68). The picture is muddied, however, by his youthful ambition to axiomatize probability himself (Popper, 1938) and his later effort to say something original about propensity (Popper, 1959). In *Realism and the Aim of Science* in 1983, he mentions Cournot's principle in passing, but suggests somehow replacing it with a theorem (*sic*) of Doob's on the futility of gambling strategies (Popper, 1983, p. 379). Recasting Cournot's principle as a principle about the futility of gambling is the very project to which I now turn, but I cannot support this with an appeal to Popper's authority, for he never seems to have appreciated the principle's historical importance and continuing potential.

2. COURNOT'S PRINCIPLE IN GAME-THEORETIC FORM

As I have explained, Shafer and Vovk (2001) revive Cournot's principle in a game-theoretic form: a strategy for placing bets without risking bankruptcy will not multiply the bettor's capital by a large or infinite factor. In the case where the bettor can buy or sell any random variable for its expected value, this is equivalent to the classical form of the principle; Jean Ville demonstrated the equivalence in 1939 (Ville, 1939). The game-theoretic principle, however, can also be applied to real markets, where only some payoffs are priced.

This section discusses some of the implications of the game-theoretic principle. After reviewing Ville's theorem (section 2.1), I sketch the main contribution of Shafer and Vovk (2001), the aim of which was to show how the game-theoretic principle extends from classical probability games to more general games and to generalize classical limit theorems accordingly (sections 2.2 and 2.3). Then I review more recent work, which shows that good forecasts can be obtained by using a quasi-universal test as a foil (sections 2.4 and 2.5). This has profound implications for the interpretation of probability, the practice of statistics and our understanding of markets. I look at some of the implications for markets in section 2.6.

2.1   Ville's Theorem

Consider a sequence $Y_1, Y_2, \ldots$ of binary random variables with a joint probability distribution P. Suppose, for simplicity, that P assigns every finite sequence $y_1, \ldots, y_n$ of 0s and 1s positive probability, so that its conditional probabilities for Y_n given values of the preceding variables are always unambiguously defined. Following Jean Ville (1939), consider a gambler who begins with $1 and is allowed to bet as he pleases on each round, provided that he does not risk bankruptcy. We can formalize this with the following protocol, where betting on Y_n is represented as buying some number s_n (possibly zero or negative) of tickets that cost $\$P\{Y_n = 1 \mid Y_1 = y_1, \ldots, Y_{n-1} = y_{n-1}\}$ and pay $\$Y_n$.

Binary Probability Protocol

Players

Reality, Sceptic

Protocol:
   $K_0 := 1$.
   For $n_0 := 1, 2, \ldots$:
       Sceptic announces $s_n \in \mathfrak{R}$.
       Reality announces $y_n \in \{0, 1\}$.
       $K_n := K_{n-1} + s_n(y_n - P\{Y_n = 1 \mid Y_1 = y_1, \ldots, Y_{n-1} = y_{n-1}\})$.

Restriction on Sceptic
Sceptic must choose the s_n so that his capital is always non-negative ($K_n \geq 0$ for all n) no matter how Reality moves.

This is a perfect-information sequential protocol; moves are made in the order listed, and each player sees the other player's moves as they are made. The sequence $K_0, K_1, \ldots$ is Sceptic's capital process.
   Ville showed that Sceptic's getting rich in this protocol is equivalent to an event of small probability happening, in the following sense:

1.   When Sceptic follows a measurable strategy (a rule that gives s_n as a function of $y_1, \ldots, y_{n-1}$),

$$P\left\{\sup_n K_n \geq \frac{1}{\varepsilon}\right\} \leq \varepsilon, \tag{4.1}$$

for every $\varepsilon > 0$. (This is because the capital process K_0, K_1, ... is a non-negative martingale; equation (4.1) is sometimes called 'Doob's inequality'.)

2. If A is a measurable subset of $\{0, 1\}^\infty$ with $P(A) \leq \varepsilon$, then Sceptic has a measurable strategy that guarantees

$$\liminf_{n\to\infty} K_n \geq \frac{1}{\varepsilon},$$

whenever $(y_1, y_2, \ldots) \in A$.

We can summarize these results by saying that Sceptic's being able to multiply his capital by a factor of $1/\varepsilon$ or more is equivalent to the happening of an event with probability ε or less.

Although Ville spelled out his theory only for the binary case, he made its generality clear. It applies to the following more general protocol, where prices are regular conditional expected values for a known joint probability distribution P for a sequence of random variables $Y_1, Y_2, \ldots$:

Probability Protocol

Players

Reality, Sceptic

Protocol
    $K_0 := 1$.
    For $n := 1, 2, \ldots$:
        Sceptic announces $s_n \in \mathfrak{R} \to \mathfrak{R}$ such that

$$E(s_n(Y_n) | Y_1 = y_1, \ldots, Y_{n-1} = y_{n-1})$$

    exists.
    Reality announces $y_n \in \mathfrak{R}$.
    $K_n := K_{n-1} + s_n(y_n) - E(s_n(Y_n) | Y_1 = y_1, \ldots, Y_{n-1} = y_{n-1})$.

Restriction on Sceptic
Sceptic must choose the s_n so that his capital is always non-negative ($K_n \geq 0$ for all n), no matter how Reality moves.

Here Sceptic can buy any measurable function of Y_n on the nth round for its conditional expected value, provided this expected value exists. In this general protocol, as in the binary protocol, there is a probability of ε or less that the capital process for a particular strategy will reach $1/\varepsilon$ times its initial value, and there is a zero probability that it will diverge to infinity. Conversely, for any event of probability less than ε, there is a strategy whose capital process reaches $1/\varepsilon$ times its initial value if the event happens, and for any event of probability zero, there is a strategy whose capital process diverges to infinity if the event happens (Shafer and Vovk, 2001, ch. 8).

In light of these results, we can put both the finitary and infinitary versions of Cournot's principle in game-theoretic terms:

- **The finitary principle**   Instead of saying that an event of small probability singled out in advance will not happen, we say that a strategy chosen by Sceptic, if it avoids risk of bankruptcy, will not multiply his capital by a large factor.
- **The infinitary principle**   Instead of saying that an event of zero probability singled out in advance will not happen, we say that a strategy chosen by Sceptic, if it avoids risk of bankruptcy, will not make him infinitely rich.

As we will see shortly, the game-theoretic principles can be used in more general protocols, where prices are limited and are not necessarily related to a meaningful probability measure for Reality's moves.

Ville's work was motivated by von Mises's notion of a collective (von Mises, 1919, 1928, 1931). Von Mises had argued that a sequence $y_1, y_2, \ldots$ of 0s and 1s should be considered random if no subsequence with a different frequency of 1s can be picked out by a gambler to whom the ys are presented sequentially; this condition, von Mises felt, would keep the gambler from getting rich by deciding when to bet. Ville showed that von Mises's condition is insufficient, inasmuch as it does not rule out the gambler's getting rich by varying the direction and amount to bet.

Ville was the first to use the concept of a martingale as a tool in probability theory. For him, a martingale was a strategy for the player I have been calling Sceptic. He also began using the word for the player's capital process, for once the initial capital is fixed, the strategies and the capital processes are in a one-to-one correspondence. Doob, who borrowed the concept from Ville (Doob, 1940, 1949), made it apparently more suitable for general use by stripping away the betting story; for him, a martingale was merely a sequence $K_1, K_2, \ldots$ of random variables, such that

$$E(K_{n+1} | K_1 = k_1, \ldots, K_n = k_n) = k_n.$$

In Doob's later formulation (1953), which is now standard in the theory of stochastic processes and the theory of finance, we begin with a filtration $\mathfrak{I}_1 \subseteq \mathfrak{I}_2 \subseteq \ldots$ in a probability space $(P, \Omega, \mathfrak{I})$, and we say that random variables $K_1, K_2, \ldots$ form a martingale if K_n is measurable with respect to $\mathfrak{I}_n$ and

$$E(K_{n+1} | \mathfrak{I}_n) = K_n$$

for all n.

2.2 The Game-theoretic Framework

The framework of Shafer and Vovk (2001) returns to Ville's game-theoretic version of classical probability theory and generalizes it. The generalization has three aspects.

1. Instead of beginning with a probability measure and using its conditional probabilities or expected values as prices on each round, we allow another player, Forecaster, to set the prices as play proceeds. This makes the framework 'prequential' (Dawid, 1984); there is no need to specify what the price on the nth round would be had Reality moved differently on earlier rounds.
2. When convenient, we make explicit additional information, say x_n, that Reality provides to Forecaster and Sceptic before they make their nth moves.
3. We allow the story to be multi-dimensional, with Reality making several moves and Forecaster pricing them all.

A convenient level of generality for the present discussion is provided by the following protocol, where $\mathfrak{R}^k$ is a k-dimensional Euclidean space, $\mathbf{Y}$ is a subset of $\mathfrak{R}^k$, and $\mathbf{X}$ is an arbitrary set.

Linear Forecasting Protocol

Players

Reality, Forecaster, Sceptic

Protocol
  $K_0 := 1$.
  For $n := 1, 2, \ldots N$:
    Reality announces $x_n \in \mathbf{X}$.
    Forecaster announces $f_n \in \mathfrak{R}^k$.

Sceptic announces $s_n \in \mathfrak{R}^k$.
Reality announces $y_n \in \mathbf{Y}$.
$K_n := K_{n-1} + s_n \cdot (y_n - f_n)$.

Restriction on Sceptic

Sceptic must choose the s_n so that his capital is always non-negative ($K_n \geq 0$ for all n) no matter how the other players move.

Here $s_n \cdot (y_n - f_n)$ is the dot product of the k-dimensional vectors s_n and $(y_n - f_n)$. Notice also that play stops on the Nth round rather than continuing indefinitely. This is a convenient assumption in this section, where we emphasize the finitary picture; we will return to the infinitary picture later.

The linear forecasting protocol covers many prediction problems considered in statistics (where x and y are often called *independent* and *dependent* variables, respectively) and machine learning (where x is called the *object* and y the *label*) (Hastie et al., 2001; Vapnik, 1996; Vovk et al., 2005a). Market games can be included by taking f_n to be a vector of opening prices and y_n the corresponding vector of closing prices for the nth trading period.

A strategy for Sceptic in the linear forecasting protocol is a rule that gives each of his moves s_n as a function of the preceding moves by Reality and Forecaster, $(x_1, f_1, y_1), \ldots, (x_{n-1}, f_{n-1}, y_{n-1}), x_n, f_n$. A strategy for Forecaster is a rule that gives each of his moves f_n as a function of the preceding moves by Reality and Sceptic, $(x_1, s_1, y_1), \ldots, (x_{n-1}, s_{n-1}, y_{n-1}), x_n$. One way of prescribing a strategy for Forecaster is to choose a probability distribution for $(x_1, y_1), (x_2, y_2) \ldots$ and set f_n equal to the conditional expected value of y_n given $(x_1, y_1), \ldots, (x_{n-1}, y_{n-1}), x_n$. We will look at other interesting strategies for Forecaster in section 2.5.

How can one express confidence in Forecaster? The natural way is to assert Cournot's principle: say that a legal strategy for Sceptic (one that avoids $K_n < 0$ no matter how the other players move) will not multiply Sceptic's initial capital by a large factor.

Once we adopt Cournot's principle in this form, it is natural to scale the implications of our confidence in Forecaster the same way we do in classical probability. This means treating an event that happens only when a specified legal strategy multiplies the capital by $1/\varepsilon$ as no more likely than an event with probability ε.

To formalize this, consider a possible sequence of moves by Reality and Forecaster,

$$(x_1, f_1, y_1), \ldots, (x_N, f_N, y_N) \tag{4.2}$$

The space of all such sequences, $\{\mathbf{X} \times \mathfrak{R}^k \times \mathbf{Y}\}^N$, is the *sample space* for our protocol, and a subset of it is an *event*. The *upper probability* of an event E is

$\overline{PE} :=$ inf $\{\varepsilon |$. Sceptic has a strategy that guarantees $K_N \geq 1/\varepsilon$ if
Forecaster and Reality satisfy E and $K_N \geq 0$ otherwise$\}$.

Roughly, $\overline{PE}$ is the smallest ε, such that Sceptic can multiply his capital by $1/\varepsilon$ if E happens without risking bankruptcy if E fails. When $\overline{PE}$ is small, we say that E is *morally impossible*.

The *lower probability* of an event E is

$$\underline{PE} = 1 - \overline{PE^c},$$

where E^c is E's complement with respect to the sample space. When $\underline{PE}$ is close to one, we say that E is *morally certain*.

As in classical probability, we can combine Cournot's principle with a form of Bernoulli's theorem to obtain a statement about relative frequency in a long sequence of events. In a sufficiently long sequence of events with upper probability 0.1 or less, for example, it is morally certain that no more than about 10 per cent of the events will happen (Shafer and Vovk, 2002, section 5.3). This is a martingale-type result; rather than insist that the events be independent in some sense, we assume that the upper probability for each event is calculated at the point in the game where the previous event is settled.

2.3   Extending the Classical Limit Theorems

One of the main contributions of Shafer and Vovk (2001) was to show that game theory can replace measure theory as a foundation for classical probability. We showed in particular that classical limit theorems, especially the strong law of large numbers and the law of the iterated logarithm, can be proven constructively within a purely game-theoretic framework. From Ville's work, we know that for any event with probability zero, there is a strategy for Sceptic that avoids bankruptcy for sure and makes him infinitely rich if the event fails. But constructing the strategy is another matter. In the case of the events of probability zero associated with the classical theorems, we did construct the requisite strategies; they are computable and continuous.

We provided similar constructions for classical results that do not require an infinite number of rounds of play to be meaningful: the weak law of large numbers, finitary versions of the law of the iterated logarithm, and the central limit theorem. The game-theoretic central limit theorem gives conditions under which upper and lower probabilities for the value of an average of many outcomes will approximately coincide and equal the usual probabilities computed from the normal distribution.

The game-theoretic results are more powerful than the measure-theoretic ones in the respects I listed at the beginning of section 2.2: the prices can be provided by Forecaster (an actual forecaster or a market) rather than by a probability distribution known in advance, and Forecaster and Sceptic can use information *x* that is not itself priced or probabilized. In addition, new results emerge when betting is restricted in some way. A new one-sided central limit theorem arises if Forecaster makes only one-sided betting offers (Shafer and Vovk, 2001, ch. 5), and laws of large numbers can be established for market prices (ibid., ch. 15).

2.4   Is There a Universal Test?

Within the measure-theoretic formalization of probability, it is axiomatic that the union of a countable number of events of probability zero itself has probability zero. In the early twentieth century, there was considerable hesitation about this axiom. Even Émile Borel, who introduced it, was uncomfortable with it. Maurice Fréchet and Bruno de Finetti debated it (de Finetti, 1930; Fréchet, 1930). It was finally accepted by most mathematicians, because it is useful (in proving the limit theorems, for example) and apparently harmless. Because only a finite number of events can be observed, an assumption about infinite collections of events, being untestable, should not get us into trouble (Kolmogorov, 1933, p. 14).

Once the countable additivity of probability was more or less universally accepted, it became natural to discuss universal statistical tests. If we imagine that we can observe an infinite sequence of random variables Y_1, Y_2, ..., then any subset of $\mathfrak{R}^\infty$ that is assigned probability zero by a probability measure P on $\mathfrak{R}^\infty$ defines a test of the hypothesis that P is the joint probability distribution for Y_1, Y_2, ... Given that we have only a finite number of mathematical and logical symbols and can combine them in at most a countable number of ways, we can define at most a countable number of subsets of $\mathfrak{R}^\infty$ that have measure zero. Their union, say E, seems to define a universal test: reject P if and only if the observed sequence y_1, y_2, ... falls in E. This idea was advanced by Abraham Wald in the 1930s, in defence of von Mises's and Ville's idea of using batteries of tests to define randomness for sequences (Wald, 1936, 1937, 1938; de Finetti, 1939, pp. 15–16). It was given definitive form within measure-theoretic probability in 1966 by Per Martin-Löf, who demonstrated the existence of what he called universal tests of stochasticity (Martin-Löf, 1966–7). More recently, this concept has been elaborated in the theory of algorithmic complexity (Li and Vitányi, 1997, section 2.5).

The thesis that one can find a universal test appears less plausible when we abandon the infinitary picture for the more realistic finitary picture, where we test using events of small probability rather than events of zero probability. When we consider two events E_1 and E_2 whose probabilities are so small as to make them morally impossible, we will surely say that their disjunction $E_1 \cup$

E_2 is also morally impossible, for the sum of two small numbers is also small, even if not quite as small.[6] But we cannot count on the sum of many small numbers being small, and so we cannot say that the union of many morally impossible events is always morally impossible.

The picture is similar in the game-theoretic framework. In this framework, we are testing not a probability distribution but the hypothesis that Forecaster is a good forecaster. A test for Sceptic is not an event with small probability, but a strategy for Sceptic that does not risk bankruptcy. We reject the hypothesis when the strategy makes Sceptic sufficiently rich (infinitely rich or many times richer than he was initially). We combine tests not by taking unions of events, but by averaging strategies.

Suppose, as usual, that Sceptic starts with 1, and suppose S_1 and S_2 are strategies for Sceptic that do not risk bankruptcy. Then $(S_1 + S_2)/2$ does not risk bankruptcy, and we can say the following.

- **Infinitary case** If S_1 or S_2 make Sceptic infinitely rich, then $(S_1 + S_2)/2$ will also make him infinitely rich.
- **Finitary case** If S_1 or S_2 increases Sceptic's capital from 1 to some large number C, then $(S_1 + S_2)/2$ will also increase it to a large number, at least C/2.

This is parallel to the way testing using $E_1 \cup E_2$ is related to testing using E_1 or E_2. In the infinitary case, we can combine two tests perfectly, obtaining a test that rejects Forecaster's being a good forecaster if either of the separate tests rejects this hypothesis. In the finitary case, the combination is not so perfect; the combined test does reject if either of the separate tests rejects, but perhaps not so strongly.

When we look closer, however, the game-theoretic approach provides some new insights. Consider first the infinitary case. In the measure-theoretic approach pioneered by Borel, Fréchet and Kolmogorov, we use countable additivity to prove limit theorems such as the law of large numbers. In the game-theoretic approach, we have no such arbitrary general axiom, but there is an obvious way to try to combine a countable number of strategies $S_1, S_2, \ldots$. We try to form a strategy S by taking the linear combination of these strategies using positive coefficients $\alpha_1, \alpha_2, \ldots$ that add to one. This means that S's move in the situation $(x_1, f_1, y_1), \ldots, (x_{n-1}, f_{n-1}, y_{n-1}), x_n, f_n$ should be

$$S((x_1, f_1, y_1), \ldots, (x_{n-1}, f_{n-1}, y_{n-1}), x_n, f_n)$$
$$= \sum_{j=1}^{\infty} \alpha_j S_j((x_1, f_1, y_1), \ldots, (x_{n-1}, f_{n-1}, y_{n-1}), x_n, f_n). \tag{4.3}$$

As it turns out, this works for the strategies we need to combine to prove the classical limit theorems (see, for example, Shafer and Vovk, 2001, p. 67), but it does not work for arbitrary strategies $S_1, S_2, \ldots$ in arbitrary instances of the linear forecasting protocol, because there is no guarantee that the right-hand side of (4.3) will converge. This vindicates, in some respects, the critics of countable additivity. The general axiom turns out not to be necessary after all.

The new insights provided by the game-theoretic approach in the finitary case are more complicated to explain, but also more important. As it turns out, the aspects of disagreement between forecasts f_n and outcomes y_n that we really want to test are relatively limited. To see this, consider binary probability forecasting again:

Binary Probability Protocol With Forecaster and Objects

Players

Reality, Forecaster, Sceptic

Protocol
$K_0 := 1$.
For $n := 1, 2, \ldots$:
   Reality announces $x_n \in \mathbf{X}$.
   Forecaster announces $p_n \in [0, 1]$.
   Sceptic announces $s_n \in \mathfrak{R}$.
   Reality announces $y_n \in \{0, 1\}$.
   $K_n := K_{n-1} + s_n(y_n - p_n)$.

Restriction on Sceptic
Sceptic must choose the s_n so that his capital is always non-negative ($K_n \geq 0$ for all n) no matter how the other players move.

In this protocol, where Forecaster gives a probability p_n on each round, taking into account the previous outcomes $y_1, \ldots, y_{n-1}$ and auxiliary information $x_1, \ldots, x_n$, we are mainly interested in two aspects of the agreement between the probabilities p_n and the outcomes y_n:

- **Calibration** Whenever there is a large number of rounds on which p_n is close to some fixed probability p^*, we want the frequency with which $y_n = 1$ on those rounds to be approximately equal to p^*.
- **Resolution** We want this approximate equality between frequency and p^* to remain true when we consider only rounds where p_n is close to p^* and also x_n is close to some fixed value x^* in the object space $\mathbf{X}$.

As it turns out (Vovk et al., 2005b), we can often average strategies that reject Forecaster's performance over a grid of values of (x^*, p^*) that are sufficiently dense to capture all deviations of practical interest. This average strategy, which is testing for calibration and resolution, will not necessarily test for more subtle deviations by $y_1, y_2, \ldots$ from the forecasts $p_1, p_2, \ldots$, such as those associated with the law of the iterated logarithm or Ville's refutation of von Mises's theory, but these more subtle deviations may hold little interest. So the average strategy can be regarded, for practical purposes, as a universal test. To avoid confusion, I call it a *quasi-universal strategy*.

2.5 Defensive Forecasting

In cases where we have a quasi-universal strategy, a new opportunity opens up for Forecaster. Forecaster will do well enough if he can avoid rejection by that strategy. Formally, he needs a winning strategy in a version of the game where Sceptic is required to follow the quasi-universal strategy, but Reality is free to move as she pleases. Does Forecaster have such a winning strategy? The surprising answer is yes.

This is easiest to see in the case where the quasi-universal strategy gives a move for the nth round that is continuous in the forecast p_n. As it happens, this is not an unreasonable requirement. We can construct quasi-universal strategies for calibration and resolution that are continuous in this respect, and there is even a philosophical argument for ruling out any discontinuous strategy for Sceptic: discontinuous functions are not really computable (Brouwer, 1918; Martin-Löf, 1970).

As it turns out, it is easy to show that for any forecast-continuous strategy for Sceptic, there exists a strategy for Forecaster that does not allow Sceptic's capital to grow, regardless of what Reality does. Let me repeat the simple proof given in Vovk, Nouretdinov et al. (2005) and Vovk et al. (2005b). It begins by simplifying so that Forecaster's job seems to be even a little harder. Instead of requiring that the entire forecast-continuous strategy for Sceptic be announced at the beginning of the game, we ask only that Sceptic announce his strategy for each round before Forecaster's move on that round. In addition, we drop the restriction that Sceptic avoid risk of bankruptcy. The following protocol results.

Binary Forecasting against Continuous Tests

Players

Reality, Forecaster, Sceptic

Protocol

$K_0 := 1.$

For $n := 1, 2, \ldots :$

　Reality announces $x_n \in \mathbf{X}$.

　Sceptic announces continuous $S_n : [0, 1] \to \mathfrak{R}$.

　Forecaster announces $p_n \in [0, 1]$.

　Reality announces $y_n \in \{0, 1\}$.

　$K_n := K_{n-1} + S_n(p_n)(y_n - p_n).$

Here S_n is Sceptic's strategy for the nth round; it gives his move as a function of Forecaster's not-yet-announced move p_n.

Theorem 1　Forecaster has a strategy that ensures $K_0 \geq K_1 \geq K_2 \geq \ldots$.

Proof　Because S_n is continuous, Forecaster can use the following strategy:

- if the function $S_n(p)$ takes the value 0, choose p_n so that $S_n(p_n) = 0$;
- if S_n is always positive, take $p_n := 1$;
- if S_n is always negative, take $p_n := 0$.

This guarantees that $S_n(p_n)(y_n - p_n) \leq 0$, so that $K_n \leq K_{n-1}$.

Some readers may question the philosophical rationale for requiring that S_n be continuous. As it turns out, dropping this requirement does not cost us much; Forecaster can still win if we allow him to randomize (Vovk and Shafer, 2005). This means that instead of telling Reality his probability p_n, Forecaster may give Reality only a probability distribution P_n for p_n, with the value p_n to be drawn from P_n out of sight of Reality or perhaps after Reality has selected y_n.

　A strategy for Forecaster is what one usually calls a probability model; given the previous outcomes $y_1, \ldots, y_{n-1}$ and auxiliary information $x_1, \ldots, x_n$, it gives a probability p_n for $y_n = 1$. Such probabilities can be used in any repetitive decision problem (Vovk, 2005). So Theorem 1's guarantee that they are valid, in the sense that they pass any reasonable test of calibration and resolution, has immense practical significance.

　When he follows the strategy described by Theorem 1, is Forecaster using experience of the past to predict the future? He is certainly taking the past into consideration. The moves for Sceptic recommended by the quasi-universal strategy signal emerging discrepancies that Sceptic would like to take advantage of, and the strategy for Forecaster chooses his p_n to avoid extending these discrepancies. Because they succeed regardless of the y_n, however, it is awkward to call the p_n predictions. They are really only descriptions of the past, not predictions of the future.

The fact that we can always make good probability forecasts undermines some popular ideas about stochasticity. Indeed, to the extent that everything is stochastic, stochasticity has no content. We can still point to quantum mechanics as an extraordinarily successful stochastic theory, whose probabilities appear to withstand all tests, not just tests of calibration and resolution. Less extreme but also remarkable, there are cases where relatively simple probability models – exchangeable models or Markov models, for example – are successful. In these cases, which go beyond merely being able to give sequential probabilities that beat tests of calibration and resolution, it is reasonable to claim predictive insight; perhaps it is even reasonable to claim that we have caught a glimpse of causal regularities (Shafer, 1996). It seems, however, that bare stochasticity is no regularity at all.

2.6 Implications for Market Prices

Organized exchanges, in which a buyer or seller can always find a ready price for a particular commodity or security, are forecasting games. So we can ask whether Cournot's principle holds in such exchanges, and we can consider the implications of its holding. It is often said that in an efficient market, an investor cannot make a lot of money without taking undue risk. Cournot's principle makes this precise by saying that he will not make a lot of money without risking bankruptcy; he starts with a certain initial capital, and on each round of trading he risks at most a portion of his current capital. In the next section, I will say more about how this formulation relates to established formulations of the efficient-markets hypothesis. Here, in preparation, I explain how Cournot's principle alone can explain certain stylized facts about prices that are often explained using stochasticity.

2.6.1   The $\sqrt{dt}$ effect

Consider first the stylized fact that changes in market prices over an interval of time of length dt scale as $\sqrt{dt}$. In a securities market where shares are traded 252 days per year, for example, the typical change in price of a share from one year to the next is $\sqrt{252}$, or about 16 times as large as the typical change from one day to the next. There is a standard way of explaining this. We begin by assuming that price changes are stochastic, and we argue that successive changes must be uncorrelated; otherwise someone who knew the correlation (or learned it by observation) could devise a trading strategy with positive expected value. The uncorrelatedness of 252 successive daily price changes implies that their sum, the annual price change, is about $\sqrt{252}$ times as large, on average, as the daily changes. This is a simple argument, but stochastic ideas intervene in two places, first when price changes are assumed to be stochastic, and then when market efficiency is interpreted as the absence of a trading strategy with positive expected value. As I now explain, we can replace this stochastic argument with a purely game-theoretic argument in which Cournot's principle expresses the assumption of market efficiency.

For simplicity, consider the following protocol, which describes a market in shares of a corporation. Investor plays the role of Sceptic; he tries to make money, and Cournot's principle says he cannot get very rich following the rules, which do not permit him to risk bankruptcy. Market plays the roles of Forecaster (by giving opening prices) and Reality (by giving closing prices). For simplicity, we suppose that today's opening price is yesterday's closing price, so that Market gives only one price each day, at the end of the day. When Investor holds s_n shares during day n, he makes $s_n(y_n - y_{n-1})$, where y_n is the price at the end of day n.

The Market Protocol

Players

Investor, Market

Protocol

$\quad K_0 := 1.$
$\quad$ Market announces $y_0 \in \mathfrak{R}$.
$\quad$ For $n := 1, 2, \ldots N$:
$\quad\quad$ Investor announces $s_n \in \mathfrak{R}$.
$\quad\quad$ Market announces $y_n \in \mathfrak{R}$.
$\quad\quad K_n := K_{n-1} + s_n(y_n - y_{n-1}).$

Restriction on Investor

Investor must choose the s_n so that his capital is always non-negative ($K_n \geq 0$ for all n) no matter how Market moves.

For simplicity, we ignore the fact that the price y_n of a share cannot be negative. Since there is no stochastic assumption here, we cannot appeal to the idea of the variance of a probability distribution for price changes to explain what $\sqrt{dt}$ scaling means, but we can use

$$\sqrt{\frac{1}{N}\sum_{n=1}^{N}(y_n - y_{n-1})^2} \qquad (4.4)$$

as the typical daily change, and we can compare it to the magnitude of the change we see over the whole game, say

$$\max_{0<n\leq N} |y_n - y_0|.$$

(4.5)

The quantity (4.5) should have the same order of magnitude as $\sqrt{N}$ times the quantity (4.4). Equivalently, we should have

$$\sum_{n=1}^{N}(y_n - y_{n-1})^2 \sim \max_{0<n\leq N}(y_n - y_0)^2,$$

(4.6)

where $\sim$ is understood to mean that the two quantities are of the same order of magnitude.

Does Cournot's principle give us any reason to think that (4.6) should hold? Indeed it does. As it turns out, Investor has a legal strategy (one avoiding bankruptcy) that makes a lot of money if (4.6) is violated. Market (who here represents all the other investors and speculators) wants to set prices so that Investor will not make a lot of money, and we just saw in section 2.5 that he can more or less do so. So we may expect (4.6) to hold.

The strategy that makes money if (4.6) is violated is an average of two strategies, one a momentum strategy (holding more shares after the price goes up), the other a contrarian strategy (holding more shares after the price goes down).

1. The momentum strategy is based on the assumption that Investor can count on $\Sigma(y_n - y_{n-1})^2 \leq E$ and $\max(y_n - y_0)^2 \geq D$, where D and E are known constants. On this assumption, the strategy is legal and turns \$1 into \$$D/E$ or more for sure.
2. The contrarian strategy is based on the assumption that Investor can count on $\Sigma(y_n - y_{n-1})^2 \geq E$ and $\max(y_n - y_0)^2 \leq D$, where D and E are known constants. On this assumption, the strategy is legal and turns \$1 into \$$E/D$ or more for sure.

If the assumptions about $\Sigma(y_n - y_{n-1})^2$ and $\max(y_n - y_0)^2$ fail, then the strategy fails to make money, but Investor can still avoid bankruptcy. For details, see Vovk and Shafer (2003a).

2.6.2 The game-theoretic CAPM
The Capital Asset Pricing Model (CAPM), popular in finance theory for almost 40 years, assumes that a firm whose shares are traded in a securities market has a stable level of risk relative to the market as a whole. The risk for a security s is defined in terms of a probability model for the returns of all the securities in the market; it is the theoretical regression coefficient

$$\beta_s = \frac{Cov(R_s, R_m)}{Var(R_m)},$$

(4.7)

where R_s is a random variable whose realizations are s's returns, and R_m is a random variable whose realizations are a market index's returns.[7] The CAPM says that

$$E(R_s) = r + \beta_s (E(R_m) - r), \qquad (4.8)$$

where r is the rate of interest on government debt, assumed to be constant (Copeland and Weston, 1988, p. 197). Because $E(R_m) - r$ is usually positive, this equation suggests that securities with higher β have higher average returns. The equation has found only weak empirical confirmation, but it continues to be popular, because it suggests plausible ways of analysing decision problems faced by financial managers.

As it turns out, a purely game-theoretic argument based on Cournot's principle leads to an analogous equation involving only observed returns, with no reference to a probability distribution. The game-theoretic equation is where

$$\bar{r}_s \sim r' + b_s (\bar{r}_m - r'), \qquad (4.9)$$

where

$$\bar{r}_s := \frac{1}{N} \sum_{n=1}^{N} s_n, \qquad \bar{r}_m := \frac{1}{N} \sum_{n=1}^{N} m_n,$$

and

$$b_s := \frac{\sum_{n=1}^{N} s_n m_n}{\sum_{n=1}^{N} m_n^2}, \qquad r' := \bar{r}_m - \frac{1}{N} \sum_{n=1}^{N} m_n^2,$$

s_n and m_n being the actual returns of s and the market index, respectively, over period n. This is analogous to (4.8), inasmuch as r' measures the performance of the market as a whole, and the other quantities are empirical analogues of the theoretical quantities in (4.8).

The interpretation of (4.9) is similar to the interpretation of the game-theoretic version of $\sqrt{dt}$ scaling, equation (4.6): a speculator can make money to the extent it is violated. Given the approximations in the derivation of (4.9), as well as the existence of transaction costs and other market imperfections, we can expect the relation to hold only loosely, but we can ask whether it is any looser in practice than the empirical relations implied by CAPM. If not, then the very approximate confirmation of CAPM that has been discerned in data might be attributed to (4.9), leaving nothing that can be interpreted as empirical justification for the stochastic assumptions in CAPM. For details, see Vovk and Shafer (2002).

3. THE RETURN OF COURNOT'S PRINCIPLE

In this concluding section, I discuss what probability, economics and finance can gain from a revival of Cournot's principle.

3.1 Why Probability Needs Cournot's Principle

Until the middle of the twentieth century, specialists in mathematical probability generally assumed that any probability can be known, either *a priori* or by observation. Those who understood probability as a measure of belief did not question the presumption that one can know one's beliefs. Those who understood probability as relative frequency assumed that one can observe frequencies. Those who interpreted probability using Cournot's principle did so on the assumption that they would know the probabilities they wanted to test; you would not check whether an event of small probability happened unless you had conjectured it had small probability.

The observations necessary for estimating a numerical probability may be hard to come by, but at worst, Cournot suggested, they could be made by a superior intelligence that represents the limits of what humans can observe (Martin, 1996, pp. 146–50). Here Cournot was drawing an analogy with the classical understanding of determinism. Classical determinism required more than the future being determined in some theological sense; it required that the future be predictable by means of laws that can be used by a human, or at least by a superior intelligence whose powers of calculation and observation are human-like.

The presumption that probabilities are knowable leads to the apprehension that some events may not have probabilities. Perhaps there are three categories of events:

1. those we can predict with certainty;
2. those we can predict only by giving their probability;
3. those that we can predict neither with certainty nor probabilistically.

Most probabilists did think that there are events in the third category. Kolmogorov said so explicitly, and he did not speak of them as events whose probabilities cannot be known; he spoke of them as events that do not have probabilities (Kolmogorov, 1983, p. 1). John Maynard Keynes and R.A. Fisher, each in his own way, also insisted that not every event has a numerical probability (Fisher, 1956; Keynes, 1921, 1937).

Doob's success in formalizing the concept of a probability measure for an arbitrary stochastic process destabilized this consensus. As I have already emphasized, there are many cases where we cannot repeat an entire stochastic process, cases where there is only one realization, one time series. In these cases, the probability measure assigns probabilities to many events that are not repeated. Having no direct frequency interpretation, these probabilities cannot be verified in any direct way. Because Doob did not appeal to Cournot's principle or provide any other guidance about its meaning, his followers looked in other directions for understanding. Many looked towards mechanisms, such as well-balanced dice that produce or at least simulate randomness. As they saw it, phenomena must be produced in some way. Deterministic phenomena are produced by deterministic mechanisms, indeterministic phenomena by chance mechanisms. The probabilities, even if unverifiable and perhaps unknowable, are meaningful, because they have this generative task.

The growing importance of this way of seeing the world is evidenced by a pivotal article published by Jerzy Neyman in 1960. According to Neyman, science was moving into a period of dynamic indeterminism,

> characterized by the search for evolutionary chance mechanisms capable of explaining the various frequencies observed in the development of phenomena studied. The chance mechanism of carcinogenesis and the chance mechanism behind the varying properties of the comets in the Solar System exemplify the subjects of dynamic indeterministic studies. One might hazard the assertion that every serious contemporary study is a study of the chance mechanism behind some phenomena. The statistical and probabilistic tool in such studies is the theory of stochastic processes. (Neyman, 1960, p. 625)

As this quotation confirms, Neyman was a frequentist. His rhetoric, however, suggests that the initial meaning of probabilities lies in their relation to how phenomena are generated rather than in their relation to frequencies. He wants to explain frequencies, but he does not ask that every probability have a frequency interpretation. Perhaps it is enough that successive probability predictions be well calibrated and have good resolution in the sense explained in section 2.4.

What is most striking about Neyman's vision is that stochastic processes appear as the only alternative to deterministic models. The third category of phenomena, those we can predict neither with certainty nor probabilistically, has disappeared. This way of thinking has become ever more dominant since 1960. In many branches of science, we now hear casual references to 'true', 'physical' or 'objective' probabilities, without any hesitation about their existence. An indeterministic process is assumed to be a stochastic process, regardless of whether we do or even can know the probabilities. The naïveté derided by von Kries 120 years ago is once again orthodoxy.

The game-theoretic results reported in section 2 provide a framework for regaining the philosophical sophistication of Keynes, Fisher and Kolmogorov, without abandoning the successes achieved by the theory of stochastic processes. Whenever we test a stochastic process empirically, we are applying Cournot's principle to known (hypothetical) probabilities. When we have less than a stochastic process, a model giving only limited prices or probabilities, we can still test it via Cournot's principle, without regarding it as part of some unknowable yet somehow still meaningful full stochastic process.

The results on defensive forecasting reviewed in section 2.5 also provide new insights. They show that, in a certain limited sense, our third category is indeed empty. Any quantity or event that can be placed in a series (in a time series, not necessarily a series of independent repetitions) can be predicted probabilistically, at least with respect to that series. This suggests that talk about chance mechanisms is also empty. Defensive forecasting works for any time series, regardless of how it is generated. The idea of a chance mechanism adds nothing.

3.2 Why Economics Needs Cournot's Principle

The suggestion that market prices are expected values goes back at least to Cournot (Cournot, [1843] 1984, ch. 5). But whose expected values are they? Does the market have a mind? And how do we learn more details about the probabilities that presumably accompany these expected values? These questions scarcely troubled Cournot, who still lived in a Laplacean world where one did not fret too much about mankind's ability to discern the proper measure of its ignorance. As critiques such as that of von Kries accumulated, however, this tranquillity became less and less tenable. By the beginning of the twentieth century, it seemed to require either the philosophical naïveté of a Bachelier (1900) or the obscurity of an Edgeworth (Mirowski, 1994).

So far as probability is concerned, today's economists are descendants not of Edgeworth and Keynes, but of Doob, Neyman and de Finetti. It was Paul Samuelson, perhaps, who first brought Doob's measure-theoretic version of martingales into economics, in the 1965 article now recognized as a first step in the formulation of the concept of informational efficiency (Samuelson, 1965). Doob's mathematics was not enough to bring Samuelson back to Cournot's tranquillity, as we see in the conclusion of the article:

> I have not here discussed where the basic probability distributions are supposed to come from. In whose minds are they *ex ante*? Is there any *ex post* validation of them? Are they supposed to belong to the market as a whole? And what does that mean? Are they supposed to belong to the "representative individual," and who is he? Are

they some defensible or necessitous compromise of divergent expectation patterns? Do price quotations somehow produce a Pareto-optimal configuration of *ex ante* subjective probabilities? This paper has not attempted to pronounce on these interesting questions. (Ibid., p. 790)

These questions point towards a deconstruction of probability, but Samuelson's profession has moved in the opposite direction, resolutely embracing, under the slogan of 'rational expectations', the hypothesis that the world of trade has true probabilities in the sense of Neyman, happily congruent with its inhabitants' subjective probabilities in the sense of de Finetti (Lucas and Prescott, 1971). The effect may be bullheadedness rather than tranquillity, but economics has reimposed a unity on objective and subjective probability.

The game-theoretic framework allows us to give up this wilful reunification, renouncing Cournot's tranquillity, but retaining Cournot's principle. Once we reclaim Cournot's principle as a way of interpreting probabilities, we can interpret prices directly in the same way: neither a representative individual nor a mind for the market is needed. There is no need to posit probabilities, objective or subjective, that go beyond the prices. These prices are no one's opinions. They are created by competition (Hayek, 1978). They form a martingale not in Doob's sense, but in Ville's sense. Because they are the prices at which investors can trade, they generate other martingales in Ville's sense, even though no probabilities intervene. Moreover, because the finitary version of the game-theoretic treatment produces error bounds that tighten as the number of instances grows, we can regain the Knightian distinction between risks faced by an insurance company, which competes in evaluating average outcomes in a long series of trails it observes along with competitors, and the uncertainties faced by an entrepreneur or venture capitalist, who encounters a smaller number of opportunities in a series more privately observed (Knight, 1921).

3.3   Why Finance Needs Cournot's Principle

We can always invent a probability distribution with respect to which prices form a martingale. As Eugene Fama explained in his celebrated 1970 article (Fama, 1970), the central problem in understanding market efficiency is to explain what it means for this probability distribution to reflect fully all available information. Some have questioned whether he ever provided an explanation, but his 1976 finance text (Fama, 1976) added a gloss that has endured: the probabilities should correspond to rational expectations (LeRoy, 1989). Somehow, the probabilities should be right. They should connect properly with what really happens in the future.

This brings us back again to Cournot's principle, and to the thesis of this chapter, that we can test market prices directly using the game-theoretic version of Cournot's principle, without positing full probability distributions.

The results on defensive forecasting that I reported in section 2.5 tell us that it is possible to set prices that will foil nearly any trading strategy that does not risk bankruptcy. In markets with reasonable liquidity, there are many speculators trying to do exactly that, and so it is reasonable to hypothesize that they have succeeded. In other words, the game-theoretic version of Cournot's principle is a very plausible hypothesis. It predicts, however, only a sort of equilibrium in speculation, not equilibrium among rational investors with well-founded probabilities concerning the risks of different investments and well-defined preferences over those risks (Bourghelle et al., 2005).

Does it tell us that prices fully reflect all available information? In one sense, yes. It tells us that there is no information available that will allow a speculator to beat the prices. It does not say, however, that the available information determines prices. It does not rule out there being prices just as consistent with all available information that differ from the actual prices by a factor of 2, or a factor of 3, or a factor of 10. It does not rule out there being prices just as consistent with all the available information that would result in vastly different allocations of capital among competing projects (Stiglitz, 1981). It does not rule out long slow swings in prices based on no information at all or variability far beyond that justified by the flow of new information (Poterba and Summers, 1988; Shiller, 1989).

Future empirical work on the hypothesis of informational efficiency in capital markets should, I believe, try to unbundle the game-theoretic hypothesis expressed by Cournot's principle from the quite distinct hypothesis that price changes are largely due to new information. Much empirical work that has already been done, related to the anomalies I have just mentioned, may in the future be seen as first steps in this direction.

NOTES

1. This chapter draws on collaboration with Vladimir Vovk and has benefited from correspondence and conversation with innumerable colleagues, many of whom are thanked in earlier books and papers cited here. The author has also benefited from the discussion of the chapter in the form of a paper given at the 8th Conference of the Cournot Centre for Economic Studies in Paris, 1–2 December 2005, especially discussion by André Orléan, Bernard Walliser and John Vickers. Comments by Alain de Fontenay and Marietta Peytcheva were also helpful.
2. Most of them did not call it 'Cournot's principle', but this name, due to Fréchet, was used in the 1950s (see p. 59) and may be the most reasonable and convenient name available today.
3. In German, *Spiel* means 'game' or 'play', and *Raum* (plural *Räume*) means 'room' or 'space'. In most contexts, *Spielraum* can be translated as 'leeway' or 'room for maneuver'. For von Kries, the *Spielraum* for each case was the set of all arrangements of the circumstances that produce it.
4. More precisely, he did not do this for the case of continuous time. He did show, in section I.6 of the *Grundbegriffe*, how to construct a probability measure representing a discrete Markov chain.
5. Of course, hardly any experiment can be repeated exactly, for chances always vary. This point

haunted probability theory from its very beginning with Bernoulli (Bru, [1981] 2005, section 1.3).

6. Kolmogorov made the same point by saying that if two events are both practically certain, then their simultaneous happening is also practically certain, but not quite as certain (Kolmogorov, 1992, pp. 4–5). After the decline of Cournot's principle, this came to be seen as paradoxical, as in Kyburg's 'lottery paradox' (Kyburg, 1961).

7. Here 'return' means simple return $R = (p_{n+1} - p_n)/p_n$, where p_n is the price of the share (or the level of the market index) at time n. All expected values, variances and covariances are with respect to probabilities conditional on information known at time n.

REFERENCES

Aldrich, J. (2003), 'The language of the English biometric school', *International Statistical Review*, **71** (1), 109–29.

Anderson, O.N. (1935), *Einführung in die mathematische Statistik*, Vienna: Springer.

Anderson, O.N. (1949), 'Die Begründung des Gesetzes der grossen Zahlen und die Umkehrung des Theorems von Bernoulli', *Dialectica*, **3** (9/10), 65–77.

Anonymous (1954), 'Account in Russian of a conference on statistics in Moscow in 1954', Вестник статистики (*Bulletin of Statistics*), **5**, 39–95.

Bachelier, L. (1900), 'Théorie de la spéculation', *Annales scientifiques de l'École Normale Supérieure, 3e série*, **17**, 21–86. Bachelier's doctoral dissertation. Reprinted in facsimile, Paris: Editions Jacques Gabay, 1995. An English translation, by A. James Boness, appears on pp. 17–78 of *The Random Character of Stock Market Prices*, ed. Paul H. Cootner, Cambridge, MA: MIT Press, 1964.

Bernoulli, J. (1713), *Ars conjectandi*, Basel: Thurnisius. Edith Sylla's English translation, *The Art of Conjecturing, together with Letter to a Friend on Sets in Court Tennis*, Johns Hopkins University Press, 2005. Oscar Sheynin's English translation of Part IV, dated 2005, is at www.sheynin.de.

Bernstein, F. (1912), 'Über eine Anwendung der Mengenlehre auf ein aus der Theorie der säkularen Störungen herrührendes Problem', *Mathematische Annalen*, **71**, 417–39.

Bohlmann, G. (1901), 'Lebensversicherungs-Mathematik', *Encyklopädie der mathematischen Wissenschaften*, I/2, Leipzig: Teubner, pp. 852–917.

Borel, É. (1906), 'La valeur pratique du calcul des probabilités', *Revue du mois*, **1**, 424–37. Reprinted in É. Borel (1972), *Oeuvres de Emile Borel*, Paris: Centre National de la Recherche Scientifique, vol. 2, pp. 991–1004.

Borel, É. (1909), *Éléments de la théorie des probabilités*, Paris: Gauthier-Villars, 3rd edn 1924. The 1950 edition was translated into English by John E. Freund and published as *Elements of the Theory of Probability*, Englewood Cliffs: Prentice-Hall, 1965.

Borel, É. (1914), *Le Hasard*, Paris: Alcan. The first and second editions both appeared in 1914, with later editions in 1920, 1928, 1932, 1938 and 1948.

Borel, É. (1930), 'Sur les probabilités universellement négligeables', *Comptes rendus hebdomadaires des séances de l'Académie des Sciences*, **190**, 537–40. Reprinted as Note IV of É. Borel (1939), *Valeur pratique et philosophie des probabilités*, Paris: Gauthier-Villars. Reprinted Paris: Éditions Jacques Gabay, 1991.

Borel, É. (1941), *Le jeu, la chance et les théories scientifiques modernes*, Paris: Gallimard.

Borel, É. (1943), *Les probabilités et la vie*, Paris: Presses Universitaires de France. Later editions in 1946, 1950, 1958 and 1967. The 1958 edition was translated into English by Maurice Baudin and published as *Probabilities and Life*, New York: Dover, 1962.

Borel, É. (1950), *Probabilité et certitude*, Paris: Presses Universitaires de France. English translation, *Probability and Certainty*, New York: Walker, 1963.

Bourghelle, D., O. Brandouy, R. Gillet and A. Orléan (eds) (2005), *Croyances, Représentations Collectives et Conventions en France*, Paris: Economica.

Brissaud, M. (ed.) (2002), *Écrits sur les processus aléatoires: Mélanges en hommage à Robert Fortet*, Paris: Lavoisier.

Brouwer, L.E.J. (1918), 'Begründung der Mengenlehre unabhängig vom logischen Satz vom ausgeschlossenen Dritten. Erster Teil. Allgemeine Mengelehre', *Koninklijke Nederlandse Akademie van Wetenschschappen Verhandelingen*, **5**, 1–43.

Bru, B. (1981), 'Poisson, le calcul des probabilités et l'instruction publique', in M. Métivier, P. Costabel and P. Dugac (eds), *Siméon Denis Poisson et la science de son temps*, Palaiseau: Éditions de l'École Polytechnique, pp. 51–94. Translated as 'Poisson, the probability calculus, and public education', in the *Electronic Journal for History of Probability and Statistics*, www.jehps.net, **1** (2), November 2005.

Bru, B. (1999), 'Borel, Lévy, Neyman, Pearson et les autres', *MATAPLI*, (60), 51–60.

Bru, B. (2002), 'Présentation de l'œuvre de Robert Fortet', in M. Brissaud (ed.), *Écrits sur les processus aléatoires: Mélanges en hommage à Robert Fortet*, Paris: Lavoisier, pp. 19–48.

Buffon, G.-L. (1777), 'Essai d'arithmétique morale', in *Supplément à l'Histoire naturelle*, Paris: Imprimerie Royale, 4, pp. 46–148.

Carnap, R. (1950), *Logical Foundations of Probabililty*, Chicago, IL: University of Chicago Press.

Castelnuovo, G. (1919), *Calcolo delle probabilitá*, Milan, Rome and Naples: Albrighi e Segati, 2nd edn in 2 vols, 1926 and 1928; 3rd edn 1948.

Chuprov, A.A. (1910), Очерки по теории статистики (*Essays on the theory of statistics*), Saint Petersburg: Sabashnikov, 1st edn 1909; 2nd edn reprinted Moscow: State Publishing House, 1959.

Copeland, T.E. and J.F. Weston (1988), *Financial Theory and Corporate Policy*, Reading, MA: Addison-Wesley.

Cournot, A.A. (1843), *Exposition de la théorie des chances et des probabilités*, Paris: Hachette. Reprinted in 1984 as Vol. I (Bru, B.) (ed.) of A.A. Cournot (1973–84), *Œuvres complètes*, Paris: Vrin, 10 vols, 11th to appear.

Cramér, H. (1946), *Mathematical Methods in Statistics*, Princeton, NJ: Princeton University Press.

D'Alembert, J. (1761), 'Réflexions sur le calcul des probabilités', in J. d'Alembert (1761–80), *Opuscules mathématiques*, Paris, vol. 2, pp. 1–25.

D'Alembert, J. (1767), 'Doutes et questions sur le calcul des probabilités', in J. d'Alembert (1759–67), *Mélanges de littérature, d'histoire, et de philosophie*, Paris, vol. 5, pp. 275–304.

Daston, L. (1979), 'D'Alembert's critique of probability theory', *Historia Mathematica*, **6**, 259–79.

Daston, L. (1994), 'How probabilities came to be objective and subjective', *Historia Mathematica*, **21**, 330–44.

Dawid, A.P. (1984), 'Statistical theory: The prequential approach (with discussion)', *Journal of the Royal Statistical Society*, Series A, **147**, 278–92.

Dawid, A.P. (2004), 'Probability, causality and the empirical world: A Bayes–de Finetti–Popper–Borel synthesis', *Statistical Science*, **19**, 44–57.

De Finetti, B. (1930), 'A proposito dell'estensione del teorema delle probabilità totali alle classi numerabili', *Rendiconti del Reale Istituto Lombardo di Scienze e Lettere*, **63**, 901–5, 1063–9.

De Finetti, B. (1939), *Compte rendu critique du colloque de Genève sur la théorie des probabilités*, Paris: Hermann; 8th fascicule of R. Wavre (1938–39), *Colloque consacré à la théorie des probabilités*, Paris: Hermann. The colloquium held October 1937 at the University of Geneva. Proceedings published by Hermann in eight fascicules in the series *Actualités Scientifiques et Industrielles*. The first seven fascicules appeared in 1938 as numbers 734 through 740; the eighth, de Finetti's summary of the colloquium, appeared in 1939 as number 766.

De Finetti, B. (1951), 'Recent suggestions for the reconciliation of theories of probability', in J. Neyman (ed.) (1951), *Proceedings of the Second Berkeley Symposium on Mathematical Statistics and Probability*, Berkeley and Los Angeles, CA: University of California Press, pp. 217–25.

De Finetti, B., 'Notes de M. B. de Finetti sur le "Rapport général"', in M. Fréchet, (1955), *Les mathématiques et le concret*, Paris: Presses Universitaires de France, pp. 232–41.

De Morgan, A. (1838), *An Essay on Probabilities, and on their application to Life Contingencies and Insurance Offices*, London: Longman, Orme, Brown. Reprinted New York: Arne Press, 1981.

Doob, J.L. (1940), 'Regularity properties of certain families of chance variables', *Transactions of the American Mathematical Society*, **47**, 455–86.

Doob, J.L. (1941), 'Probability as measure', *Annals of Mathematical Statistics*, **12**, 206–14. This article stems from a discussion with Richard von Mises at a meeting of the Institute of Mathematical Statistics in Hanover, NH, September 1940.

Doob, J.L. (1949), 'Application of the theory of martingales', in *Le Calcul des Probabilités et ses Applications*, Colloques Internationaux, Paris: Centre National de la Recherche Scientifique, pp. 23–7.

Doob, J.L. (1953), *Stochastic Processes*, New York: Wiley.

Edgeworth, F.Y. (1887), *Metretike, or the Method of Measuring Probabilities and Utility*, London: Temple.

Edgeworth, F.Y. (1996), *Writings in Probability, Statistics, and Economics*, Cheltenham, UK and Northampton, MA, USA: Edward Elgar, 3 vols, ed. Charles R. McCann, Jr.

Ellis, R.L. (1849), 'On the foundations of the theory of probabilities', *Transactions of the Cambridge Philosophical Society*, **8** (1), 1–6. The paper was read on 14 February 1842. Part 1 of Vol. 8 was published in 1843 or 1844, but Vol. 8 was not completed until 1849.

Fama, E.F. (1970), 'Efficient capital markets: A review of theory and empirical work', *Journal of Finance*, **25**, 383–417.

Fama, E.F. (1976), *Foundations of Finance*, New York: Basic Books.

Fisher, R.A. (1922), 'On the mathematical foundations of theoretical statistics', *Philosophical Transactions of the Royal Society of London*, A, **222**, 309–68.

Fisher, R.A. (1925), *Statistical Methods for Research Workers*, Edinburgh: Oliver and Boyd, 13th edn 1958.

Fisher, R.A. (1956), *Statistical Methods and Scientific Inference*, Edinburgh: Oliver and Boyd.

Fréchet, M. (1930), 'Sur l'extension du théorème des probabilités totales au cas d'une suite infinie d'événements', *Rendiconti del Reale Istituto Lombardo di Scienze e Lettere*, **63**, 899–900, 1059–62.

Fréchet, M. (1937–38), *Recherches théoriques modernes sur la théorie des probabilités*,

Paris: Gauthier-Villars. This work consists of two books: M. Fréchet (1937), *Généralités sur les probabilités. Variables aléatoires*, Paris: Gauthier-Villars, and Fréchet, M. (1938), *Méthode des fonctions arbitraires. Théorie des événements en chaîne dans le cas d'un nombre fini d'états possibles*, Paris: Gauthier-Villars. The two books together constitute fascicule 3 of Vol. 1 of Émile Borel's *Traité du calcul des probabilités et ses applications*.

Fréchet, M. (1938), 'Exposé et discussion de quelques recherches récentes sur les fondements du calcul des probabilités', in R. Wavre (ed.) (1938), *Les fondements du calcul des probabilités*, pp. 23–55, 2nd fascicule of R. Wavre (1938–39), *Colloque consacré à la théorie des probabilités*, Paris: Hermann.

Fréchet, M. (1951), 'Rapport général sur les travaux du Colloque de Calcul des Probabilités', in R. Bayer (ed.), 'XVIIIe Congrès International de Philosophie des Sciences, Paris, 1949', *Actualités Scientifiques et Industrielles*, 1146, Paris: Hermann, pp. 3–21.

Fréchet, M. (1955), *Les mathématiques et le concret*, Paris: Presses Universitaires de France.

Fréchet, M. and M. Halbwachs (1924), *Le calcul des probabilités à la portée de tous*, Paris: Dunod.

Gnedenko, B.V. (1950), Курс теории вероятностей (*Theory of Probability*), Moscow: Nauka, 1st edn 1950; 6th edn 1988.

Hadamard, J. (1922), 'Les principes du calcul des probabilités', *Revue de métaphysique et de morale*, **39**, 289–93. A slightly longer version of this note, with the title 'Les axiomes du calcul des probabilités', was included in *Oeuvres de Jacques Hadamard*, Tome IV, pp. 2161–2. Paris: Centre National de la Recherche Scientifique, 1968.

Hastie, T., R. Tibshirani and J. Friedman (2001), *The Elements of Statistical Learning Theory: Data Mining, Inference, and Prediction*, New York: Springer.

Hayek, F.A. (1978), 'Competition as a discovery procedure', in *New Studies in Philosophy, Politics, Economics and History of Ideas*, Chicago, IL: University of Chicago Press, pp. 179–90.

Howie, D. (2002), *Interpreting Probability: Controversies and Developments in the Early Twentieth Century*, Cambridge: Cambridge University Press.

Jevons, W.S. (1874), *The Principles of Science: a Treatise on Logic and Scientific Method*, London, New York: Macmillan, 2 vols; 2nd edn 1887. Reprinted New York: Dover, 1958.

Kamlah, A. (1983), 'Probability as a quasi-theoretical concept; J. V. Kries' sophisticated account after a century', *Erkenntnis*, **19**, 239–51.

Keynes, J.M. (1921), *A Treatise on Probability*, London: Macmillan.

Keynes, J.M. (1937), 'The general theory of employment', *Quarterly Journal of Economics*, **51**, 209–33.

Knight, F.H. (1921), *Risk, Uncertainty and Profit*, Boston, MA: Houghton Mifflin.

Kolmogorov, A.N. (1931), 'Über die analytischen Methoden in der Wahrscheinlichkeitsrechnung', *Mathematische Annalen*, **104**, 415–58. Translated into English in *Selected Works of A. N. Kolmogorov. Volume II: Probability Theory and Mathematical Statistics*, Dordrecht: Kluwer, 1992, pp. 62–108.

Kolmogorov, A.N. (1933), *Grundbegriffe der Wahrscheinlichkeitsrechnung*, Berlin: Springer. English trans. Nathan Morrison, *Foundations of the Theory of Probability* (Chelsea, New York) 1950; 2nd edn 1956.

Kolmogorov, A.N. (1948), 'The main problems of theoretical statistics (abstract)', in Второе всесоюзное совещание по математической статистике (*Second National Conference on Mathematical Statistics*), Tashkent, pp. 216–20. English trans. in O.

Sheynin (ed.) (1998), *From Davidov to Romanovsky. More Russian papers on probability and statistics. S.N. Bernstein, B.V. Gnedenko, A.N. Kolmogorov, A.M. Liapunov, P.A. Nekrasov, A.A. Markov, Kh.O. Ondar, T.A. Sarymsakov, N.V. Smirnov*, Egelsbach: Hänsel-Hohenhausen, pp. 216–24.

Kolmogorov, A.N. (1954), Summary, in Russian, of his address to a conference on statistics in Moscow in 1954, in Anonymous (1954), 'Account in Russian of a conference on statistics in Moscow in 1954', Вестник статистики (*Bulletin of Statistics*), **5**, 46–7. English trans. in O. Sheynin (ed.) (1998), *op. cit.*, pp. 225–6.

Kolmogorov, A.N. (1956), 'Теория вероятностей' ('Probability theory'), in A.D. Aleksandrov, A.N. Kolmogorov and M.A. Lavrent'ev (eds), Математика, ее содержание, методы и значение, Moscow: Nauka, ch. XI, 252–84, 33–71 of Part 4 in the 1963 English edn; 229–64 of Vol. 2 in the 1965 English edn.

Kolmogorov, A.N. (1983), 'Combinatorial foundations of information theory and the calculus of probabilities', *Russian Mathematical Surveys*, **38** (4), 29–40.

Kolmogorov, A.N. (1992), *Selected Works of A. N. Kolmogorov. Volume II: Probability Theory and Mathematical Statistics*, Dordrecht: Kluwer.

Kotz, S. (1965), 'Statistics in the USSR', *Survey*, **57**, 132–41.

Kyburg Jr, H.E. (1961), *Probability and the Logic of Rational Belief*, Middletown, CT: Wesleyan University Press.

Le Lionnais, F. (ed.) (1948), *Les grands courants de la pensée mathématique*, Paris: Cahiers du Sud. Reprinted by Blanchard in 1962 and by Hermann in 1998. English transl., *Great Currents of Mathematical Thought*, New York: Dover, 1971.

LeRoy, S.F. (1989), 'Efficient capital markets and martingales', *Journal of Economic Literature*, **27**, 1583–621.

Lévy, P. (1925), *Calcul des probabilités*, Paris: Gauthier-Villars.

Lévy, P. (1937), *Théorie de l'addition des variables aléatoires*, Paris: Gauthier-Villars, 2nd edn 1954.

Li, M. and P. Vitányi (1997), *An Introduction to Kolmogorov Complexity and Its Applications*, New York: Springer.

Loève, M. (1955), *Probability Theory: foundations, random sequences*, Princeton, NJ: Van Nostrand, 2nd edn 1960.

Lorentz, G.G. (2002), 'Mathematics and politics in the Soviet Union from 1928 to 1953', *Journal of Approximation Theory*, **116**, 169–223.

Loveland, J. (2001); 'Buffon, the certainty of sunrise, and the probabilistic reductio ad absurdum', *Archive for History of Exact Sciences*, **55**, 465–77.

Lucas Jr, R.E. and E.C. Prescott (1971), 'Investment under uncertainty', *Econometrica*, **39**, 659–81.

Malkiel, B.G. (2003), 'The efficient market hypothesis and its critics', *Journal of Economic Perspectives*, **17**, 59–82.

Markov, A.A. (1912), *Wahrscheinlichkeitsrechnung*, Leipzig: Teubner. Translation of the second edition of A.A. Markov, (1900), Исчисление вероятностей (*Calculus of Probability*), Типография Императорской Академии Наук, Saint Petersburg, 2nd edn 1908, 4th edn 1924.

Martin, T. (1996), *Probabilités et critique philosophique selon Cournot*, Paris: Vrin.

Martin, T. (1998), *Bibliographie cournotienne*, Besançon: Annales littéraires de l'Université Franche-Comté.

Martin, T. (2003), 'Probabilité et certitude' in T. Martin (ed.) (2003), *Probabilités subjectives et rationalité de l'action*, Paris: CNRS Éditions, pp. 119–34.

Martin-Löf, P. (1966–67), *Statistics from the point of view of statistical mechanics*, Notes by Ole Jørsboe. Matematisk Institut. Aarhus University.

Martin-Löf, P. (1970), *Notes on Constructive Mathematics*, Stockholm: Almqvist & Wiksell.

Meinong, A. (1915), *Über Möglichkeit und Wahrscheinlichkeit: Beiträge zur Gegenstandstheorie und Erkenntnistheorie*, Leipzig: Barth.

Mirowski, P. (ed.) (1994), *Edgeworth on Chance, Economic Hazard, and Statistics*, Lanham, MD: Rowman & Littlefield.

Nagel, E. (1939), *Principles of the Theory of Probability*, Chicago, IL: University of Chicago Press.

Neyman, J. (1960), 'Indeterminism in science and new demands on statisticians', *Journal of the American Statistical Association*, **55**, 625–39.

Ondar, Kh.O. (ed.) (1981), *The Correspondence Between A. A. Markov and A. A. Chuprov on the Theory of Probability and Mathematical Statistics*, New York: Springer.

Poincaré, H. (1890), 'Sur le problème des trois corps et les équations de la dynamique', *Acta Mathematica*, **13**, 1–271.

Poisson, S.-D. (1837), *Recherches sur la probabilité des jugements en matière criminelle et en matière civile, précédés des règles générales du calcul des probabilités*, Paris: Bachelier.

Popper, K.R. (1935), *Logik der Forschung: Zur Erkenntnistheorie der modernen Naturwissenschaft*, Vienna: Springer. English trans., *The Logic of Scientific Discovery*, London: Hutchinson, 1959.

Popper, K.R. (1938), 'A set of independent axioms for probability', *Mind*, **47**, 275–77.

Popper, K.R. (1959), 'The propensity interpretation of probability', *British Journal for the Philosophy of Science*, **37**, 25–42.

Popper, K.R. (1983), *Realism and the Aim of Science*, London: Hutchinson.

Porter, T.M. (1986), *The Rise of Statistical Thinking, 1820–1900*, Princeton, NJ: Princeton University Press.

Porter, T.M. (2004), *Karl Pearson: The Scientific Life in a Statistical Age*, Princeton, NJ: Princeton University Press.

Poterba, J.M. and L. Summers (1988), 'Mean reversion in stock prices: evidence and implications', *Journal of Financial Economics*, **22**, 27–59.

Prokhorov, Y.V. and B.A. Sevast'yanov (1987), 'Probability theory', in M. Hazewinkel (ed.), *Encyclopaedia of Mathematics* (updated and annotated translation of the *Soviet Mathematical Encyclopaedia*), Dordrecht: Kluwer.

Reichenbach, H. (1916), *Der Begriff der Wahrscheinlichkeit für die mathematische Darstellung der Wirklichkeit*, Leipzig: Barth.

Reichenbach, H. (1949), *The theory of probability: an inquiry into the logical and mathematical foundations of the calculus of probability*, Berkeley, CA: University of California Press. English trans., by Ernest H. Hutten and Maria Reichenbach, of *Wahrscheinlichkeitslehre: eine Untersuchung über die logischen und mathematischen Grundlagen der Wahrscheinlichkeitsrechnung*, Leiden: A.W. Sijthoff, 1935.

Richter, H. (1954), 'Zur Begründung der Wahrscheinlichkeitsrechnung', *Dialectica*, **8**, 48–77.

Richter, H. (1956), *Wahrscheinlichkeitstheorie*, Berlin: Springer.

Samuelson, P.A. (1965), 'Proof that properly anticipated prices fluctuate randomly', *Industrial Management Review*, **6**, 41–50.

Seneta, E. (1997) 'Boltzmann, Ludwig Edward', in N.L. Johnson and S. Kotz (1997), *Leading Personalities in Statistical Sciences*, New York: Wiley, pp. 353–4.

Shafer, G. (1996), *The Art of Causal Conjecture*, Cambridge, MA: The MIT Press.

Shafer, G. and V. Vovk (2001), *Probability and Finance: It's Only a Game!*, New York: Wiley.

Shafer, G. and V. Vovk (2002), 'On a review by V.N. Tutubalin', http://www.probability andfinance.com/reviews/tut_response1.pdf.

Shafer, G. and V. Vovk (2005), 'The origins and legacy of Kolmogorov's *Grundbegriffe*', Working Paper No. 4, http://www.probabilityandfinance.com.

Shafer, G. and V. Vovk (2006), 'The sources of Kolmogorov's *Grundbegriffe*', *Statistical Science*, **21** (1), 70–98.

Sheynin, O. (1996), *Aleksandr A. Chuprov: Life, Work, Correspondence. The making of mathematical statistics*, Göttingen: Vandenhoeck & Ruprecht.

Shiller, R.J. (1989), *Market Volatility*, Cambridge, MA: The MIT Press.

Shiller, R.J. (2003), 'From efficient markets theory to behavioral finance', *Journal of Economic Perspectives*, **17**, 83–104.

Stigler, S.M. (1986), *The History of Statistics: The Measurement of Uncertainty before 1900*, Cambridge, MA: Harvard University Press.

Stiglitz, J.E. (1981), 'The allocation role of the stock market: Pareto optimality and competition', *Journal of Finance*, **36**, 235–51.

Stumpf, K.F. (1892), 'Ueber den Begriff der mathematischen Wahrscheinlichkeit', *Sitzungsberichte der philosophisch-philologischen und der historischen Classe der k. b. Akademie der Wissenschaften zu München*, 37–120.

Vapnik, V. (1996), *The Nature of Statistical Learning Theory*, New York: Springer.

Venn, J. (1888), *The Logic of Chance*, London and New York: Macmillan, 3rd edn.

Ville, J.-A. (1939), *Étude critique de la notion de collectif*, Paris: Gauthier-Villars.

Von Bortkiewicz, L. (1901), 'Anwendungen der Wahrscheinlichkeitsrechnung auf Statistik', in *Encyklopädie der mathematischen Wissenschaften*, Leipzig: Teubner, Bd. I, Teil 2, pp. 821–51.

Von Hirsch, G. (1954), 'Sur un aspect paradoxal de la théorie des probabilités', *Dialetica*, **8**, 125–44.

Von Kries, J. (1886), *Die Principien der Wahrscheinlichkeitsrechnung. Eine logische Untersuchung*, Freiburg: Mohr; 2nd edn 1927.

Von Mises, R. (1919), 'Grundlagen der Wahrscheinlichkeitsrechnung', *Mathematische Zeitschrift*, **5**, 52–99.

Von Mises, R. (1928), *Wahrscheinlichkeitsrechnung, Statistik und Wahrheit*, Vienna: Springer, 2nd edn 1936, 3rd edn 1951; posthumous 4th edn, ed. Hilda Geiringer, 1972. English editions, under the title *Probability, Statistics and Truth*, 1939 and 1957.

Von Mises, R. (1931), *Wahrscheinlichkeitsrechnung und ihre Anwendung in der Statistik und theoretischen Physik*, Leipzig and Vienna: Deuticke.

Von Plato, Jan (1994), *Creating Modern Probability: Its Mathematics, Physics, and Philosophy in Historical Perspective*, Cambridge: Cambridge University Press.

Vovk, V. (2005), 'Competitive on-line learning with a convex loss function', Working Paper No. 14, http://www.probabilityandfinance.com.

Vovk, V. and G. Shafer (2002), 'The game-theoretic capital asset pricing model', Working Paper No. 1, http://www.probabilityandfinance.com.

Vovk, V. and G. Shafer (2003a), 'A game-theoretic explanation of the $\sqrt{dt}$ effect', Working Paper No. 5, http://www.probabilityandfinance.com.

Vovk, V. and G. Shafer (2003b), 'Kolmogorov's contributions to the foundations of probability', *Problems of Information Transmission*, **39** (1), 21–31. Extended version: Working Paper No. 6, http://www.probabilityandfinance.com.

Vovk, V. and G. Shafer (2005), 'Good randomized sequential probability forecasting is always possible', *Journal of the Royal Statistical Society, Series B*, **67**, 747–64. Extended version: Working Paper No. 7, http://www.probabilityandfinance.com.

Vovk, V., A. Gammerman and G. Shafer (2005a), *Algorithmic Learning in a Random World*, New York: Springer.

Vovk, V., A. Takemura and G. Shafer (2005b), 'Defensive forecasting', in *Algorithmic Learning Theory: Proceedings of the 16th International Conference, ALT 2005*, Singapore, 8–11 October, New York: Springer-Verlag, p. 459. Also in *Lecture Notes in Computer Science*, **3734**. Extended version: Working Paper No. 8, http://www.probabilityandfinance.com.

Vovk, V., I. Nouretdinov, A. Takemura and G. Shafer (2005), 'Defensive forecasting for linear protocols', in *AISTATS 2005: Proceedings of the 10th International Workshop on Artificial Intelligence and Statistics*, Barbados, 6–8 January, pp. 365–72. http://www.gatsby.ucl.ac.uk/aistats/proceedings.htm. Extended version: Working Paper No. 10, http://www.probabilityandfinance.com.

Wald, A. (1936), 'Sur la notion de collectif dans le calcul des probabilités', *Comptes rendus hebdomadaires des séances de l'Académie des Sciences*, **202**, 180–83.

Wald, A. (1937), 'Die Widerspruchfreiheit des Kollectivbegriffes der Wahrscheinlichkeitsrechnung', *Ergebnisse eines Mathematischen Kolloquiums*, **8**, 38–72.

Wald, A. (1938), 'Die Widerspruchfreiheit des Kollectivbegriffes', in R. Wavre (ed.) (1938), *Les fondements du calcul des probabilités*, pp. 79–99. This is the second fascicule of R. Wavre, (1938–39), *Colloque consacré à la théorie des probabilités*, Paris: Hermann. The colloquium was held in October 1937 at the University of Geneva. The proceedings were published by Hermann in eight fascicules in their series *Actualités Scientifiques et Industrielles*.

D74 C71
F51 C73

5. War and peace*

Robert J. Aumann

Prefatory Note: In 1994, John Nash, Reinhard Selten and John Harsanyi were awarded the Bank of Sweden Prize in Economic Sciences in Memory of Alfred Nobel for their pioneering analysis of non-cooperative games. Fundamental to their work is the concept of strategic equilibrium, an idea initiated by Augustin Cournot in 1838 in connection with duopolies. In 1996, William Vickrey was awarded the Prize for applying this concept to the theory of auctions. In 2005, Robert Aumann shared the Prize with Thomas Schelling; in large part, Aumann's share was for applying the equilibrium concept to repeated games.

According to Aumann, if Augustin Cournot had still been alive, he could have won the prize on at least three different occasions.

In the text that follows, Robert Aumann illustrates the roles that different sorts of strategic equilibria play in repeated games applied to war and peace.

'Wars and other conflicts are among the main sources of human misery.' Thus begins the *Advanced Information* announcement of the 2005 Bank of Sweden Prize in Economic Sciences in Memory of Alfred Nobel, awarded for Game Theory Analysis of Conflict and Cooperation. So it is appropriate to devote this lecture to one of the most pressing and profound issues that confront humanity: that of War and Peace.

I would like to suggest that we should perhaps change direction in our efforts to bring about world peace. Up to now all the effort has been put into resolving specific conflicts: India–Pakistan, North–South Ireland, various African wars, Balkan wars, Russia–Chechnya, Israel–Arab, etc., etc. I'd like to suggest that we should shift emphasis and study war in general.

Let me make a comparison. There are two approaches to cancer. One is clinical. You have, say, breast cancer. What should you do? Surgery? Radiation?

*   Prize Lecture, 8 December 2005. This text is a very lightly edited version of the 40-minute lecture delivered at the Royal Swedish Academy of Sciences in Stockholm. We are grateful to Prof. Nicolaus Tideman for pointing out an error in a previous version.

The lecture appeared in *Les Prix Nobels 2005*, edited by K. Grandin, Stockholm: The Nobel Foundation, pp. 350–58 © The Nobel Foundation, 2006.

Chemotherapy? Which chemotherapy? How much radiation? Do you cut out the lymph nodes? The answers are based on clinical tests, simply on what works best. You treat each case on its own, using your best information. And your aim is to cure the disease, or to ameliorate it, in the specific patient before you.

And, there is another approach. You don't do surgery, you don't do radiation, you don't do chemotherapy, you don't look at statistics, you don't look at the patient at all. You just try to understand what happens in a cancerous cell. Does it have anything to do with the DNA? What happens? What is the process like? *Don't* try to cure it. Just try to *understand* it. You work with mice, not people. You try to make them sick, not cure them.

Louis Pasteur was a physician. It was important to him to treat people, to cure them. But Robert Koch was not a physician; he didn't try to cure people. He just wanted to know how infectious disease works. And eventually, his work became tremendously important in treating and curing disease.

War has been with us ever since the dawn of civilization. Nothing has been more constant in history than war. It's a phenomenon, it's not a series of isolated events. The efforts to resolve specific conflicts are certainly laudable, and sometimes they really bear fruit. But there's also another way of going about it – studying war as a general phenomenon, studying its general, defining characteristics, what the common denominators are, what the differences are. Historically, sociologically, psychologically, and – yes – *rationally*. Why does *homo economicus* – rational man – go to war?

What do I mean by 'rationality'? It is this:

A person's behavior is **rational** *if it is in* **his** *best interests, given* **his** *information.*

With this definition, can war be rational? Unfortunately, the answer is yes; it can be. In one of the greatest speeches of all time – his second inaugural – Abraham Lincoln said: 'Both parties deprecated war; but one would make war rather than let the nation survive; and the other would accept war rather than let it perish. And the war came.'

It is a big mistake to say that war is irrational. We take all the ills of the world – wars, strikes, racial discrimination – and dismiss them by calling them irrational. They are not necessarily irrational. Though it hurts, they may be rational. If war is rational, once we understand that it is, we can at least somehow address the problem. If we simply dismiss it as irrational, we can't address the problem.

Many years ago, I was present at a meeting of students at Yale University. Jim Tobin, who later was awarded the Prize in Economic Sciences in Memory of Alfred Nobel, was also there. The discussion was freewheeling, and one question that came up was: Can one sum up economics in one word? Tobin's answer was 'yes'; the word is *incentives*. Economics is all about incentives.

So, what I'd like to do is an economic analysis of war. Now this does *not* mean what it sounds like. I'm not talking about how to finance a war, or how to rebuild after a war, or anything like that. I'm talking about the *incentives* that lead to war, and about building incentives that prevent war.

Let me give an example. Economics teaches us that things are not always as they appear. For example, suppose you want to raise revenue from taxes. To do that, obviously you should raise the tax rates, right? No, wrong. You might want to *lower* the tax rates. To give people an incentive to work, or to reduce avoidance and evasion of taxes, or to heat up the economy, or whatever. That's just one example; there are thousands like it. An economy is a game: the incentives of the players interact in complex ways, and lead to surprising, often counter-intuitive results. But as it turns out, the economy really works that way.

So now, let's get back to war, and how *homo economicus* – rational man – fits into the picture. An example, in the spirit of the previous item, is this. You want to prevent war. To do that, obviously you should disarm, lower the level of armaments. Right? No, wrong. You might want to do the exact opposite. In the long years of the cold war between the USA and the Soviet Union, what prevented 'hot' war was that bombers carrying nuclear weapons were in the air 24 hours a day, 365 days a year. Disarming would have led to war.

The bottom line is – again – that we should start studying war, from all viewpoints, for its own sake. Try to understand what makes it happen. Pure, basic science. *That* may lead, eventually, to peace. The piecemeal, case-based approach has not worked too well up to now.

Now I would like to get to some of my own basic contributions, some of those that were cited by the Prize Committee. Specifically, let's discuss repeated games, and how they relate to war, and to other conflicts, like strikes, and indeed to all interactive situations.

Repeated games model long-term interaction. The theory of repeated games is able to account for phenomena such as altruism, cooperation, trust, loyalty, revenge, threats (self-destructive or otherwise) – phenomena that may at first seem irrational – in terms of the 'selfish' utility-maximizing paradigm of game theory and neoclassical economics.

That it 'accounts' for such phenomena does not mean that people deliberately choose to take revenge, or to act generously, out of consciously self-serving, rational motives. Rather, over the millennia, people have evolved norms of behavior that are by and large successful, indeed optimal. Such evolution may actually be biological, genetic. Or, it may be 'memetic'; this word derives from the word 'meme', a term coined by the biologist Richard Dawkins to parallel the term 'gene', but to express social, rather than biological, heredity and evolution.

One of the great discoveries of game theory came in the early 1970s, when the biologists John Maynard Smith and George Price realized that strategic equilibrium in games and population equilibrium in the living world are defined by the same equations. Evolution – be it genetic or memetic – leads to strategic equilibrium. So what we are saying is that in *repeated* games, strategic equilibrium expresses phenomena such as altruism, cooperation, trust, loyalty, revenge, threats, and so on. Let us see how that works out.

What do I mean by 'strategic equilibrium'? Very roughly, the players in a game are said to be in *strategic equilibrium* (or simply *equilibrium*) when their play is *mutually optimal*: when the actions and plans of each player are rational in the given strategic environment – i.e., when each knows the actions and plans of the others.

For formulating and developing the concept of strategic equilibrium, John Nash was awarded the 1994 Prize in Economic Sciences in Memory of Alfred Nobel, on the fiftieth anniversary of the publication of John von Neumann and Oskar Morgenstern's *Theory of Games and Economic Behavior*. Sharing that Prize were John Harsanyi, for formulating and developing the concept of *Bayesian* equilibrium, i.e., strategic equilibrium in games of incomplete information; and Reinhard Selten, for formulating and developing the concept of *perfect* equilibrium, a refinement of Nash's concept, on which we will say more below. Along with the concepts of *correlated* equilibrium (Aumann, 1974, 1987), and *strong* equilibrium (Aumann, 1959), both of which were cited in the 2005 Prize announcement, the above three fundamental concepts constitute the theoretical cornerstones of non-cooperative game theory.

Subsequent to the 1994 prize, two Prizes in Economic Sciences in Memory of Alfred Nobel were awarded for *applications* of these fundamental concepts. The first was in 1996, when William Vickrey was awarded the Prize posthumously for his work on auctions. (Vickrey died between the time of the Prize announcement and that of the ceremony.) The design of auctions and of bidding strategies are among the prime practical applications of game theory; a good – though somewhat dated – survey is Wilson, 1992.

The second came this year – 2005. Professor Schelling will, of course, speak and write for himself. As for your humble servant, he received the prize for applying the fundamental equilibrium concepts mentioned above to *repeated* games. That is, suppose you are playing the same game G, with the same players, year after year. One can look at this situation as a single big game – the so-called *supergame* of G, denoted G^∞ – whose rules are, 'play G every year'. The idea is to apply the above equilibrium concepts to the supergame G^∞, rather than to the one-shot game G, and to see what one gets.

The theory of repeated games that emerges from this process is extremely rich and deep (good – though somewhat dated – surveys are Sorin, 1992, Zamir, 1992 and Forges, 1992). In the few minutes that are available to me, I can barely scratch its surface. Let me nevertheless try. I will briefly discuss just one aspect: the *cooperative*. Very roughly, the conclusion is that

Repetition enables cooperation.

Let us flesh this out a little. We use the term *cooperative* to describe any possible outcome of a game, as long as no player can *guarantee* a better outcome for himself. It is important to emphasize that in general, a cooperative outcome is *not* in equilibrium; it's the result of an agreement. For example, in the well-known 'prisoner's dilemma' game, the outcome in which neither prisoner confesses is a cooperative outcome; it is in neither player's best interests, though it is better for both than the unique equilibrium.

An even simpler example is the following game *H*: There are two players, Rowena and Colin. Rowena must decide whether both she and Colin will receive the same amount – namely 10 – or whether she will receive ten times more, and Colin will receive ten times less. Simultaneously, Colin must decide whether or not to take a punitive action, which will harm both Rowena and himself; if he does so, the division is cancelled, and instead, each player gets nothing. The game matrix is

	Acquiesce	Punish
Divide Evenly	10 10	0 0
Divide Greedily	1 100	0 0

The outcome (**E,A**), yielding 10 to each player, is a cooperative outcome, as no player can guarantee more for himself; but as in the prisoner's dilemma, it is not achievable in equilibrium.

Why are cooperative outcomes interesting, even though they are not achievable in equilibrium? The reason is that they are achievable by contract – by agreement – in those contexts in which *contracts are enforceable*. And there are many such contexts: for example, a national context, with a court system. The Talmud (Avot 3, 2) says,

הוי מתפלל בשלומה של מלכות, שאלמלא מוראה, איש את רעהו חיים בלעו.

'Pray for the welfare of the government, for without its authority, man would swallow man alive.' If contracts are enforceable, Rowena and Colin can achieve the cooperative outcome (**E,A**) by agreement; if not, (**E,A**) is for practical purposes unachievable.

The cooperative theory of games that has grown from these considerations pre-dates the work of Nash by about a decade (von Neumann and Morgenstern,

1944). It is very rich and fruitful, and in my opinion, has yielded *the* central insights of game theory. However, we will not discuss these insights here; they are for another Prize in Economic Sciences in Memory of Alfred Nobel, in the future.

What I do wish to discuss here is the relation of cooperative game theory to repeated games. The fundamental insight is that repetition is like an enforcement mechanism, which enables the emergence of cooperative outcomes *in equilibrium* – when everybody is acting in his own best interests.

Intuitively, this is well known and understood. People are much more cooperative in a long-term relationship. They know that there is a tomorrow, that inappropriate behavior will be punished in the future. A businessman who cheats his customers may make a short-term profit, but he will not stay in business long.

Let's illustrate this with the game *H*. If the game is played just once, then Rowena is clearly better off by dividing **Greedily**, and Colin by **Acquiescing**. (Indeed, these strategies are *dominant*.) Colin will not like this very much – he is getting nothing – but there is not much that he can do about it. Technically, the *only* equilibrium is (**G,A**).

But in the supergame H^∞, there *is* something that Colin can do. He can *threaten* to **P**unish Rowena for ever afterwards if she ever divides **Greedily**. So it will not be worthwhile for her to divide greedily. Indeed, in H^∞ this is actually an equilibrium in the sense of Nash. Rowena's strategy is 'play **E** for ever'; Colin's strategy is 'play **A** as long as Rowena plays **E**; if she ever plays **G**, play **P** for ever afterwards'.

Let's be quite clear about this. What is maintaining the equilibrium in these games is the *threat of punishment*. If you like, call it 'MAD' – mutually assured destruction, the motto of the cold war.

One caveat is necessary to make this work. The discount rate must not be too high. Even if it is anything over 10 percent – if \$1 in a year is worth less than 90 cents today – then cooperation is impossible, because it's still worthwhile for Rowena to be greedy. The reason is that even if Colin punishes her – and himself! – for ever afterwards, then when evaluated today, the entire eternal punishment is worth less than \$90, which is all that Rowena gains today by dividing greedily rather than evenly.

I don't mean just the monetary discount rate, what you get in the bank. I mean the personal, subjective discount rate. For repetition to engender cooperation, the players must not be too eager for immediate results. The present, the now, must not be too important. If you want peace now, you may well never get peace. But if you have time – if you can wait – that changes the whole picture; *then* you may get peace now. It's one of those paradoxical, upside-down insights of game theory, and indeed of much of science. Just a week or two ago, I learned that global warming may cause a cooling of Europe, because it may cause a change in the direction of the Gulf Stream. Warming may bring about cooling. Wanting peace now may cause you never to get it – not now, and not in the future. But if you can wait, maybe you will get it now.

The reason is as above: the strategies that achieve cooperation in an equilibrium of the supergame involve punishments in subsequent stages if cooperation is not forthcoming in the current stage. If the discount rates are too high, then the players are more interested in the present than in the future, and a one-time coup now may more than make up for losses in the sequel. This vitiates the threat to punish in future stages.

To summarize: in the supergame H^∞ of the game H, the cooperative outcome $(\mathbf{E},\mathbf{A})$ is achievable in equilibrium. This is a special case of a much more general principle, known as the *Folk Theorem*, which says that *any* cooperative outcome of *any* game G is achievable as a strategic equilibrium outcome of its supergame G^∞ – even if that outcome is not an equilibrium outcome of G. Conversely, every strategic equilibrium outcome of G^∞ is a cooperative outcome of G. In brief, for any game G, we have

The Folk Theorem: The cooperative outcomes of G coincide with the equilibrium outcomes of its supergame G^∞.

Differently put, repetition acts as an enforcement mechanism: it makes cooperation achievable when it is not achievable in the one-shot game. Of course, the above caveat continues to apply: in order for this to work, the discount rates of all agents must be low; they must not be too interested in the present as compared with the future.

There is another point to be made, and it again relates back to the 1994 Prize. John Nash got the Prize for his development of equilibrium. Reinhard Selten got the Prize for his development of *perfect* equilibrium. Perfect equilibrium means, roughly, that the threat of punishment is *credible;* that *if* you have to go to a punishment, then after you punish, you are still in equilibrium – you do not have an incentive to deviate.

That certainly is *not* the case for the equilibrium we have described in the supergame H^∞ of the game H. If Rowena plays **G** in spite of Colin's threat, then it is *not* in Colin's best interest to punish forever. That raises the question: in the repeated game, can $(\mathbf{E},\mathbf{A})$ be maintained not only in strategic equilibrium, but also in *perfect* equilibrium?

The answer is yes. In 1976, Lloyd Shapley – whom I consider to be the greatest game theorist of all time – and I proved what is known as the *Perfect Folk Theorem*; a similar result was established by Ariel Rubinstein, independently and simultaneously. Both results were published only much later (Aumann and Shapley, 1994; Rubinstein, 1994). The Perfect Folk Theorem says that in the supergame G^∞ of any game G, any cooperative outcome of G is achievable as a *perfect* equilibrium outcome of G^∞ – again, even if that outcome is not an equilibrium outcome of G. The converse of course also holds. In brief, for any game G, we have

The Perfect Folk Theorem: The cooperative outcomes of G coincide with the perfect equilibrium outcomes of its supergame G^∞.

So again, repetition acts as an enforcement mechanism: it makes cooperation achievable when it is not achievable in the one-shot game, even when one replaces strategic equilibrium as the criterion for achievability by the more stringent requirement of *perfect* equilibrium. Again, the caveat about discount rates applies: in order for this to work, the discount rates of all agents must be low; they must not be too interested in the present as compared with the future.

The proof of the Perfect Folk Theorem is quite interesting, and I will illustrate it very sketchily in the game H, for the cooperative outcome **(E,A)**. In the first instance, the equilibrium directs playing **(E,A)** all the time. If Rowena deviates by dividing **G**reedily, then Colin punishes her – plays **P**. He does not, however, do this forever, but only until Rowena's deviation becomes unprofitable. This in itself is still not enough, though; there must be something that motivates Colin to carry out the punishment. And here comes the central idea of the proof: if Colin does not punish Rowena, then Rowena must punish Colin – by playing **G** – for not punishing Rowena. Moreover, the process continues – any player who does not carry out a prescribed punishment is punished by the other player for not doing so.

Much of society is held together by this kind of reasoning. If you are stopped by a policeman for speeding, you do not offer him a bribe, because you are afraid that he will turn you in for offering a bribe. But why should he not accept the bribe? Because he is afraid that you will turn him in for accepting it. But why would you turn him in? Because if you don't, he might turn you in for not turning him in. And so on.

This brings us to our last item. Cooperative game theory consists not only of delineating all the possible cooperative outcomes, but also of choosing among them. There are various ways of doing this, but perhaps best known is the notion of *core*, developed by Lloyd Shapley in the early 1950s. An outcome x of a game is said to be in its 'core' if no set S of players can *improve* upon it – i.e., assure to each player in S an outcome that is better for him than what he gets at x. Inter alia, the concept of core plays a central role in applications of game theory to economics; specifically, the core outcomes of an economy with many individually insignificant agents are the same as the competitive (a.k.a. Walrasian) outcomes – those defined by a system of prices for which the supply of each good matches its demand (see, e.g., Debreu and Scarf, 1963; Aumann, 1964).

Another prominent application of the core is to *matching* markets (see, e.g., Gale and Shapley, 1962; Roth and Sotomayor, 1990). The core also has many other applications (for surveys, see Anderson, 1992; Gabszewicz and Shitovitz, 1992; Kannai, 1992; Kurz, 1994; Young, 1994).

Here again, there is a strong connection with equilibrium in repeated games. When the players in a game are in (strategic) equilibrium, it is not worthwhile for any one of them to deviate to a different strategy. A *strong* equilibrium is defined similarly, except that there it is not worthwhile for any *set* of players to deviate – at least one of the deviating players will not gain from the deviation. We then have the following

Theorem (Aumann, 1959): The core outcomes of G coincide with the strong equilibrium outcomes of its supergame G^∞.

In his 1950 thesis, where he developed the notion of strategic equilibrium for which he got the Prize in Economic Sciences in Memory of Alfred Nobel in 1994, John Nash also proposed what has come to be called the *Nash Program* – expressing the notions of cooperative game theory in terms of some appropriately defined non-cooperative game; building a bridge between cooperative and non-cooperative game theory. The three theorems presented above show that repetition constitutes precisely such a bridge – it is a realization of the Nash Program.

We end with a passage from the prophet Isaiah (2, 2–4):

והיה באחרית הימים. נכון יהיה הר בית יי בראש ההרים. ונישא מגבעות. ונהרו אליו כל הגוים.
והלכו עמים רבים ואמרו, לכו ונעלה אל הר יי. אל בית אלהי יעקב. וירנו מדרכיו, ונלכה בארחותיו; כי
מציון תצא תורה. ודבר יי מירושלם. ושפט בין הגוים, והוכיח לעמים רבים: וכיתתו חרבותם לאיתים.
וחניתותיהם למזמרות; לא ישא גוי אל גוי חרב, ולא ילמדו עוד מלחמה.

'And it shall come to pass ... that ... many people shall go and say, ... let us go up to the mountain of the Lord, ... and He will teach us of His ways, and we will walk in His paths. ... And He shall judge among the nations, and shall rebuke many people; and they shall beat their swords into ploughshares, and their spears into pruning hooks; nation shall not lift up sword against nation, neither shall they learn war any more.'

Isaiah is saying that the nations can beat their swords into ploughshares when there is a central government – a Lord, recognized by all. In the absence of that, one *can* perhaps have peace – no nation lifting up its sword against another. But the swords must continue to be there – they cannot be beaten into ploughshares – and the nations must continue to *learn* war, in order *not* to fight!

REFERENCES

Anderson, R.M., 1992, 'The Core in Perfectly Competitive Economies', in Aumann and Hart 1992, pp. 413–57.

Aumann, R.J., 1959, 'Acceptable Points in General Cooperative *n*-Person Games', in *Contributions to the Theory of Games IV*, Annals of Mathematics Study 40, edited by A.W. Tucker and R.D. Luce, Princeton: Princeton University Press, pp. 287–324.

Aumann, R.J., 1964, 'Markets with a Continuum of Traders', *Econometrica* **32**, 39–50.

Aumann, R.J., 1974, 'Subjectivity and Correlation in Randomized Strategies', *Journal of Mathematical Economics* **1**, 67–96.

Aumann, R.J., 1987, 'Correlated Equilibrium as an Expression of Bayesian Rationality', *Econometrica* **55**, 1–18.

Aumann, R.J. and Hart, S. (eds), 1992, 1994, 2002, *Handbook of Game Theory, with economic applications*, Vols 1, 2, 3, Amsterdam: Elsevier.

Aumann, R.J. and Shapley, L.S., 1994, 'Long-Term Competition: A Game-Theoretic Analysis', in *Essays in Game Theory in Honor of Michael Maschler*, edited by N. Megiddo, New York: Springer, pp. 1–15.

Debreu, G. and Scarf, H., 1963, 'A Limit Theorem on the Core of an Economy', *International Economic Review* **4**, 235–46.

Forges, F., 1992, 'Repeated Games of Incomplete Information: Non-Zero-Sum', in Aumann and Hart 1992, pp. 155–77.

Gabszewicz, J.J. and Shitovitz, B., 1992, 'The Core in Imperfectly Competitive Economies', in Aumann and Hart 1992, pp. 459–83.

Gale, D. and Shapley, L.S., 1962, 'College Admissions and the Stability of Marriage', *American Mathematical Monthly* **69**, 9–15.

Kannai, Y., 1992, 'The Core and Balancedness', in Aumann and Hart 1992, pp. 355–95.

Kurz, M., 1994, 'Game Theory and Public Economics', in Aumann and Hart 1994, pp. 1153–92.

Peleg, B., 1992, 'Axiomatizations of the Core', in Aumann and Hart 1992, pp. 397–412.

Roth, A. and Sotomayor, M., 1990, *Two-Sided Matching: A Study in Game-Theoretic Modeling and Analysis*, Econometric Society Monograph Series, Cambridge: Cambridge University Press.

Rubinstein, A., 1994, 'Equilibrium in Supergames', in *Essays in Game Theory in Honor of Michael Maschler*, edited by N. Megiddo, New York: Springer, pp. 17–28.

Sorin, S., 1992, 'Repeated Games with Complete Information', in Aumann and Hart 1992, pp. 71–107.

von Neumann, J., and Morgenstern, O., 1944, *Theory of Games and Economic Behavior*, Princeton: Princeton University Press.

Wilson, R., 1992, 'Strategic Analysis of Auctions', in Aumann and Hart 1992, pp. 227–79.

Young, H.P., 1994, 'Cost Allocation', in Aumann and Hart 1994, pp. 1193–236.

Zamir, S., 1992, 'Repeated Games of Incomplete Information: Zero-Sum', in Aumann and Hart 1992, pp. 109–54.

6.   Cournot and the social income

Robert M. Solow

Like any English-speaking economist, all I ever knew of Cournot is the 1897 English translation of *The Mathematical Principles of the Theory of Wealth*. More accurately, Cournot was always identified with his theory of duopoly, or more generally of markets with a small number of sellers, along with the alternative theories proposed later by Bertrand and von Stackelberg.

There is a large literature on Cournot and the theory of oligopoly, and an enormous literature on the more general notion that came to be called the Cournot–Nash equilibrium in the theory of n-person non-cooperative games. This has never been a special interest of mine, so it would be foolish for me to pursue that central theme in a conference devoted to Cournot and his work. So I looked further.

I had not actually reread the *Mathematical Principles* since my graduate-student days 60 years ago. When I picked it up again, I was struck – even in translation – by the force and clarity of Cournot's mind, and the natural modernity of the way he approached mathematical economics. Irving Fisher made the same observation in his 1898 review of the Bacon translation. I also noticed the existence of two chapters that were new to me, or that I had forgotten: Chapter 11, 'Of the Social Income', and Chapter 12, 'Of Variations in the Social Income, Resulting from the Communication of Markets' (by which Cournot means international or interregional trade). These chapters seem not to have been much discussed. They appear to point beyond the theory of a single market, in the direction of macroeconomics, which is a special interest of mine. So I decided to discuss them here.

Chapter 11 begins very impressively with a general discussion of a system of many markets. It is worth quoting at length:

> So far we have studied how, for each commodity by itself, the law of demand in connection with the conditions of production of that commodity, determines the price of it and regulates the income of its producers. We considered as given and invariable the prices of other commodities and the incomes of other producers; but in reality the economic system is a whole of which all the parts are connected and react on each other. An increase in the income of the producers of commodity A will affect the demand for commodities B, C, etc., and the incomes of their producers, and, by its

reaction, will involve a change in the demand for commodity A. It seems, therefore, as if, for a complete and rigorous solution of the problems relative to some parts of the economic system, it were indispensable to take the entire system into consideration. But this would surpass the powers of mathematical analysis and of our practical methods of calculation, even if the values of all the constants could be assigned to them numerically. The object of this chapter and of the following one is to show how far it is possible to avoid this difficulty, while maintaining a certain kind of approximation, and to carry on, by the aid of mathematical symbols, a useful analysis of the most general questions which this subject brings up. (Cournot, 1897 [1838], pp. 127–8)

This remarkable statement points clearly ahead to Walras and the theory of general equilibrium. At a certain level of abstraction, 'the powers of mathematical analysis' were able to produce a coherent model of a competitive economic system with any number of goods, markets and consumers, and eventually to state sufficient conditions for an equilibrium to exist. (There was a brief correspondence between Cournot and Walras in 1873–75 (Jaffé and Théodule, [1952] 1965). It is mostly just a polite exchange. Walras gladly recognizes that Cournot was 'the only writer who had up to now occupied himself seriously with [the mathematical theory of exchange]', and addresses him once as '*veneré Maître*'. In the only letter of real substance, Walras outlines the equations of consumer equilibrium with n goods. Cournot was then 72 years old, with failing eyesight – he needed someone to read to him, which made absorbing mathematics especially difficult – and did not really respond. He did not much care for ratios of marginal utilities anyway.)

The 'powers of our practical methods of calculation' have now expanded to the point where 'computable general equilibrium' models have been created, provided with estimated parameters, and operated for some developing economies. Cournot was right to emphasize the difficulty of assigning numerical values to the many constants as a major stumbling-block in the practical application of general-equilibrium theory to complex economic systems. It still is. In my mind, that difficulty is the main impulse behind the need for a real-time aggregative approach to empirical economics, in short for the development of the sort of miniature general-equilibrium models we call macroeconomics. Cournot wrote 100 years before J.M. Keynes started macroeconomics on its way. How far was Cournot able to go?

The answer, I have to say, is not very far at all. I found Chapters 11 and 12 to be rather disappointing, although this may simply reflect unrealistically high expectations; in fact I will make a more generous judgement later on. In his generally admiring review of the book, Fisher says, 'The two concluding chapters on "Social Income" are the most unsatisfactory in the book. They form one of those innumerable and futile attempts to define the income of a community and analyze its variations. Cournot here loses his accustomed perspicuity' (Fisher, 1898, p. 130). This is too harsh. In the course of his life, Irving Fisher devoted a lot of subtle thought to the proper definition of income. He could justly point to the – after all, inevitable – crudity of Cournot's concept, but it is unfair to expect a lot more. I want to focus on other limitations in Cournot's treatment of social income and its variations, but I will have to mention some elementary flaws in his definitions, though not the ones that Fisher probably had in mind.

In particular, Cournot defines the social income initially from the income side, as the sum of wages, profits, rents and so on, including the stipends of so-called 'unproductive' workers. No problem there. But then, going over to the product side, he defines the contribution of a particular commodity to the social income as pD, where p is its price and D is 'the number of units annually supplied for consumption' (Cournot, 1897 [1838], p. 128). It is quite clear that he means annual sales, not 'final' consumption in the modern national-accounting sense. But of course, when these many pDs for different commodities are added up, the value of all intermediate goods (those that are the output of one firm and an input to another firm) will be double-counted and more. On the product side it is value added for each commodity that should be summed, not sales. Only then can the product side be built up by addition and decomposed, as Cournot wishes, into 'the incomes of landlords and of capitalists who furnished the raw materials and the instruments for utilizing them, and the profits and wages of the various industrial agents who have cooperated in producing the commodity and in bringing it to market' (ibid., p. 128). We know that then the two totals must match.

Why did Cournot make this mistake? Naturally, the concept of 'value added' had not yet been developed. Maybe he visualized each of his producers as being vertically integrated, or maybe he reckoned, in the conditions of 1838, that intermediate goods could be neglected as a first approximation without substantial error. The list of cooperating participants in production just quoted is consistent with neither of these possibilities. Apparently he did not see the problem. We can go on to consider the rest of his ideas by making either of these assumptions for him, even if he did not.

Cournot then sets himself the following problem, for a particular commodity A. Suppose the initial price and output are p_0 and D_0; some exogenous event then causes the price to change to p_1, the corresponding quantity to D_1. For concreteness, he supposes that the price has gone up and the quantity gone down, but that revenue has fallen, $p_1 D_1 < p_0 D_0$. (We would say that the elasticity of demand exceeds one; Cournot has the concept, but not that locution.) What will be the ultimate effect on the social income?

He does a rather opaque calculation to confirm the obvious fact that consumers of commodity A will have $p_0 D_0 - p_1 D_1$ more to spend on other goods than they had spent in the initial situation. (The opaqueness seems to come from the assumption that the reduction in the demand for A comes about through the refusal by consumers to buy any A at all, while the others continue to buy the old amount, with nobody in between.) This is exactly the amount by which the revenues of the producers of commodity A have been reduced by the change in price. All incomes are presumed to be spent, so there is no net impact on expenditures in the rest of the economy. There will, however, be changes in the consumption of commodities B, C, D and so on, induced by the change in the price of A, and therefore in the incomes earned by producers of those goods, and therefore also in the demand for commodity A. But these effects will all be small; some of them will be positive and others negative. So they can be neglected. To a first-order approximation, says Cournot, the (small) rise in the price of A from p_0 to p_1 has diminished the social income by $p_0 D_0 - p_1 D_1$. It should be kept in mind that Cournot – unsurprisingly – always takes it for granted that all income is spent; there is no net saving.

I suppose a purist would turn up his nose and say that, after those fine Walras-sounding words at the beginning of the chapter, Cournot has simply abandoned the whole idea of general equilibrium. From a puristic point of view that is so. But a sophisticated and pragmatic macroeconomist might cheer Cournot on. He had found his way to the simplification that makes macroeconomics possible. To treat the economy as if it were a one-commodity (or perhaps two-commodity) world is to hope that changes in relative prices, though they will change relative quantities, may have only second-order effects on aggregates such as the social income. No one believes that such good luck could hold all the time, even in non-extreme cases. But it may hold often enough to provide a basis for macroeconomics.

The next step in Cournot's argument is interesting, again with modern overtones. He observes that purchasers of A in the new situation are paying a higher price for a smaller quantity, and are thus worse off than in the initial state of affairs. In fact, he says it as if they have been deprived of $(p_1 - p_0)D_1$ worth of income and the price had not changed. (J.R. Hicks would have put it slightly differently and more completely, but Hicks was comfortable with marginal utilities.) Cournot goes on to say that this implicit loss of income, added to the income reduction suffered by producers of A, $p_0 D_0 - p_1 D_1$, gives the quantity $p_0(D_0 - D_1)$, and he calls this the real reduction in social income, in contrast to the *nominal* reduction $p_0 D_0 - p_1 D_1$. Notice that the real loss is the change in quantity valued at the base-year price; one might think of it as a Laspeyres-type measurement. Suppose that commodity A had a relatively inelastic demand, so that a higher price leads to $p_1 D_1 > p_0 D_0$: Cournot goes on to show that the nominal social income will *increase*, but *real* social income is still reduced by the rise in price from p_0 to p_1.

Cournot's conclusions about the change in real social income that follow from a price increase make most sense when the source of the price increase is an increase in cost. Common sense would be shocked if a higher cost anywhere could lead, in principle, to a benefit everywhere. Cournot applies the same reasoning to the quite different case in which the rise in the price of commodity A is caused by the imposition of a tax on purchases of A. He had analysed this situation at length earlier in the book, when he is dealing with competition and oligopoly in a single isolated market. When it comes to the social income, however, his analysis is incomplete. A tax gives rise to a revenue; and so far as I can tell, he pays no attention to the *use* that is made of the tax revenue, and the social benefit that may result. His argument applies to a situation in which the tax revenue is spent on useless things or otherwise wasted. But then, of course, the tax is exactly analogous to an increase in cost.

Suppose there is a decrease in the cost of production of commodity A and thus a fall in its price. Then the earlier argument works with a change in sign, and real social income increases (though as before nominal social income could go either way, depending on circumstances). Cournot then adds an interesting remark:

> In estimating the real increase in the social income caused by a fall in price, no account is made of the advantage for the new consumers of the commodity, which consists in employing a part of their incomes in a manner more to their taste; for this advantage is not capable of numerical appreciation, and is not a new source of wealth in itself, although it may finally lead to an increase in wealth, if the commodity A is the raw material of other products, or an instrument which serves for other products. (Cournot, 1897 [1838] p. 138)

I am not sure what the author has in mind here. He may be conceding the importance of marginal utilities; remember that this is 1838 and 'utility' had not yet been introduced into economic theory. The other point, about a lower price of A opening up investment opportunities in other industries, would be just as effective – in the reverse direction, of course – in case the cost of production of A had increased.

Cournot is quite aware that essentially everything he has said in Chapter 11 comes from calculating with prices and quantities before and after, with no appeal to deeper sources of behaviour. So next he tries something a little more ambitious, but still using the same technique. Consider two commodities A and B, whose prices and quantities change for whatever reason. (The changes are both exogenous; the markets for A and B do not interact.) All other prices and quantities are assumed to be unchanged, according to the simplification already used. The notation for prices and quantities of A is as before; prices and quantities of B are similar, except with a prime, as in p', D'.

The particular experiment Cournot wants to conduct is one in which expenditure on A is reduced by an amount h, and expenditure on B is increased by the same amount. Thus

$$p_0 D_0 - p_1 D_1 = h = p_1' D_1' - p_0' D_0'.$$

In Cournot's vocabulary, the nominal social income is unchanged. But, he says, invoking a previous result, real social income has fallen by $p_0(D_0 - D_1)$ on account of commodity A, and has risen by $p_1'(D_1' - D_0')$ in respect of commodity B. What happens to real social income can be ascertained by comparing these two value expressions. And using the preceding statement about nominal social income, an equivalent comparison can be made in terms of the expressions $(p_0' - p_1')D_0'$ and $(p_1 - p_0)D_1$.

But there is something peculiar here. Cournot's first expression for the change in real social income on account of A is exactly the 'Laspeyres' expression he had deduced before: the change in quantity valued at base-period price. But when it comes to B he goes over to a 'Paasche' expression: the change in quantity valued at second- or 'given'-period price. He offers no explanation for this switch, nor does there appear to be one. A and B are just labels, after all. It should make no difference if we were to interchange their roles. Using the base-year price consistently gives a slightly different and slightly neater condition for an increase in real social income, but no drastic change.

There are a few more exercises of this kind in Chapter 11, but there is no need to list them. I do want to mention one other modern touch: at the end of the chapter, Cournot makes a point of insisting that, so far as the social income is concerned, there is no special distinction between goods and services. Commodity A could be alcoholic beverages and commodity B could be theatrical representations. It is all the same to Cournot's arithmetic. Even today there is a tendency to overstate the difference between material goods and immaterial services. Cournot was not tempted.

Before I go on to sketch Chapter 12, I should say why I found this part of the *Mathematical Principles* disappointing. One way to see it is to compare what Cournot has to say about variations in the social income with what he has to say in earlier chapters about monopoly, duopoly and competition. There he analyses with skill and originality how a market economy works. It is all about the mechanics of a market with few sellers and many buyers; and the result is a statement about the likely outcomes in price and quantity terms, and the characteristics of the environment that control the particular outcome that emerges.

Macroeconomics tries to do much the same thing for the economy as a whole rather than for a single market. It faces the problem of doing this in the realization that aggregate outcomes are determined by thousands of interrelated markets, but that this process is too complicated to be dealt with concretely on its own terms.

That is not at all what goes on in Chapters 11 and 12. As we have seen, there are essentially no moving parts, no 'behaviour equations'. The interrelations among markets are suspended by assumption. The earlier focus on mechanics disappears; instead we are given a more or less arbitrary and unmotivated change in price and quantity in one or two markets, and we are led to think about the arithmetic of the before and after situations.

I realize that the 'disappointment' is of my own making, a sort of misreading of what Cournot is after. His use of the phrase 'social income' is not a premature reference to macroeconomics a century before its time. That would have been a miracle. He is really making an excursion into welfare economics. His reference to social income is a foreshadowing of Samuelson's 1950 paper, 'Evaluation of Real National Income'.

It may not be a miracle, but it is certainly an example of Cournot's originality. More or less in the spirit of 'revealed preference', it is an attempt to base explicit judgements about changes in social welfare on observable prices and quantities. It does not quite succeed, mainly because it lacks the theoretical underpinnings that came, almost half a century later, with the subjective theory of value. But Cournot's sturdy focus on observables is attractive; and it could be said to point, as I have hinted earlier, in the direction of index-number theory.

I turn now to Chapter 12, on international trade. There has to be some new notation. 'A' now refers to the country that exports commodity M, and B is the importing country. In an initial state of when trade is impossible, p_a, D_a, p_b, D_b are the prices and quantities of M in the respective countries; the same symbols with primes represent prices and quantities of M produced in the two countries after trade is opened. In this post-trade situation, A exports an amount E of commodity M to country B; and buyers in A consume an amount Δ, so $D'_a = \Delta + E$.

In the normal case, if A exports M when trade opens, both the local price of M and its production will increase. The slightly 'opaque' calculation I mentioned earlier applies here too; it is a little more transparent the second time around. It shows that consumers in A have to spend more on M than they did in autarchy, and so have less to spend on non-tradables N, P, Q, and so on. But the 'more' that consumers spend on M accrues as income to producers of M, who can only spend it on N, P, Q. Cournot concludes that aggregate spending on other goods in country A will be unchanged by the opening of trade. He then invokes the same 'simplification' – or surrender – that I criticized earlier to argue that further reactions are likely to be negligible. Therefore 'the national income at A, or the sum total of the incomes of the producers at A, has increased, in consequence of the exportation of commodity M, by a value exactly equal to $p'_a D'_a - p_a D_a$' (Cournot, 1897 [1838], p. 153).

This is what Cournot calls a change in nominal income, and is always positive. He converts it to a change in real income, as in Chapter 11, and shows that it too is always positive. (The same peculiar – as I think – choice of prices occurs in the conversion; but consistent use of base-year prices leads to the same qualitative result.) So the opening up of trade, in one commodity only, has increased the 'real national income' of the exporting country.

Cournot then turns his attention to *B*, the importing country. He finds, by the same methods, that the nominal national income of *B* has decreased by exactly as much as the nominal national income of *A* has increased. From this he calculates real national income in *B*; it has decreased, but not by the same amount as the increase in *A*. There follows a paragraph worth quoting:

> We do not consider, as an amount to be deducted from this actual diminution of income, the advantage resulting to consumers, who buy as a consequence of the reduction, from their thus being able to use a part of their incomes more to their liking. This advantage is incapable of valuation, and can only increase the mass of wealth indirectly, in case the article which falls in price is the raw material or the instrument for further products, a condition which must be independently considered for each particular application. (Cournot, 1897 [1838], p. 156)

Cournot's methods are simply too limited to encompass the now-standard 'gains from trade' calculation. The 'advantage' to country *B* that he ignores cannot be discussed seriously without making use of two developments that came along well after his work: explicit general equilibrium, and the subjective theory of value. Cournot sees the point clearly, and deserves admiration for that, but he lacks the tools to deal with it.

It is a digression, but I want to take a few sentences to give Cournot credit for another small piece of analysis that shows how well he does what he can do. He points out that the goods exported are worth more in the importing country than in the exporting country, by the amount $(p_b' - p_a')E$. This amount will accrue as transportation costs or merchants' profits to the carrying trade, which may be carried out by residents of *A*, of *B*, or of third countries. He calculates that if it all appears as income in *B*, the importing country, the change in its real national income goes from negative to positive.

This is very neat, and Cournot generalizes it: 'the highest development of commun[i]cations between fractions of the same territory ... conditions remaining otherwise the same, ... does necessarily raise the real value of the national income to a maximum, and brings about the most advantageous working' (Cournot, 1897 [1838], p. 160). Then he rather tartly remarks that the 'school of Adam Smith' made the same claim, 'although there is a fundamental disparity between the example offered as proof and the case to which it is desired to apply it' (ibid., p. 160). Yes, Monsieur Cournot, you win this competition.

But then comes a passage that would be of great interest to a student of debating tactics. Cournot is aware that he has produced an argument that seems to favour protectionism on the part of the importing country *B*, whose real national income has likely decreased as a result of the opening of trade. The 'school of Adam Smith' would reply that, when all is said and done, trade between *A* and

B has to balance, treating them as the only traders. So the asymmetry between *A* and *B* must disappear. Each will be to the same extent importer and exporter, 'which would greatly complicate the question and lead to a complex result' (ibid., p. 162).

Now come the debating tactics. Cournot rejoins: that was not our assumption; our assumption was that trade between *A* and *B* opens only in connection with commodity *M*. 'What will be the effect of this removal of barriers which affects only a single commodity?' Under our assumptions, 'markets *A* and *B* are not placed under symmetrical conditions, [so] it is not surprising that we find formulas for the two markets which are unsymmetrical, and which even give results of opposite tendencies' (ibid., p. 163). In effect, he continues, I have shown why a government might have an interest in promoting exports or preventing imports of a commodity that is produced at home. If there were a likelihood of retaliation, he concedes, then the situation between *A* and *B* would in fact be symmetric, and all bets are off. In any case this leaves the modern argument about the gains from trade untouched.

The final half-dozen pages of the *Mathematical Principles* continue this one-person debate between Cournot on the one hand and Smith and Say on the other. For reasons which must have to do with the politics of the time, Cournot seems to want to strengthen the hand of protectionism, while the mathematical economist in him wants to limit him to what he can prove. In the end he resorts to the lame but familiar dodge: 'If we have tried to overthrow the doctrine of Smith's school as to [trade] barriers, it was only from theoretical considerations, and not in the least to make ourselves the advocates of prohibitory and restrictive laws' (ibid., p. 171). And then comes an extraordinary statement: 'Moreover, it must be recognized that such questions as that of commercial liberty are not settled either by the arguments of scientific men or even by the wisdom of statesmen. A higher power drives nations in this direction or that, and when the day of a system is past, good reasons cannot restore its lost vitality any more than sophisms' (ibid.). I much prefer the answer that Laplace is said to have given when Bonaparte asked where was the hand of God in Laplace's equations of motion: 'Sire, I have no need of that hypothesis.'

In the main hallway of the Department of Economics at MIT hangs a series of photographs of great economists. Antoine Augustin Cournot is there between John Stuart Mill and Léon Walras, and across from John von Neumann. I am no good at reading intellect and character from faces, and I doubt that any of you are good at it either; but rereading the *Mathematical Principles* has convinced me that Cournot belongs there. The book is a monument for its time; more than that, there is nothing antique about Cournot's energetic way of arguing his points.

Yes, Chapters 11 and 12 are disappointing. I had hoped to find that Cournot had made more headway towards modern macroeconomics or towards modern welfare economics than he was actually able to do. But those were my hopes or expectations, and thus of little significance. It is more important that those chapters could make one feel pretty good about the progress of economics as a discipline. The variations in the social income and the gains from international trade, and even duopoly, oligopoly and competition, are better understood now than Cournot could possibly understand them, in part because economics has built on his work. I am less sure that we have learned to be better than Cournot in the business of applying the results of economic research to policy debates, not because he was so good at it but because we are so bad. That is supposed to be the main objective of the Cournot Centre, and it was well named.

REFERENCES

Cournot, A.A. (1838), *Recherches sur les principes mathématiques de la théorie des richesses*, reprinted in G. Jorland (ed.) (1980), *Œuvres complètes*, Tome VIII, Paris: Vrin.

Cournot, A.A. (1897) [1838], *Researches into the Mathematical Principles of the Theory of Wealth* [*Recherches sur les principes mathématiques de la théorie des richesses*], translated by N.T. Bacon, with a Bibliography of Mathematical Economics by I. Fisher, New York: Macmillan.

Fisher, I. (1898), 'Cournot and mathematical economics', *Quarterly Journal of Economics*, January, 119–38.

Jaffé, W. and G. Théodule (1952), 'La correspondance complète de Cournot et Walras (1873–1875)', reprinted in W. Jaffé (ed.) (1965), *Correspondence of Leon Walras and related papers*, vol. 1, Amsterdam: North-Holland.

Samuelson, P. (1950), 'Evaluation of Real National Income', *Oxford Economic Papers, New Series*, **2** (1), 1–29.

7. Comparing the incomparable: the sociology of statistics

Alain Desrosières

INTRODUCTION

Augustin Cournot (1801–77) is frequently presented as one of the founding fathers of mathematical modelling in economics. In contemporary terms, mathematical modelling of economic phenomena involves either purely theoretical or hypothetico-deductive constructions, or, more commonly, the testing of theoretical hypotheses against statistical data, using econometric tools. Yet the combination of theory and empirical data in this way is a recent development. Modern econometrics in its unified form took off only in the 1930s (Morgan, 1990; Armatte, 1995). Cournot's work in economic modelling, by contrast, divided into two separate parts, each represented by a book. His first book, from 1838, concerned the 'theory of wealth', whereas the second book treated a different topic, the 'theory of chance and probability', and there was no connection between the two. The same dichotomy appeared in the case of other authors, such as Edgeworth and Keynes. Claude Ménard (1977) has examined the 'resistance to statistics' of three nineteenth-century economists: Say, Cournot and Walras. In Cournot's treatise of 1843, which broke new ground in the theory of knowledge, Ménard found 'an epistemological representation in which the method of investigation and the object of knowledge are perceived as independent'. Cournot, however, did not see in statistics a satisfactory instrument for the support of theoretical hypotheses. Statistics presupposed conventions and comparisons that could not be replicated fully. Paraphrasing Cournot, Ménard remarks:

> If the exact same experiment can never be repeated, how can the specificity of social facts be compared? These insoluble problems have been the cause of an 'exuberant proliferation' of statistical information … . The importance of space and time, that is to say, history, in social phenomena, only serves to accentuate the difficulties. … How can one compare data collected in human contexts and environments that are so completely heterogeneous? … How can the observer's contribution be circumscribed? On the basis of which tools? (Ménard, 1977, p. 422)

Drawing support from the notion of an 'equivalence convention', I shall describe how researchers and more generally social policy makers since Cournot have handled, if not resolved, these difficulties. This notion will serve to show that since that period, the objections of nineteenth-century economists and their resistance to statistics have been overcome, not logically, in the epistemological universe that Cournot inhabited, but socially, in a world where people *agree* to compare incomparables, treating heterogeneous situations as equivalent *for practical ends*.

COMPARING THE INCOMPARABLE[1]

In the first half of the nineteenth century, the pioneers of the so-called moral sciences (the future social sciences) took a lively interest in the probabilistic and quantitative modes of reasoning that had originated in the traditions of the eighteenth-century philosophers and astronomers. Two figures symbolize this historical moment: the Belgian statistician Adolphe Quetelet (1796–1874), and the French philosopher and mathematician Augustin Cournot (1801–77). However, unlike Quetelet who was the advocate of offices of national statistics, Cournot devoted himself less to the effective implementation of quantitative methods in science and society, and more to the study of the philosophical implications, in terms of the theory of knowledge, of recourse to these new ways of reasoning and argumentation. His work of 1843, *Exposition de la théorie des chances et des probabilités*, treats these questions in detail.

The modern reader cannot fail to observe that Cournot distances his position subtly from the scientistic objectivist interpretation adopted by frequentist statisticians, led by Quetelet.[2] From the frequentist perspective (popularized in the phrase 'the law of large numbers'), quantification is presented as the paradigmatic tool of 'objectivity', 'common language' and 'shared diagnosis' between observers or agents, who, through quantification, can communicate with each other, overcoming subjective differences, and consequently, substituting rational language for passionate speech. At several points, Cournot evokes the central question of interpretation, which underpins simultaneously the construction, format and conclusions of quantitative arguments. In this way, he places this mode of reasoning within an open reflection on the means of knowledge, whereas, more commonly, these arguments are advanced in order to close a debate. In particular, he applies this process to two questions. On the one hand, he introduces the distinction between so-called *objective* and *subjective* probabilities. On the other hand, he discusses the interpretation of *segmentation* or *cuts*: the latter are the categories organized by statisticians according to equivalence conventions, with the aim of ordering and comparing the objects of study. Following a brief review of the legacy of these two intuitions of Cournot, I shall examine how they can be implemented in three contexts where quantitative arguments are often mobilized: risk management, macroeconomic policies and the evaluation of public policies. The chapter will revisit, although with different tools, certain questions that Cournot raises in his *Exposition*. How should probabilistic tools and statistical methods be integrated with other means of knowledge and action? What conventions does this integration imply? How should one 'compare incomparables'? Can one complete Cournot's rigorous logical examination with an empirical study of the social uses of these instruments, as they have developed over two centuries?

Cournot was the first to place strong insistence on the *dual* character of the calculus of probabilities, which, on the one hand, quantifies *reasons for belief*, and, on the other hand, often (but not always) relies on *observed frequencies*. Since its earliest appearance in the 1660s (Hacking, 1975), this duality has been described in different ways. Condorcet distinguished 'reasons to believe' and 'facility'. Cournot spoke of 'chance' and 'probability'. Carnap contrasted 'inductive' with 'statistical' probabilities. In the eighteenth century, the decision-theoretic aspect, based on 'reasons to believe', predominated (Daston, 1989), particularly in procedures stemming from Bayes's theorem. This theorem set out a way of taking account of partial information about unknown situations, in order to estimate a 'causal probability' enabling one to support a decision. The nineteenth-century frequentist perspective contested this way of reasoning. It distinguished radically decisions based on non-quantifiable judgements (for example, those of a trial jury) from those that relied on repeated observations, in particular those provided by the new statistical offices advocated by Quetelet. For frequentists, Bayesian procedures, combining a small number of observations with a purely conjectural '*a priori* probability' to infer a stronger '*a posteriori* probability', seemed like a fantasy. As the choice of *a priori* probabilities was often arbitrary, the reasoning appeared built on sand. In the twentieth century, by contrast, the question of decision making under uncertainty attracted new interest with the work of Keynes, de Finetti and Savage. Discussions of Bayesianism and its interpretation assumed primary importance. Yet in 1843, Cournot had already sensed the significance of Bayesian reasoning, at the very moment when it was being discredited:

> A rule, first formulated by the Englishman Bayes, and on which Condorcet and Laplace wished to build the doctrine of a posteriori probabilities, has become the source of numerous equivocations which must first be clarified, and of serious errors that must be rectified, and which disappear as soon as one is made aware of the fundamental distinction between those probabilities that have an objective existence, which give a measure of the possibility of things, and subjective probabilities, relative in part to our knowledge, in part to our ignorance, and which *vary from one individual to another*,[3] according to their capacities and the data provided to them. (Cournot, [1843] 1984, p. 155)

In the twentieth century, the idea that subjective probabilities 'vary from one individual to another' became a topic of research in experimental psychology, in particular in the works of Kahneman and Tversky (1973), who showed that the human mind does not function according to Bayesian assumptions. In turn, these results were contested by Gigerenzer and Murray (1987), who criticized the poor experimental framework and the weakness of the interpretations (Amossé et al., 2001). The interest of these controversies is to centre the debate on an empirical question: how does the human mind combine quantitative information with *other information* that is temporally prior or of another kind? This approach differs from research that was limited to studies of putatively comprehensive data files. The advances of the latter reflect the fact that since the 1930s and the work of Ronald Fisher, William Gosset (*alias* Student), Jerzy Neyman and Egon Pearson, inferential statistics had made remarkable progress in parameter estimation and hypothesis testing using data files.

EXPLORING THE CONTACT ZONES BETWEEN PROPOSITIONS INVOLVING DIFFERENT REGISTERS

Mathematical statisticians have handled less well the question of interpretation, that is to say, the articulation of knowledge produced in terms of *what one knows (or thinks one knows) from other sources*. Yet this type of question was suggested by Cournot in 1843. Of interest here are the *contact zones*, or mediation points, between the rhetoric of statistics and other rhetorics.[4] Progress in mathematical statistics and econometric models in particular[5] has enlarged the space within which interlinked and mutually reinforcing statistical styles of reasoning come to appear self-sufficient, and have less and less contact with other types of argumentation. This development accompanied the increased professionalization of statisticians and econometrists. Matters were different in the nineteenth century, when methods of analysis were less sophisticated, and the cognitive and professional divisions of labour were less clearly delineated. The questions raised by zone border crossings were more visible, and hence often more discussed and rendered more explicit.

The point is neither to criticize or denigrate current uses of quantitative methods, nor to deepen the epistemological questions that these uses throw up, nor to make normative proposals for an improved methodology. I wish simply to provide some pointers for empirical studies of statistical practices and, more precisely, of transactions in the contact zones, in which quantified assertions inscribed in more or less formal models replace non-quantified assertions formulated in natural language. How is the world altered by the production and circulation of these quantified formal assertions? To what extent do they enable or prevent the production of unified incontestable interpretations, as their producers and users wish and even claim? If they do not do this, how should variations of interpretation be analysed?

When Cournot observed that subjective probabilities 'vary from one individual to another', he did not venture to explore the forms and causes of this variability: are they psychological, cultural, or biographical? Subsequent research has expanded these questions. Nevertheless, Cournot did see an aspect of statistical work for which the question of articulation in terms of pre-existing knowledge is crucial: what he called the 'choice of segments', that is to say, nomenclature. Remarking that if one classifies French administrative departments according to some variable (alphabetical order, crime rate), he asks whether the 'top classes' and 'bottom classes' are the result of random chance, or, on the contrary, of some relevant feature? Today's means of rapid calculation enable the savvy statistician (or, in the eyes of some, the less-than-honest dataminer) to calculate all possible correlations in a file, to choose the 'best', and *then* to formulate hypotheses which are miraculously confirmed by the data in the file. Cournot explicated this precise question in 1843, when he spoke of the 'prior judgement that orients the gaze towards the segments' (i.e., the nomenclature), and the interpretation of the 'spreads observed':

> A further element lies in the prior judgement, through which we perceive the nomenclature giving rise to the spreads observed, as one that is natural to employ out of the multitude of possible divisions, and not as one that catches our attention merely on account of the spreads observed. This prior judgement, by which statistical experience appears obliged to fix on one nomenclature rather than another, results from motives whose significance cannot be rigorously estimated and *may be very differently estimated by different minds*.[6] It is a conjectural judgement, itself based on probabilities, but on probabilities that cannot be resolved into an enumeration of chances, the discussion of which does not properly belong to the doctrine of mathematical probability. (Cournot, 1843 [1984], p. 196)

According to this reasoning, 'segmentation' (in this case the French administrative departments) is a given, but one cannot pretend prior complete ignorance about the specificities of the departments of the Seine, which includes Paris, or Corsica, which is an island. Cournot, however, does not raise the question of the genesis of the 'segments'. Yet the construction, coding and interpretation of statistical nomenclature constitute privileged moments in the study of the contact zones mentioned above. A statistical category is the result of an equivalence convention. The verb *convene*,[7] from which the word *convention* is derived, evokes the social procedure that yields the category. This procedure is a key element of the contact zone.[8]

The methodological doubt that Cournot articulated was not, however, the product of an arbitrary relativist scepticism, claiming (as is sometimes done in polemical contexts) that 'statistics can be made to say anything ...'. On the contrary, in a perspective that finally brings him close to Quetelet, he considered that belief in certain truths rested on a rational order, above individual subjectivities. Thus the variability of perceptions and interpretations is imputed to individual error, as was the case in the language of the eighteenth-century astronomers. Objectivity is induced through averaging, which, through the magic of the law of large numbers, enabled one to base contingent individual observations on 'chains of interlinking truths', closer to the 'rational order':[9]

> Our belief in certain truths is therefore founded solely neither on the repetition of the same judgements nor on unanimous or near unanimous assent: it rests principally on the perception of a rational order according to which these truths are interlinked, and on the conviction that the causes of error are abnormal, irregular and subjective causes, which could not give rise to such a regular and objective coordination. (Cournot, [1843] 1984, p. 421)

Cournot's idea combines, on the one hand, a methodological doubt justifying his attention to individual subjectivity, and, on the other hand, the conviction that there exists a rational order transcending individual subjectivity. This ambivalence is echoed in the controversies raised in recent sociology of science, polarized between different forms of *realism* and *constructivism* (Hacking, 1999). Taking these observations as the point of departure, I shall study in what sense quantification can be said to create objectivity. In one fell swoop, quantification appears to constrain, reduce and delimit the space of possible interpretations of the world, but at the same time, it *creates another world*, with new possibilities of interpretation and action. Quantification reconfigures the world, creating new objects that enter human social circulation.

QUANTIFY = CONVENE + MEASURE

In an experimental spirit, I shall suggest a framework in which to examine quantification procedures and their cognitive and social effects. The framework differs slightly from realist epistemology coming from the natural sciences, which often prevails in the social sciences. I shall test the framework using examples of problems drawn from current debates: risk management, macroeconomic analysis and public management indicators. In order to carry out this experiment, it will be indispensable to distinguish two commonly confused ideas: the idea of *quantification*, and the idea of *measurement*. The verb *quantify* is used here in a broad sense: *to express and realize in numerical form that which was previously expressed in words and not in numbers*. By contrast, the idea of *measurement*, drawn from the natural sciences, implies that something already exists in a form that is measurable using a realist metrology, for example, the height of Mont Blanc. In the case of the social sciences or the evaluation of public services, profligate use of the term *measure* and its cognates leads to error, by leaving in the shadows the *conventions of quantification*. The verb *quantify*, in its transitive form (*make* into a number, *put a figure on*, numeri-cize), presupposes that a series of prior equivalence conventions has been developed and made explicit,[10] involving comparisons, negotiations, compro-mises, translations, registrations, encodings, codifiable and replicable procedures, and calculations leading to numericization. Measurement, strictly understood, comes afterwards, as the rule-based implementation of these con-ventions. From this viewpoint, quantification splits into two moments: *convention* and *measurement*.

The use of the verb *quantify* draws attention to the socially and cognitively creative dimension of the activity. This activity does not just provide a *reflection* of the world (the common viewpoint), but it transforms the world, by reconfigur-ing it differently. The distinction between *quantify* and *measure* is not 'relativist' in the pejorative sense occasionally attributed to the word. It aims at separating analytically two moments that are historically and socially distinct. The distinc-tion is convincingly illustrated by examples such as 'intelligence', when the 'intelligence quotient (IQ)' was initially conceived, 'public opinion', when 'Gallup'-style polls first appeared (introduced into France by Jean Stoetzel), or the more recent debates about the quantification of the effects of public pro-grammes. The invention of the notion of *probability* in the seventeenth century, in order to *quantify the uncertain* by means of a number lying between 0 and 1, is an illustrious precedent in this domain. The 'reality' and the ontological status of the concept of probability were discussed at length, in particular by Cournot, whose distinction between objective and subjective probability was a cunning way of dealing with the epistemological challenge.

The suspicion of relativism may arise when the real existence of the object, prior to its being measured, is put in doubt by those for whom the measure actu-ally creates the object. Intelligence is 'what is measured by IQ tests'. Opinion is 'what is measured by opinion polls'. The standing hypothesis of this chapter is that quantification, understood as the totality of socially agreed conventions and mensuration operations, creates a new way of thinking, representing and expressing the world, and of acting upon it. The recurring question whether 'a statistic reflects reality more or less well' is deceptive shorthand, contaminated by the metrological realism of the natural sciences. Statistics, and more gener-ally all forms of quantification (for example, probabilistic quantification, accounting quantification), transform the world, through their very existence, by their diffusion and use in argumentation, whether in science, politics or journalism. Once the procedures of quantification have been coded and pro-grammed, their results are reified. They tend to become 'reality', by an irreversible 'ratchet effect'. The initial conventions are forgotten, the quantified object is naturalized, so to speak, and the use of the verb 'measure' automati-cally springs to mind and into ink on the page. This naturalization remains in force until, for reasons that require case-by-case analysis, controversies erupt and the 'black boxes' are reopened. An example is provided by the recent contestation of the 'volume–price split' in the economic growth rate.

The question of the objectivity and univocity of statements formulated in quantitative terms has already been raised above, inspired by Cournot's remarks on the variability in the ways in which human minds navigate the contact zone between, on the one hand, a non-formalized world, and on the other hand, the world of formalisms, via what is referred to as a 'model'. The definition of the verb *quantify* that I propose, distinct from the definition of the verb *measure*, allows one to raise this question in a different way. Quantification provides a specific language, endowed with remarkable properties of transferability, standardized computational manipulations, and programmable systems of interpretation. Thus it makes available to researchers and policy makers 'coherent objects', in the triple meaning of intrinsic coherence (resistance to criticism), combinatorial cohesiveness, and power of social cohesion, keeping people together by encouraging (and sometimes forcing) them to use this universalizing language rather than some other language. This perspective, which differs from the common received standpoint advocated by the quantitative social sciences and, more generally, by users of statistical and accounting tools, is advanced as a hypothesis that I shall attempt to apply in exploring three areas where quantitative arguments are widely invoked: risk management, macroeconomic planning and the evaluation of public management. Three types of equivalence space will be deployed: the space of probabilities, which Cournot studied in 1843, the space of value and wealth, which he examined in 1838, and finally, the space of means and ends of public management, which, as a theoretician, Cournot scarcely envisaged at all.

WHEN PEOPLE AGREE TO SET UP EQUIVALENCE SPACES

The three examples mentioned above are intentionally disparate. They have been chosen because, in each of the three cases, something that, *a priori*, was expressed in verbal form, ended up in numerical form, despite the fact that this transition was far from evident and the translation was (and often still is) debated in various ways. What price was paid to achieve this conversion from words to numbers? The historical moments when these 'numericizations' (just as one says 'dramatizations') occurred, are entirely different: risk has been 'probabilized' since the middle of the eighteenth century, the aggregates of national accounting have been quantified since the middle of the twentieth century, and discussion of the quantified evaluation of the performance and quality of public service (also called *benchmarking*) started in the 1980s. Other examples have already been mentioned: the (highly contested) identification of intelligence with IQ, and of public opinion with Gallup polls. The decisive stage is the negotiation of the conventions that make things *commensurable*, that is to say, comparable according to a numerical scale, whereas, *a priori*, this comparison was judged 'impossible' by many: 'You are comparing things that are not comparable; it *cannot be quantified.*' These criticisms are frequently heard from those who contest the commensurability in question. The objections are centuries old; they invariably surface, at some moment or other, in relation to the cases mentioned above.

The ambivalence of these objections lies in the French infinitive *pouvoir*. The French verb has two meanings: 'to be physically possible', and 'to be permitted'. In English, the ambivalence is expressed by two distinct verbs: *can* and *may*. The former is quasi-physical: it appears to stem from the nature of the thing in question. By contrast, the latter relates to the moral, social or political order. To compare (that is to say, *see together*) is a political act: in certain societies, one could not (in the sense of 'it was inconceivable to') compare slaves and free men, women and men, commoners and nobles, black people and white people. 'Social inequalities', as this expression is understood today, in terms of a reference to a common equivalence space, were thought of in this way at the end of the nineteenth century only in connection with inequalities of income, and (with rare exceptions) in the middle of the twentieth century in connection with other types of inequality, such as consumption, access to education, or social mobility. To postulate and construct an equivalence space enabling quantification, and hence mensuration, is an act that is at once both political and technical. It is political in that it *changes the world*: to compare commoners and nobles required the night of 4 August 1789,[11] to compare blacks and whites required the abolition of slavery, to compare women and men required truly universal suffrage including women.

American sociologists have put forward the related idea of *commensuration*. Under the title *Commensuration as a Social Process*, the idea of which is close to what I am proposing here, Wendy Espeland and Mitchell Stevens (1998) analyse the social processes that aim increasingly to *monetize* human acts, as an effect of the extension of market mechanisms. In this case, the equivalence space is money, the antiquity and generality of which should not be ignored. From a closely related perspective, Viviana Zelizer (2001) describes how, in divorce cases in the USA, previous amorous relationships, which it would have been inconceivable to valorize, suddenly become the object of bitter negotiations with the aim of quantifying them in dollar terms, in order to fix levels of compensation, generally for women injured by the separation. In these diverse cases, the authors study the *resistances* of all sorts that these commensurations encounter and must overcome. Their case studies are interesting for the proposal I am advancing, but they have nevertheless the disadvantage of restricting commensuration to *monetization* (within a perspective that is perhaps unsurprising in the US context).[12] The passage to a cash equivalent is one case (certainly historically important) among other constructions of equivalence spaces that have marked the history of humankind. Of the three cases presented here, the second (the evaluation of macroeconomic aggregates) involves the question of monetization, of course, but this is not necessarily so for the two others: risk management, and public service performance evaluation, using benchmarking, where the quantifications employed may or may not be monetary.

PROBABILITY IN THE EIGHTEENTH CENTURY: A DARING INTELLECTUAL CONSTRUCTION

Many of the problems raised by contact zone border crossings had already catalysed in the eighteenth century with the use of the calculus of probabilities. At that time, probability seemed an astonishing construction, uniting in a single cognitive space, quantified by a number between 0 and 1, three forms of 'degrees of belief' that were *a priori* very different (Daston, 1989): (1) forms issuing from geometric constructions such as games of coin tossing or dice; (2) forms deduced from regularities observed in a large number of events, such as the sex ratio or mortality; and (3) forms resulting from a bundle of clues and conjectures about a unique event that was not comparable to any other, such as the guilt of a crime suspect. The fact of collecting and indexing in this way, within the same equivalence space, three entirely heterogeneous ways of knowing or believing, appeared a daring intellectual feat. It is true that in his *Ars Conjectandi*, published in 1713 eight years after his death, Jacob Bernoulli, using his model of successive drawings of black and white balls from an urn, had proposed an ingenious way of linking the first and second of the three forms of degrees of belief. His 'law of large numbers' suggested a convergence of the frequencies observed of black and white balls, as the number of drawings increased. It created the possibility of assimilating the sex ratio or the suicide rate to the drawing of a ball from a Bernoulli urn. However, the same was not true of the subjective probability of a unique event, of which Cournot could say that it 'varied from one intelligence to another'. This brought about the relative discredit that both this type of probability and Bayesian reasoning experienced for almost a century, from the 1830s until 1930, to the advantage of the frequentist interpretation of probability.

Frequentist reasoning, originating from the model of Bernoulli urns, enjoyed great success in the nineteenth century, with the spread of so-called moral statistics, collected by the new offices of statistics promoted by Quetelet. Observed regularities induced a form of statistical determinism (even fatalism), and thereby, the idea that it is possible to *predict* at the collective macro-social level, phenomena that are unpredictable at the individual level, such as crime or suicide. This manner of reasoning, dubbed *the taming of chance* by Ian Hacking (1990), is at the origin of several types of activity. On one hand, the *quantitative social sciences* (sociology since Durkheim, econometrics since Frisch and Tinbergen) could share the ambition of being able to predict the future course of the world, like their big sisters astronomy and physics. On the other hand, *insurance* could now ground its rates (premia) and future repayments on the basis of the frequency of accidents observed in the past. But to do this, it is necessary to *agree* on the definition and scope of the Bernoulli urn (the risks to be covered), the identity of the balls (the elementary events), the nomenclature of the colours of the balls (the accident categories) and the coding procedures (once an accident is reported and a repayment made). Hence, prior to any risk measurement, risk quantification involves a complex game of conventions, negotiated in the contact zone. Recurrent controversies are normal, because the choices enumerated above involve *judgements* that are variable not only 'according to each intelligence' as Cournot thought, but also according to the interests of the actors. In this way, quantification is not sufficient to unite the various diagnoses around a univocal objectivity, although this may be the aim, in all good faith, of some (but not all) of the actors involved.

The notion of risk, associated with frequentist reasoning, has become essential in medical fields, on the one hand, in epidemiology (preventative intervention), and, on the other hand, in clinical medicine (therapeutic effectiveness). Some of the research on the subject is contemporaneous with Cournot: in France, the work of Docteur Louis, whose 'numerical method' aimed at comparing the effects of various treatments of typhoid, and the studies of the English epidemiologist William Farr on the prevention of cholera epidemics (Desrosières, 2000). The criticisms encountered by these applied quantitative methods are typical of what is played out in the contact zone. Resistance was of two sorts. The first 'traditionalist' criticism invoked the singularity of the patient–doctor consultation, and the impossibility of reducing the complexity of a person to a family of 'equivalence classes' by 'segmenting the former into slices'.[13] The other 'modernist' criticism was more interested in 'the' precise direct cause of a symptom or treatment effect, and not in statistical regularities or average causes. This was the position of Claude Bernard, and later of Pasteurian microbiologists. The latter sought 'the' cholera bacterium, or 'the' AIDS virus. The same battle was replayed (and quickly resolved) during the AIDS epidemic at the beginning of the 1980s, when blinkered epidemiology led to talk of an ill that, statistically, hit 'the 4 Hs' (Haitians, haemophiliacs, heroine addicts and homosexuals), before the HIV virus was identified. If, in our time, the two perspectives – the first 'macro' and statistical, and the second 'micro' (in the sense of an individual case, but also in the sense of microscope) – are perceived as complementary, the opposition, reflected in the history of medicine, refers back to a more general question, central in the analysis of what happens in the contact zone, concerning the kind of 'causality' that quantitative methods suggest.

STATISTICAL REGULARITIES AND CAUSALITY

Karl Pearson (1857–1936), one of the founders of mathematical statistics, was the first to formulate the ideas of correlation and regression. Drawing inspiration from the theories of the German physicist and anti-realist philosopher of science Ernst Mach (1838–1916), he emphasized the fact that statistics merely showed distributions, co-occurrences, regularities and 'contingency tables' (that is to say, joint distributions), but *in no case causes* (Pearson, 1912). Pearson thought causality was a 'metaphysical notion'. Even if, at a philosophical level, this position is conceivable, it certainly does not work for a man of action. Chased out the door, causality simply slips in again by the window, under a different, or even the same, name. Modern uses of the notions of 'risk', 'risk factor' and 'risk category' in epidemiology or the treatment of delinquency or drug dependence, provide examples of these metamorphoses of causality, torn between an anodyne epistemology and sets of practices, which, in these fields, grab any means available to integrate economic, social and political observations and objectives of all sorts more or less coherently. By an irony of history, despite his anti-causalist *credo*, Karl Pearson himself furnished a formalism that through its very terminology induced an apparently causalist interpretation. Linear regression models, which put the 'dependent variable' on the left-hand side of the equals sign and the 'explanatory variables' on the right-hand side, lend themselves to such a reading, despite whatever possible precautionary admonitions the statistician may utter.[14] The verb *explain* is sufficiently ambiguous to suggest a causality without explicitly affirming its existence. This lies at the core of questions about contact zone crossings. The contact zone is a translation area, like a canal lock, a decompression chamber or a corridor between two cognitive universes.

In linear regression models, the notion of a *variable* constitutes the core of the transformation that takes place in the transition from one world to another. It works like 'The Purloined Letter' of Edgar Allan Poe, that no one can see, although it is clearly visible on the chimney. The subjects of verbs, and thus of actions, cease to be persons or social groups, and become variables, which are new entities, resulting from a series of equivalence conventions, taxonomies, codings, and evaluations according to various frameworks. People are decomposed into *items*, which are recomposed into *variables*. The crucible of this transformation is the *table*, which crosses *rows* containing persons (or any other kind of beings, be they individuals or groups), against *columns* containing normalized coded items concerning each of these beings. In the first world, the table is read horizontally across the rows, and the individuals or groups are the subjects of verbs. Stories are told. In the second world, that of statistics, the gaze undergoes a perpendicular swivel: the table is vertically read down the columns, the variables become the actors. They are now the verb subjects. They are related, explained, and positively or negatively correlated. Each variable acts in a uniform way, provided that all the other variables are held constant. Thus one seeks to separate and isolate their *pure effects* (under a *ceteris paribus* assumption) using econometric methods, involving logistic regression, that generalize the rationale of linear models. The coefficients of these regressions are assumed to provide the man of action with the means of quantifying the marginal effects of the different levers that he controls.

This statistical language has two related properties. On the one hand, it is inspired by the natural sciences, which are ahistorical, and in which putative universal substances or concepts interact according to equally universal mechanisms. On the other hand, it lends itself well to the rationalization and optimization of action sought by executives in administration, politics and economics. For the latter, a *variable* defines the brief of a ministerial office, an objective to be attained, an indicator, a dial on a control panel. Linear economic models relate, on one side of the equation, those variables, often expressed in terms of *risks*, on which the executive *wishes to act* (the rate of unemployment, delinquency, road accidents, alcoholism) and, on the other side, other variables, expressed as *risk factors* (an alcohol limit, a speed limit), on which the executive *can act* through regulation, taxes or (a more recent solution) mechanisms of judicious incentive. The two properties are related. They are suitable for engineering models of intervention, which look for experimental regularities of a general scope, to orient, optimize and evaluate interventions.

The separation of *risks* and *risk factors*, a defining characteristic of causal linear models, results from explicitly discussed conventions. Patrick Peretti-Watel (2004) speaks of the 'porousness' of the equations of these models, in the sense that there may be some hesitation regarding the status of certain variables. In investigations into hard-drug use or teenage suicide, are alcohol consumption, nicotine ingestion or hashish smoking merely 'risk factors' or in fact 'risks'? The problem is more complicated, when, in so-called 'multi-factor' models, the aim is to isolate the 'pure effect, *ceteris paribus*', of certain factors, using econometric methods, the results of which depend crucially on the sets of dependent and explanatory variables chosen. The idea of separating the two categories of variable is less obvious in the first world than in the second world of assessable effective intervention, conceived according to the mechanistic model of cause and effect. Several controversies concerning the use of quantitative methods feed on this tension. They start in the system of concepts and conventions according to which the problem is defined, and in terms of which probability estimates can be made. Very frequently, the protagonists do not share a consensus about the appropriate system. Insoluble dialogues of the deaf are the result. Three recent examples (among many) are the notion of the 'precautionary principle', the potential dangerousness of genetically modified organisms (GMOs), and the possibility of evaluating various sorts of psychotherapy. Protagonists in these controversies understand and interpret the very notions of risk and uncertainty in different ways according to their positions.

RISK, UNCERTAINTY AND THE PRECAUTIONARY PRINCIPLE

The fact that, despite the wishes of eighteenth-century philosophers, not all situations of uncertainty can be probabilized, was emphasized by Knight (1921). He introduced the distinction, frequently taken up by others (notably by Keynes), between *risk*, which is probabilizable, and *uncertainty*, which is not. I have already drawn attention to the ambiguity in the word 'possibility' corresponding to the senses of can and may: is 'possibility' to be seen as a technical eventuality or a social agreement? Some insurance companies pride themselves on covering the most exceptional risks. Indeed, the business of reinsurance is to cover such risks.[15] Knight's distinction has been very useful in subsequent economic reflection. In practice, however, it assumes the aspect of a convention.[16] In recent history, marked by so-called exceptional catastrophes (9/11 in 2001, the heat wave in France in 2003, the Asian *tsunami* in 2004, Hurricane Katrina in 2005), the delimitation into risk and uncertainty in Knight's sense is once more called into question. Some commentators, such as Ulrich Beck, make risk, understood in both meanings, an essential characteristic of the current period.[17] In this context, the publication in 2005 of a report for the French General Plan Commission on the relations between 'Uncertainty, precaution and insurability', shows that the distinction between risk and uncertainty is the result, if not of assessments *'which vary from one individual to another'*, but rather of conventions relating to the argumentative and political use that is made of the distinction. The report puts forward an 'economic theory of insurability under uncertainty' (Chemarin, 2005).

The three debates mentioned above (the precautionary principle, GMOs and psychotherapy) have each been the object of an abundant literature. Within the perspective I am proposing here, these texts can be reread, with an emphasis on examining and comparing the place and role of probabilistic and statistical argument in each case, keeping in mind the notion of a 'style of reasoning' developed by Alistair Crombie (1994) and Ian Hacking (1992). Of course, the controversies bear on very different questions. Nevertheless, positional homologies are discernible. In each case, the styles of reasoning of the two adversarial camps are quasi-incommensurable. Yet, at a transversal level, analogies can be observed between the respective ways of arguing of the homological poles. On one side, that of the adversaries of the 'precautionary principle', the GMO partisans and the advocates of behavioural cognitive therapy (BCT), the probabilistic argument is seen as decisive and directed towards ending the debate. The problem is assumed to be sufficiently well defined in order that hypotheses about the probabilities of risk, or of therapeutic success, may be advanced and serve as evidence. At best, the methods of quantification and its results may be debated, but not the idea that the particular quantification brings an answer to the problem. In the three cases, this way of seeing things has the support of important scientific institutions, with arguments that are convincing within the canon or style of statistical reasoning. The French Academy of Sciences criticized the adoption of the precautionary principle, on the grounds that, in its view, the principle outlaws all risk taking. The Academy's criticism was founded on its assimilation of the principle to an outright proscription of any venture that involves potential danger. It intervened thus in the name of what it took to be freedom of research. The National Institute for Agronomic Research (INRA) endorsed experimental GMO cultivation, arguing that research was needed precisely in order to evaluate and quantify the potential risk of these crops. The National Institute for Medical Research (INSERM) compared BCTs to psychoanalysis by means of statistical 'meta-analyses' of previous evaluations of these therapies. In the three cases, quantification and the expression of risk in terms of probabilities aim to unify and aggregate radically different, even antagonistic, viewpoints within a commensurable space. They seek to gain the status of a *common language*.

In each of the three cases, the opposing side questioned the equivalences bolstering the arguments of the first camp. They returned to debating within the contact zone intermediate between the complex world of words and the world modelled by numbers and probabilities. Advocates of the precautionary principle obtained its inclusion in the Charter of the Environment attached to the Constitution. They deduced and took seriously the consequences of the notion of *non-probabilizable uncertainty*, in Knight's sense. Far from proscribing all risk-taking research, on the contrary they asked that research and consultation should take place *as far upstream as possible* when new techniques or industries emerge (Godard, 1997). They did not forbid the quantification or estimation of probabilities, but they did wish that it be done in a pluralist manner, within the framework of an enlarged universe of possibles, resulting from the confrontation of the most varied viewpoints and interests. They suggested transforming the relations between science, expertise and political decision, by including the doubts and uncertainties at the centre of democratic debate, instead of confining them within the work of experts required to deliver ready-made certainties into the hands of reassured decision makers. Procedures of this kind, such as 'consensus conferencing', gathering together diverse categories of experts and the people involved, enabling them to express their points of view, have been tested. Some have attempted to theorize (occasionally in an idyllic or even utopian fashion) these practices, under the name of 'hybrid forum', drawing attention to the diversity of actors involved in these new ways of conjugating expertise and society (Callon et al., 2001). None the less, until very recently, probabilistic and statistical tools have rarely been unfolded and discussed in these forums, except in the framework of associations.[18]

One of the difficulties in the quantification of the problems raised relating to the precautionary principle is that the confrontation frequently involves *two* equivalence spaces, which for moral reasons are judged incommensurable. The first space is public health risks, probabilized or not, which are concerned with life and death. The other space is the economy, for which, according to the analysis of Espeland and Stevens, 'commensuration' is guaranteed by monetary evaluation. Although economists have long incorporated the 'price of life' into their calculations, for example in choosing roadwork projects, the conjunction of the two spaces of quantification remains problematic. The inventors of the calculus of probabilities had, in theory, formalized a common space and a decisional criterion combining money and uncertainty (even beyond questions of life and death): mathematical expectation as the product of a potential loss or gain, multiplied by a probability. However, despite three centuries of debate and reflection on the criterion of mathematical expectation, strong reasons subsist to contest, reject or ignore it, precisely because it predicates an equivalence between beings that, for right or wrong, some people refuse to 'co-measure'. We are here at the heart of the contact zone alluded to above. The bitter debates about GMOs have to do with the difficulties in agreeing on a common equivalence space, in so far as the interests and issues, real or imagined, of farmers, seed producers and consumers are *simultaneously* uncertain and contradictory.

The reticence of psychoanalysts concerning comparative evaluations of the effectiveness of psychotherapeutic methods can also be read in terms of a refusal to accept the definition of effectiveness used in the meta-analyses undertaken at INSERM by the specialists in the field of BCTs, who concluded that the latter were superior. Psychoanalysts since Freud posit the singularity of the personal relationship that is constituted in an analysis. They refuse to circumscribe this interaction within the categories of the disappearance (in their view often momentary) of symptoms duly coded in a system of pre-established equivalences.[19] Their adversaries deplore 'this typically Gallic refusal of the culture of assessment'. Moreover, it is true that to this debate on the definition and ultimate purpose of the various methods, several economic arguments are more or less explicitly added, in terms of competition or public health economics.[20]

The project of exploring the contact zone between the worlds of words and numbers encounters along the way several controversies on the equivalence conventions necessary for quantification. After emphasizing, in memory of

Cournot, some of the controversies bearing on probability and mathematical expectation, I shall outline the recent debates involving, on the one hand, the evaluation and interpretation of macroeconomic aggregates and, on the other, the indicators promoted by so-called benchmarking techniques.

CONTROVERSIES INVOLVING THE VOLUME–PRICE SPLIT OF THE ECONOMIC GROWTH RATE

Up to this point, I have followed the lead on the equivalence convention that is provided by the calculus of probabilities, which Cournot expounded in 1843. This convention bundles together a multiplicity of conjectures into one real number lying between 0 and 1. Yet Cournot is above all best known for his work in economics. His first book, *Recherches sur les principes mathématiques de la théorie des richesses* (1838), bears on another equivalence convention, one on which economics is founded, elaborating the notions of value and wealth through the general equivalent term of money (Aglietta and Orléan, 2002). The coexistence of these two books, one from 1838, the other from 1843, by the same author, reveals a paradox. Whereas nowadays the idea of the *mathematization* of the economy seems synonymous with *quantification*, the effective synthesis of the two ways of doing economics, notably in the form of econometrics, dates only from the 1930s. The two books of 1838 and 1843 appear independent of each other, as though Cournot the economist and Cournot the probability theorist were unacquainted. It is true that the 1838 text of *Recherches* is principally devoted to the analysis of partial equilibria. Schumpeter (1983) attributes Cournot's reticence regarding more global analyses to the fact that, in his view, global analyses would exceed 'practical methods of calculation', and this leads him to envisage the use of a 'small number of aggregates' and a 'social income', which brings to mind modern national accounting:

> *Cournot recognized that* 'in the complete rigorous solution of problems relating to some components of the economic system, it is indispensable to take the whole system into consideration' (*Mathematical Principles* ... , p.127; *Recherches* ... , pp. 191–192). *This is exactly what Walras was to do. However, just like the Keynesian group of economists post Marshall, Cournot believed that* 'this would exceed the power of mathematical analysis and our practical methods of calculation' (*Mathematical Principles* ... , p.127; *Recherches* ... , p. 192). *Instead, he envisaged the possibility of dealing with the problems in terms of a small number of aggregates, in which the social income and its variants would occupy the place of honour.* (Schumpeter, 1983, vol. III, p.281)

In his partial analyses, Cournot distinguishes carefully 'real' and 'nominal' wealth and variations in quantity and price. When, a century later, public accountants *quantified* (in the sense defined above) the aggregates used to express economic growth, they ran into the problem of splitting this growth into 'volume' and 'price' (Vanoli, 2005). The ensuing controversies illustrate the irreversible ratchet effect that quantification produces. Once quantification has been programmed, debates take place in realist terms, which are the only coin plausible according to the rationale of the practical and political uses of national accounts. The question of the volume–price split has consequences on current debates on the elusive equilibrium between stability and growth. The growth rate in *volume* terms (in constant money) of an economy from one period to another is calculated by deflation (division) of the progression in *value* terms (in current money) by a price index, itself also the result of a calculation. The price index thereby plays a key role in the calculation of the growth rate.

The volume–price split provoked lively debate in the 1990s because of the difficulties of taking into account a 'quality effect' in the measurement of price progression, particularly in the case of computers, whose power had increased rapidly. How should agreement be reached on what constitutes *constant quality*? This question stimulated controversy in the United States, following a report by Michael Boskin et al. (1996) to the US Senate. The report argued that price increases were overestimated because the quality effect was insufficiently reflected. As a result, volume increases were underestimated, a fact that, according to the report, had major political and economic consequences. In this debate, all the participants, who may very well have disagreed on the report's methodology and its conclusions, were implicit realists, since the notions of 'overestimation' and 'underestimation', accepted by everyone involved, presuppose that a 'bias' exists relative to some reality that pre-exists any measurements. The language of realism was never in doubt. Incorporation of the quality effect implies a *judgement* and *conventions* (precisely concerning the said 'qualities') and is not a simple matter of a purely realist metrology. Yet this fact is rarely mentioned, even with sophisticated mathematical methods of the 'hedonic price' type.

Assessments of the consequences of European stability policies are founded on measures of the inflation rate and the volume growth rate. The European Central Bank (ECB) is frequently criticized for dealing only with the first of these rates to the detriment of the second (Fitoussi, 2002). In debate, evocation of the volume–price split problem would cloud a politically important message. Would it be possible to re-endogenize these questions of measurement conventions within scientific and social debate? In which 'hybrid forum' (in the sense of Callon et al., 2001) could this be done? Whatever one's view on such a thorny problem, it is clear that the *social division of labour* between statisticians, national accountants, university economists, ECB directors, political executives, journalists and citizens plays an essential role in the distribution of realist and conventionalist rhetorics. This suggests a programme of research and public debate, rather than abstract normative responses. It does not involve *relativizing* the work of national accountants by exhibiting their conventional, and hence judgemental, character, but rather to suggest an analogy with legal rules, decided by common agreement, with the aim of creating a *common language* between the actors.

Since the 1980s, evaluations of national accounting are taken into account in indexation procedures, European regulations and treaties, in the Growth and Stability Pact and in the decision-making processes of the ECB. The *constitutive* (even constitutional) character of national accounting is thereby accentuated.[21] The horizons of national account use have changed. Some wish to 'include in GDP' the quantification of new questions: the domestic work of women, externalities relating to destructions of the natural environment (Gadrey and Jany-Catrice, 2005). In these different cases, quantification fashions and refashions society, and does not just measure or reflect it. National accounts seem spread between increasingly different uses, from their appearance in the context of their initial employment to enthrone Keynesian policies or to guide indicative economic planning. These slippages of use prompt one to look again at a contact zone that, pre-1960, had been studied by economists such as Frisch and Hicks, but since then has been left to small teams of international expert specialists and little visited by the best-known economists (Vanoli, 2005).

Tensions such as these, resulting from the multiplicity of uses, are also visible in the case of *corporate accounting*. Thus, in order to 'value' balance sheet assets, three conventions may be employed, corresponding to three rationales of use. The *original cost* (or *historic value*) is used by the *manager* who is seeking to distribute depreciation annuities. The *resale value* is of concern to the *creditor* of the firm, who wonders what its assets are actually worth. Finally, the *sum of discounted future earnings* interests the *investor*, who wishes to allocate his or her financial assets. A comparable diversity exists in the different manners of calculating the profit of a firm, according to the objectives of the calculation. The *active* form of the verb 'value' used by accountants signifies a procedure that is implicitly more constructivist than realist. Whereas economists debate the 'foundations of value', accountants 'value', that is to say, fabricate a value according to conventions. Within the legal rules and conventions of auditing, firms have degrees of freedom that allow them to show higher or lower profits, depending on whether their concern is to convey a message to their shareholders, potential acquirers, the state, or other actors in the economy. The parameters and the effects of the techniques (sometimes called window dressing) by which firms optimize their accounting decisions in light of various constraints are the object of an elaborate mathematical branch of accounting research, which draws support from the assumptions of microeconomic theory, *Positive Accounting Theory* (Casta, 2000; Chiapello and Desrosières, [2003] 2006).

QUALIFICATION, COMPARISON, EVALUATION AND CLASSIFICATION: THE POLITICS OF STATISTICAL INDICATORS

Unlike market activities, public policies, be they national, European or local, do not have available accounting criteria such as 'market share' or profitability in order to judge their capacity to satisfy users' needs, or simply their efficiency. Traditional notions of public service and rational administration presuppose strong commitment by their members, monitored through structures of hierarchical subordination, of which the French and German states have long been the prime examples. Since the 1980s, however, this civic sense of public service has been widely judged insufficient to monitor democratically and efficiently activities that themselves are financed by the public purse. Quantified indicators were sought that could play a role more or less similar to the cost accounting, operating accounts and balance sheets of commercial firms. National accounting had exercised this role only partially, because its place was at the macroeconomic level, in a Keynesian or central planning perspective, without entering into the detail of public interventions. In this new perspective, indicators cannot be simply monetary, because the effects of interventions (schools, public health, security, foreign affairs, defence etc.) are not in general expressible in the familiar equivalence space provided by money. Thus the efforts undertaken by both the French state and the European Union can be seen as vast tentative experiments in the construction and negotiation of *new equivalence spaces*, by *agreeing* procedures for the quantification of the means and ends of intervention, using different units, amongst which money may be included but is not the sole unit. I shall discuss two examples: the Constitutional Bylaw on Budget Acts (CBBA),[22] unanimously adopted by the French Parliament in 2001, and the Open Method of Coordination (OMC) employed by the European Union.[23] The political and historical contexts of these instruments (one French, the other European) of government public policy are different, but they share the common feature of giving a central role to *statistical indicators*, that is to say, tools little discussed in public debates, although these tools constitute the actual spaces and languages that delimit and structure these debates.[24]

The CBBA is a new way of structuring the state budget, according to objectives to be achieved and not according to the means allocated. It entails that these objectives be made explicit and *quantified*, so that Parliament no longer just approves expenditure but verifies the achievement of objectives and the performance of services. This idea of the quantification of the means and ends of public intervention seems evident if Parliament is to play fully its constitutional role in voting and executing the implementation of the budget. Nevertheless, it entails important processes of objectivation and the 'equivalencing' of disparate activities within the contact zone already discussed. These activities must be articulated, discussed, named, qualified, compared, classified and evaluated. The right indicator is never evident. A pre-existing institutional and social order is often described and made explicit. In theory, this can only happen through the deep involvement of the persons concerned. Often, however, the very notion of a quantitative indicator arouses reticence, comparable to those described above in connection with medicine. The idea resurfaces that these procedures lead to the comparison of incomparables. Sometimes this idea appears absurd, and all the more so the more deeply the actors are involved in their tasks. The fact of creating categories, designed in principle to simplify the world and render it intelligible, at the same time modifies it, and makes it a different world. Actors, by changing the system of reference, are no longer the same actors, since their actions are henceforth directed by these indicators and classifications, which become criteria for intervention and evaluation.

The CBBA was presented as enabling Parliament to know better and evaluate public service interventions, within the perspective of a rebalancing of legislative and executive powers. In this context, the fact that this entails the invention and installation of a large number of quantified indicators does not seem to have attracted much attention from commentators, at least between 2001 and 2003. It seemed a technical question, to be resolved by technicians. Yet the ever more detailed discussions starting from 2004 (the law came into force in 2006) show that this moment of quantification (in the sense of the *action of quantifying*) is decisive for the course of events, although this did not precipitate any more general study of the questions mentioned above. The difficulties and perverse effects appeared *one by one*, occasionally becoming the object of denunciations or jokes. Thus, for example, the police force (under the Ministry of the Interior) and the *gendarmerie* (under the Ministry of Defence) responsible for road safety chose as indicator of their performance the percentage of positive alcohol tests out of the total of all tests effected. However, the police initially wished to evaluate its performance by an *increase* in this proportion, whereas the *gendarmerie* sought to *diminish* the proportion. Each choice had its logic. The example shows what sort of issue a political sociology of quantification could treat in a study of the methods and effects of 'indicator politics' entailed by the CBBA, or, at the European level, by the OMC.

In other certainly different contexts, similar effects have been observed. Thus the centralized planning of former communist countries failed in part because it proved impossible to fix reliable indicators for the achievement of the objectives of the Plan. The problem was caused by the perverse effects of retroaction, induced by these indicators, on the behaviour of actors. In the US context, in a study on the installation of a system of professional classification in hospitals, Bowker and Star (1999) showed how the formal explicitation of previously implicit activities resulted in their transformation. Indicators and classification are simultaneously *constraints* and *resources* that, by their very existence, change the world. Further, these management instruments, which the authors describe as boundary objects, are sufficiently ambiguous and polysemiotic to circulate from one world to another with partially different interpretations and uses. This is a sociological way of understanding the multivocity of statistical assertions, discussed in the introduction starting from Cournot's observations. The metaphor of *boundary objects* is close to what I have referred to as the *contact zone*, on condition that the latter is interpreted not just cognitively (contacts between more and less formalized languages), but also sociologically (contacts between more and less expert actors, using different languages):

> Boundary objects are those objects that both inhabit several communities of practice and satisfy the informational requirements of each of them. Boundary objects are thus both plastic enough to adapt to local needs and constraints of the several parties employing them, yet robust enough to maintain a common identity across sites. They are weakly structured in common use and become strongly structured in individual-site use. (Bowker and Star, 1999, p. 297)

The OMC is used by the European Union to try to harmonize social policies (employment, education, welfare) that do not involve monetary and economic domains falling explicitly within its sphere of competence. The first example of the method was the European Strategy for Employment (ESE) proposed at the Amsterdam Summit in 1997. The name and the procedure of the OMC were decided at the Lisbon Summit in 2000. The principle underlying the OMC is that, in an intergovernmental way, states set themselves common objectives, expressed in terms of quantified indicators, relative to which states are then classed and evaluated, as in a prize list. In theory, the results of this benchmarking exercise are purely indicative, but the simple fact that they are published serves as a powerful stimulant to guide national policies in the directions indicated at Summits (Dehousse, 2004). For example, an employment rate of 70 per cent was fixed at the Lisbon Summit in 2000. Thus, just like the CBBA, the OMC gives a key role to statistical indicators, the former for the presentation and monitoring of the state budget, the latter for the indirect guidance of European social policies.

The way in which member states of the European Union agree on methods for this quantification is therefore essential, although it is poorly known. Technically, the work is divided into two parts. The political authorities decide on the choice of indicators and define them in a succinct verbal manner. Then they transmit an order to quantify to the statisticians at Eurostat (the Office of Statistics of the European Union) and the National Institutes of Statistics. The expression 'agree' is therefore itself shared, since the political executives leave to the statisticians the business of sorting out the 'details', as for example in the precise definitions of the notions of *employment rate* (Salais, 2004), *disposable household income* (Nivière, 2005), and *homeless person* (Brousse, 2005). These three studies show that, at this stage, given the great institutional differences between countries, statisticians cannot avoid leaving vague certain sometimes important specifications in measurement procedures, and cannot harmonize them completely. The method is called 'open' because it is not binding and leaves states free to adapt it to their institutional specificities, notably by choosing as sources direct enquiries or administrative registers (Desrosières, 2005).

Indicators produced in this way can be seen as boundary objects in the sense mentioned above. These objects have a vague, non-exhaustively defined character, which allows them to serve in several universes that were previously unrelated but now become comparable. In this way, the idea of boundary objects comes close to the idea of common language. Natural language has analogous properties: it is because interlocutors do not spend their time making explicit the meaning and content of the words uttered that communication is possible. The objects produced by public statistics, the unemployment rate, the price index, GDP, share this sub-explicitness to some extent. A complete explicitation of the method of their construction and their content would risk weakening their argumentative effectiveness, not just because it would uncover the conventions and approximations that the user had not suspected, but simply for reasons of economy in the course of the exchanges, debates and demonstrations in which statistical arguments find their place. Except in the case of controversy (such as that resulting from the Boskin report), all this remains implicit. However, the idea of *vagueness* can only shock, and with perfect justification, those professionals concerned with the definition and standardization of their objects. They are caught between two contradictory requirements. On the one hand, as good engineers, they wish to specify their procedures completely, but, on the other hand, negotiations encourage them to tolerate compromises without which the indicators necessary for benchmarking would be simply impossible to provide. The equilibrium that they actually seek to maintain between these two requirements has received little formalization.[25]

SOCIAL CONDITIONS FOR RECOURSE TO THE BERNOULLI URN MODEL

The 'resistance to statistics' attributed to Cournot can be interpreted in the light of the controversies discussed here: 'how should one compare data collected in places and human contexts, in such heterogeneous environments?' The question can be juxtaposed with the criticism formulated by Baron de Keverberg in 1827 to invalidate the probabilistic sampling methods (the future 'polling') employed by Laplace since the end of the eighteenth century to estimate the French population. How, Keverberg asked, can one justify the assumption of the unicity of the Bernoulli urn when the French territory is so heterogeneous? Does the procedure of replacing the whole by a (small) part allow one to extrapolate a result obtained under these conditions? The equivalence convention of balls contained in an urn was thereby thrown into question. This criticism had such an impact (in particular on Quetelet) that the probabilistic polling method was disbarred from use until the beginning of the twentieth century (Desrosières, 2000, ch. 7).

The notion of equivalence convention articulates the social (convene–agree) and logical (the mathematical relation of equivalence) dimensions of the process of quantification. It enables one to show how the objections of Keverberg and Cournot were overcome not just logically but also socially, in a way that posed and resolved practical problems. From this standpoint, the social uses of probability and statistics have been ill served by their juxtaposition with the natural sciences, which the pioneers of the quantification of the social sciences, and more generally of the guidance and evaluation of public intervention, frequently made. They hoped to benefit from the putative objectivity of the natural sciences, according to which in the nineteenth century 'the only science is the science of the measurable'. A different and less banal rapprochement could be made with the constructions issuing from law and the political sciences. A society cannot exist without constitutive conventions that are negotiated and inscribed in stable texts. The adjective 'conventional' is not synonymous with 'arbitrary'. Since the eighteenth century, probabilistic and statistical tools have been included in the panoply of the common languages and instruments in terms of which human societies think of themselves, act, and express their projects and disagreements. Cournot was perhaps too much of a logician and an epistemologist to venture further in his fertile intuitions on the multiplicity of meanings of the probabilistic and statistical tools of his time. But then, it is true that their social uses were far less numerous than is currently the case. The questions that Cournot the philosopher treated can be dealt with today in terms of the sociology of the diverse forms of quantification and modelling that suffuse the world of action and the economic and social sciences.

NOTES

1. The expression is borrowed from the title of the book by the historian Marcel Detienne (2000), which is a critical analysis of the fact that history, often written from a nationalist perspective, considers the historian's nation as radically incomparable to other nations, blocking all historical comparativism. Statistics is precisely a conventional means, among other methods, of comparing the incomparable. Several controversies surrounding statistics bear on this exact question of comparability.
2. Although some historians see in Cournot a proponent of the frequentist interpretation, Thierry Martin (1994) shows that 'if the concept of mathematical probability is not univocally determined … , the reason is that for Cournot, it is a matter of classifying the different possible meanings, in order to appreciate the value of the results that calculation yields'. In the same spirit, the aim in the present chapter is to explore the multiplicity of meanings and interpretations that probabilistic and statistical assertions may carry.

3. My emphasis.
4. The word 'rhetoric' is not intended to have the pejorative meaning that it sometimes possesses, but the neutral meaning of a form of argumentation, or, as Hacking says, a 'style of reasoning'.
5. This reading has links with the work on the history and sociology of modelling and on the role of models, undertaken in the Anglo-American world by Mary Morgan and Margaret Morrison (1999), under the suggestive title *Models as Mediators*, and in France by Michel Armatte and Amy Dahan-Dalmedico (2004) at the Alexandre Koyré Centre. In this perspective, a *model* is a *mediator* in two ways: on the one hand, it mediates between formalism and a non-formalized world, and on the other hand, it serves as a *common language* between agents. Quantification procedures can be viewed in the same manner.
6. My emphasis.
7. The French verb *convenir* (translated above as *convene* and subsequently as *agree*) has the double sense of to agree and to convene [translator's note].
8. Various studies of these phenomena have been undertaken since the 1970s. Several are reviewed in chapter 8 of Desrosières (2000).
9. This brings to mind the references to a divine order in Quetelet, or, more recently, in the work of the French statistician Jean-Paul Benzécri, an advocate of correspondence analysis.
10. This social and logical notion of equivalence convention owes much to the early work of Bruno Latour (1984) in the supplement *Irréductions* to his book on Pasteur, and the paper of Laurent Thévenot (1983).
11. The night on which seigneurial rights and prerogatives were renounced in a session of the National Assembly, bringing to the end the *Ancien Régime* in France.
12. This approach is also related to the concern of certain sociologists to position themselves relative to economists, for whom money is *the* reference variable.
13. This perspective remains very much alive, in particular in the idea of the *patient–doctor private consultation* (*colloque singulier*) in general medical practice, and in psychoanalysis and homoeopathic medicine.
14. The question of the absence of any automatic causal link is most often raised in connection with *correlation*, although the formula for the correlation coefficient is symmetric. By contrast, in virtue of their asymmetric and hence oriented form, *regression equations* invite causal readings even more strongly.
15. In theory, one should distinguish *non-probabilizable* events from events of *very small probability*. Cournot was especially interested in the latter from a philosophical viewpoint, and a so-called 'Cournot principle' for events of very small probability became the subject of several subsequent debates (Martin, 1994).
16. The distinction is often used by economists, but infrequently adopted by statisticians, for example. The standard reference text by Stephen Stigler (1986) on the history of statistics is called: *The History of Statistics: The Measurement of Uncertainty Before 1900*. In this case, uncertainty is most certainly 'probabilized'.
17. This judgement requires some qualification since warnings of catastrophe were already expressed in comparable terms in earlier periods. For example, in the period 1820 to 1850, alarms were sounded concerning the then very new and spectacular accidents involving steam engines, gasometers and railways (Jean-Baptiste Fressoz, thesis in preparation at the Alexandre Koyré Centre under the supervision of Dominique Pestre).
18. Some associations set themselves this precise goal. In France, Pénombre, http://www.penombre.org, founded in 1993, 'offers a public space for reflection and exchanges on the use of figures in society's debates: justice, sociology, the media, statistics'. In the UK, official statistics are vigorously discussed by the association RadStats, http://www.radstats.org.uk, in existence since the 1970s: 'We believe that statistics can be used to support radical campaigns for progressive social change. Statistics should inform, not drive policies. Social problems should not be disguised by technical language.'
19. Debates around the 'numerical method' proposed by Docteur Louis in the nineteenth century set in opposition similar arguments on the theme of the private patient–doctor consultation, in which the patient 'must be treated in his or her unique wholeness'. The tension is the same between, on the one hand, the appeal to singularity and, on the other, the classification into

nosographical categories. It lies at the heart of the turbulent history of relations between medicine and statistics: the 'comparison of incomparables' is always involved.

20. The tension between an approach that is centred on the individual person and an approach that *compares and aggregates* within a perspective of the collective good, is subtly analysed from an ethical viewpoint by Anne Fagot-Largeault ([1991] 1994). In her study 'Reflections on the Notion of "Quality of Life"', she describes these two approaches as 'deontological' and 'teleological' respectively.

21. The fact that the Boskin report was commissioned and published by the US Senate shows well how the measurement conventions of the national accounts contribute to *institute* society, and not simply to *describe* it. For an update on the Boskin controversy after a decade, see http://www.csls.ca/ipm/ipm12.asp.

22. In French, this is referred to as the *Loi organique relative aux lois de finances* (LOLF).

23. There are historical precedents, that despite some differences, could be studied within this perspective: the economic planning experiments of socialist countries, and the 'rationalization of budget choices' undertaken in France in the 1970s and subsequently pursued under the name of 'public policy evaluation' (Spenlehauer, 1998). In these different cases, non-monetary quantified indicators were implemented.

24. On the instrumentation of public intervention via 'the choice and use of tools (techniques, operating methods, rules) that bring into effect and operationalize government action', see the collection *Gouverner par les instruments*, edited by Pierre Lascoumes and Patrick Le Galès (2004).

25. Some formalization is nevertheless sometimes perceptible at the level of the *meta-data* (data about data). These are sought and provided, but giving too many details would introduce an undesirable element of insidious doubt. A statistical argument is more effective if it can be invoked naked, without footnotes.

REFERENCES

Aglietta, M. and A. Orléan (2002), *La monnaie entre violence et confiance*, Paris: Odile Jacob.

Amossé, T., Y.V. Andrieux and L. Muller (2001), 'L'esprit humain est-il bayésien?', *Courrier des statistiques*, no. 100, 25–8; http://www.insee.fr/fr/ffc/docs_ffc/cs100g.pdf.

Armatte, M. (1995), *Histoire du modèle linéaire. Formes et usages en statistique et en économétrie jusqu'en 1945*, thesis, EHESS, Paris.

Armatte, M. and A. Dahan-Dalmedico (2004), 'Modèles et modélisations 1950–2000: Nouvelles pratiques, nouveaux enjeux', *Revue d'histoire des sciences*, **57** (2), Paris: PUF, 245–305.

Boskin, M., E. Dulberger, R. Gordon, Z. Griliches and D. Jorgenson (1996), *Toward a More Accurate Measure of the Cost of Living: Final Report to the Senate Finance Committee*, Washington, DC: US Government Printing Office.

Bowker, G. and L.S. Star (1999), *Sorting Things Out. Classification and Its Consequences*, Cambridge, MA: MIT Press.

Brousse, C. (2005), 'Définir et compter les sans-abri en Europe: enjeux et controverses', *Genèses*, **58** (March), 48–71.

Callon, M., P. Lascoumes and Y. Barthe (2001), *Agir dans un monde incertain. Essai sur la démocratie technique*, Paris: Seuil.

Casta, J.F. (2000), 'Théorie positive de la comptabilité', in B. Colasse (ed.), *Encyclopédie de la comptabilité, Contrôle de gestion et Audit*, Paris: Economica, pp. 1223–32.

Chemarin, S. (2005), 'Vers une théorie économique de l'assurabilité en incertitude', in C. Henry, S. Chemarin and E. Michel-Kerjean (eds) (2005), *Incertitude, Précaution et Assurabilité*, Report to the General Plan Commission; http://ceco.polytechnique. fr/CDD/PDF/2005-005.pdf.

Chiapello, E. and A. Desrosières (2003), 'La quantification de l'économie et la recherche en sciences sociales: paradoxes, contradictions et omissions. Le cas exemplaire de la *Positive Accounting Theory*', reprinted in F. Eymard-Duvernay (ed.) (2006), *L'économie des conventions, méthodes et résultats*, Paris: La Découverte.

Cournot, A.A. (1838), *Recherches sur les principes mathématiques de la théorie des richesses*, reprinted in G. Jorland (ed.) (1980), *Œuvres complètes*, Tome VIII, Paris: Vrin.

Cournot, A.A. (1843), *Exposition de la théorie des chances et des probabilités*, Paris: Hachette, reprinted in B. Bru (ed.) (1984), *Œuvres complètes*, Tome I, Paris: Vrin.

Cournot. A.A. (1897), *Researches into the mathematical principles of the theory of wealth*, trans. N.T Bacon, New York: Macmillan.

Crombie, A. (1994), *Styles of Scientific Thinking in the European Tradition: The History of Argument and Explanation Especially in the Mathematical and Biomedical Sciences and Arts*, London: Duckworth.

Daston, L. (1989), 'L'interprétation classique du calcul des probabilités', *Annales des Economies, Sociétés et Civilisations*, **3**, 715–31.

Dehousse, R. (2004), 'La méthode ouverte de coordination. Quand l'instrument tient lieu de politique', in P. Lascoumes and P. Le Galès (eds) (2004), *Gouverner par les instruments*, Paris: Presses de Sciences Po, pp. 331–56.

Desrosières, A. (2000), *La politique des grands nombres. Histoire de la raison statistique*, Paris: La Découverte/Poche; English translation (2002): *The Politics of Large Numbers: A History of Statistical Reasoning*, Cambridge, MA: Harvard University Press.

Desrosières A. (2005), 'Décrire l'Etat ou explorer la société: les deux sources de la statistique publique', *Genèses*, **58** (March), 4–27.

Detienne, M. (2000), *Comparer l'incomparable*, Paris: Seuil.

Espeland, W. and M. Stevens (1998), 'Commensuration as a Social Process', *Annual Review of Sociology*, **24**, 313–43.

Fagot-Largeault, A. (1991), 'Réflexions sur la notion de qualité de la vie', reprinted as 'Reflections on the Notion "Quality of Life"', in L. Nordenfelt (ed.) (1994), *Concepts and Measurement of Quality of Life in Health Care*, European Studies in Philosophy of Medicine Series, 47, Berlin: Springer, pp. 135–60.

Fitoussi, J.P. (2002), *La Règle et le Choix: De la souveraineté économique en Europe*, Paris: Seuil.

Gadrey, J. and F. Jany-Catrice (2005), *Les nouveaux indicateurs de richesse*, Paris: La Découverte.

Gigerenzer, G. and D.J. Murray (1987), *Cognition as Intuitive Statistics*, Hillsdale, NJ: Lawrence Erlbaum Associates.

Godard, O. (ed.) (1997), *Le principe de précaution dans la conduite des affaires humaines*, Paris: MSH and INRA.

Hacking, I. (1975), *The Emergence of Probability*, Cambridge: Cambridge University Press.

Hacking, I. (1990), *The Taming of Chance*, Cambridge: Cambridge University Press.

Hacking, I. (1992), 'Statistical Language, Statistical Truth, Statistical Reason: The Self-Authentification of a Style of Reasoning', in H. McMullin (ed.), *Social Dimensions of Science*, Indiana: Notre Dame University Press, pp. 130–57.

Hacking, I. (1999), *The Social Construction of What?*, Cambridge, MA: Harvard University Press.

Kahneman, D. and A. Tversky (1973), 'Availability: A heuristic for judging frequency and probability', *Cognitive Psychology*, **5**, 207–32.

Knight, F. (1921), *Risk, Uncertainty and Profit*, Boston, MA: Houghton Mifflin.

Lascoumes, P. and P. Le Gales (eds) (2004), *Gouverner par les instruments*, Paris: Presses de Sciences Po.

Latour, B. (1984), *Les microbes. Guerre et paix*, followed by *Irréductions*, Paris: Métailié; English translation by A. Sheridan and J. Law (1988), *The Pasteurization of France*, Cambridge, MA: Harvard University Press.

Martin, T. (1994), 'La valeur objective du calcul des probabilités selon Cournot', *Mathématiques, Informatique et Sciences humaines*, CAMS–EHESS, no. 127, 5–17.

Ménard, C. (1977), 'Trois formes de résistance aux statistiques: Say, Cournot, Walras', in *Pour une histoire de la statistique*, tome 1: *Contributions*, Paris: Economica–INSEE; reprint (1987), pp. 417–29.

Morgan, M. (1990), *The History of Econometric Ideas*, Cambridge: Cambridge University Press.

Morgan, M. and M. Morrison (1999), *Models as Mediators: Perspectives on Natural and Social Science*, Cambridge: Cambridge University Press.

Nivière, D. (2005), 'Négocier une statistique européenne: le cas de la pauvreté', *Genèses*, **58** (March), 28–47.

Pearson, K. (1912), *La Grammaire de la Science*, Paris: Alcan; English original (1911), *The Grammar of Science*, London: A. and C. Black.

Peretti-Watel, P. (2004), 'Du recours au paradigme épidémiologique pour l'étude des conduites à risque', *Revue Française de Sociologie*, **45** (1), 103–32.

Salais, R. (2004), 'La Politique des indicateurs. Du taux de chômage au taux d'emploi dans la stratégie européenne pour l'emploi (SEE)', in B. Zimmermann (ed.), *Action publique et sciences sociales*, Paris: MSH; http://www.insee.fr/fr/nom_def_met/colloques/acn/colloque_10/Salais.pdf.

Schumpeter, J. (1983), *Histoire de l'analyse économique*, vol. III, *L'âge de la science*, Paris: Gallimard.

Spenlehauer, V. (1998), *L'évaluation des politiques publiques, avatar de la planification*, thesis, Université Grenoble II – Pierre Mendès-France, Institut d'études politiques de Grenoble.

Stigler, S. (1986), *The History of Statistics. The Measurement of Uncertainty Before 1900*, Cambridge, MA: Harvard University Press.

Thévenot, L. (1983), 'L'économie du codage social', *Critiques de l'économie politique*, **23–4**, 188–222.

Vanoli, A. (2005), *A History of National Accounting*, Amsterdam: IOS Press.

Zelizer, V. (2001), 'Transactions intimes', *Genèses*, **42** (March), 121–44.

Index